HSC

ACPL ITEM
DISCARDED

671.8
BIES, JOHN L.,
SHEET METAL WORK

D1614090

DO NOT REMOVE
CARDS FROM POCKET

8H

ALLEN COUNTY PUBLIC LIBRARY

FORT WAYNE, INDIANA 46802

You may return this book to any agency, branch,
or bookmobile of the Allen County Public Library.

Sheet Metal Work

by John D. Bies

Rex Miller, Consulting Editor

Macmillan Publishing Company
New York

Collier Macmillan Publishers
London

Allen County Public Library
Ft. Wayne, Indiana

FIRST EDITION

Copyright © 1985 by G. K. Hall & Co.
Copyright © 1986 by Macmillan Publishing Company, a division of Macmillan, Inc.

All rights reserved. No part of this book may be reproduced or transmitted in any form or by any means, electronic or mechanical, including photocopying, recording or by any information storage and retrieval system, without permission in writing from the Publisher.

While every precaution has been taken in the preparation of this book, the Publisher assumes no responsibility for errors or omissions. Neither is any liability assumed for damages resulting from the use of the information contained herein.

Macmillan Publishing Company
866 Third Avenue, New York, N.Y. 10022
Collier Macmillan Canada, Inc.

Library of Congress Cataloging-in-Publication Data

Bies, John D., 1946-
    Sheet metal work.

    Reprint. Originally published: 1st ed. Boston:
T. Audel, c1985.
    1. Sheet-metal work. I. Miller, Rex, 1929-
II. Title.
[TS250.B47   1986]   671.8'23   86-8281
ISBN 0-8161-1706-3

Macmillan books are available at special discounts for bulk purchases for sales promotions, premiums, fund-raising, or educational use. For details, contact:

    Special Sales Director
    Macmillan Publishing Company
    866 Third Avenue
    New York, N.Y. 10022

10 9 8 7 6 5 4 3 2

Printed in the United States of America

Contents

CHAPTER 4

PART III

SHEET METAL PRACTICES

CHAPTER 5

CHAPTER 6

CHAPTER 7

CHAPTER 8

PART IV

FASTENING SHEET METAL

CHAPTER 15

CHAPTER 16

CHAPTER 17

PART V

FINISHING SHEET METAL PRODUCTS

CHAPTER 18

PART VI

PRODUCTION WORK

CHAPTER 19

APPENDIX

PART I

FUNDAMENTALS FOR SHEET METAL WORK

CHAPTER 1

Basic Mathematics for Sheet Metal Work

The need for skilled workers in sheet metal work has increased steadily with the growth of the manufacturing and construction industries. Examples of products that require sheet metal work are aircraft and missile bodies, electronic instrumentation chassis, appliances, heating and air-conditioning ductwork, and siding for residential or commercial buildings. In addition, a number of home owners are frequently faced with sheet metal work for improving, remodeling, or expanding their houses.

At the heart of good sheet metal work are accurate drawings, patterns, and metal layout. To ensure accuracy and precision, it is critical that one be able to apply practical mathematical concepts and principles to the processes of making drawings and patterns, laying out sheet metal stock, cutting and forming, installation, and/or assembling. The intent of this chapter is to provide a basic overview of the mathematics needed for executing accurate and precise sheet metal work.

NUMERALS

Before one can progress with the application of mathematical principles to sheet metal work, we must have a complete understanding of numbers or numerals. The system used throughout the world for expressing numerical values is known as the *Arabic system*. The Arabic system employs ten basic numerals or digits: 0, 1, 2, 3, 4, 5, 6, 7, 8, and 9. From these, any numerical value can be written, including whole numbers, fractions, and decimals.

Whole Numbers

Though whole numbers are seldom used alone in making calculations, they are at the heart of all basic mathematical processes. The
value of each digit will change, depending on where it is placed.
Hence, the word *place* has a special meaning in mathematics. The
concept of the place of a number is shown in Table 1-1 for the
number five hundred thirty-eight million, four hundred twenty-one
thousand, six hundred seventy-nine.

Table 1-1
Example of Expressing the Place of a Number

Millions			Thousands			Units		
hundred	ten	million	hundred	ten	thousand	hundreds	tens	units
5	3	8 ,	4	2	1 ,	6	7	9

Fractions

It is almost impossible to do accurate sheet metal work without
fractions, especially in the construction industry. In the vast majority
of cases, dimensions will involve a combination of whole numbers
and fractions. As such, fractions are frequently expressed in terms
of divisions of an inch, such as ¹⁄₆₄″, ¹⁄₃₂″, ¹⁄₁₆″, ¹⁄₈″, ¹⁄₄″, and ¹⁄₂″. All
fractions are made up of two numbers: a *numerator* and *denominator*. The numerator represents the top number; the denominator
is the bottom number. In the fraction ⅝, the numerator is 5 and
the denominator is 8.

The basic tool for fractional measurements is the steel rule
(Figure 1-1), which is used to make accurate measures down to the

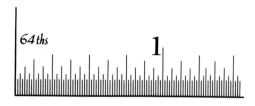

Fig. 1-1. One-sixty-fourth steel rule.

nearest ⅟₆₄″. In fractional work, most measurements will not require measures in fractions less than ⅟₆₄″; if smaller divisions are necessary, special measuring devices such as micrometers are used that express measurements in decimals. Fractional measures are almost always used in the construction industry, and frequently in production settings.

On close examination of a steel rule, one will notice that the fractional divisions represent equal divisions of an inch. Common steel rule readings are shown in Figure 1-2. That is, the ⅛″ division divides the inch into eight equal parts, ⅟₁₆″ into 16 equal parts, and so on. As a result, it is possible to identify the following equivalents:

$$\frac{1}{2} = \frac{2}{4} \qquad \frac{1}{4} = \frac{2}{8} \qquad \frac{1}{8} = \frac{2}{16} \qquad \frac{1}{16} = \frac{2}{32} \qquad \frac{1}{32} = \frac{2}{64}$$
$$= \frac{4}{8} \qquad\quad = \frac{4}{16} \qquad\quad = \frac{4}{32} \qquad\quad = \frac{4}{64}$$
$$= \frac{16}{32} \qquad\quad = \frac{8}{32} \qquad\quad = \frac{8}{64}$$
$$= \frac{32}{64} \qquad\quad = \frac{16}{64}$$

Decimals

A number used to express a division of an inch, other than fractions, is the decimal. Decimal measurements are more commonly used in manufacturing and production settings where close tolerances must be kept. When using measuring instruments such as micro-meters, decimal steel rules, and vernier calipers, one must have a

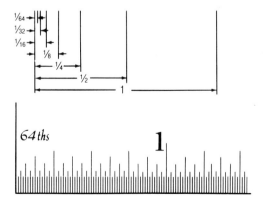

Fig. 1-2. Common steel rule readings.

thorough understanding of decimals. Figure 1-3 presents common measurements made with a decimal rule.

NOTATIONS, ABBREVIATIONS, AND SYMBOLS

A number of different notations and formulas are found in sheet metal work. The notations themselves are usually contained in formulas. The formulas are then used to obtain specific values that are useful in calculating quantities such as the amount or size of sheet metal stock to be used for a job, the total weight of the product, and the cost per unit produced.

One of the most common forms of notation is the *exponent* or *power* note, which is represented by a superscript. A superscript is a number or letter on the upper right side of another number or letter such as a^2, b^R, 3^2, and 4^A. Exponents are used to indicate how many times a number is to be multiplied by itself. Examples of this are:

$$5^1 = 5 \times 1$$
$$5^2 = 5 \times 5$$
$$5^3 = 5 \times 5 \times 5$$
$$5^4 = 5 \times 5 \times 5 \times 5$$

In exponential expressions, values that have an exponent of 2 are said to be *squared*, or raised to the second power; those with a 3 are *cubed*, or raised to the third power; after this, the power

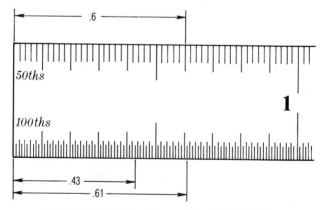

Fig. 1-3. Typical readings with a decimal rule.

14

statement is used (fourth power, fifth power, sixth power, etc.). When an exponent is used in a formula that contains several values, it is only used for the number it is next to. For example, in the expression abc^3, only c is cubed.

Another notation is the *root* expression, which is represented by the radical sign $\sqrt{}$. The index of the root is represented by a number placed at the upper left-hand corner, such as $\sqrt[3]{}$. For example, $\sqrt{4}$ means the square root of 4 (a number multiplied by itself will equal 4, in this case the square root of 4 is 2), and $\sqrt[3]{64}$ is the cubed root of 64, which is 4.

A notation that is critical in calculating many formulas is the Greek letter pi, represented as π. It has a specific numerical value, which is $^{22}\!/_7$. Because $^{22}\!/_7$ can never be expressed evenly in decimal form (22 cannot be divided evenly by 7), some individuals prefer to use the fraction in all calculation. A common practice is to use 3.14 for the value of π. For more precise calculations, the decimal equivalent can be extended to any degree, such as 3.14159.

Mathematical abbreviations and symbols are used widely, and the sheet metal worker who expects to be successful on the job should be familiar with them. An extensive coverage of every abbreviation and symbol used in mathematics would be beyond the scope of this book; however, Table 1-2 contains a summation of abbreviations and symbols that are frequently used in the sheet metal field.

TRIGONOMETRY

Sheet metal workers are often called on to determine missing dimensions for triangles. These triangles may be either right (having one angle that is 90°) or oblique (having no 90° angles). Calculations can be adapted to slanting surfaces or the location of positions for a series of holes, fasteners, or weldments.

Right Triangles

Figure 1-4 shows the trigonometric elements necessary to solve for missing dimensions for a right triangle. All right triangles are made up of one 90° angle and two acute angles (less than 90°), so that the

Table 1-2
Mathematical Abbreviations and Symbols

Abbreviations and Symbols	Meaning
A	Area
a	Vertical side of a plane figure
b	Base side of a plane figure
c	Hypotenuse of a right triangle
C	Circumference of a circle
d	Diameter
D	Large diameter
h	Vertical height
P	Perimeter
r	Radius
R	Large radius
sh	Slant height
V	Volume
W	Width
∠	Angle
⊙	Circle
∅	Diameter
÷	Divided by
:	Ratio or proportion
=	Equal to
×	Multiplied by
π	Pi
+	Plus
±	Plus or minus
▭	Rectangle
□	Square
Δ	Triangle
∴	Therefore

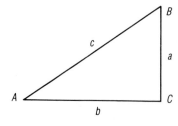

Fig. 1-4. Trigonometric elements for a right triangle.

sum of all three angles will equal 180°. As can be seen, trigonometry is used to solve linear as well as angular problems.

When solving problems dealing with triangles, it is important to have the necessary formulas available. These formulas include the use of such values as sine (sin), cosine (cos), tangent (tan), and cotangent (cot). To obtain these angular values, one must use a Table of Natural Trigonometric Functions. For accurate calculations, most shop work requires the use of tables that divide angles into degrees and minutes.

To determine the dimension of missing angles, three formulas are available. These are:

$$\tan A = a/b = \text{opposite/adjacent}$$
$$\sin A = a/c = \text{opposite/hypotenuse}$$
$$\cos A = b/c = \text{adjacent/hypotenuse}$$

Thus, if two sides of a right triangle are known, any angle can be calculated. For example, assume that we have a right triangle whose linear dimensions are: $a = 3''$, $b = 4''$, and $c = 5''$ (Figure 1-5). From this information we must calculate the size of angle A. This problem can be solved with any one of the above three formulas, by substituting the given numbers in the ratios. The possible solutions are as follows:

$$\tan A = a/b = \tfrac{3}{4} = .75000$$

Using the tangent column in the Table of Natural Trigonometric Functions, it is found that the angle nearest .75000 is 36° 52' (36 degrees 52 minutes).

$$\sin A = a/c = \tfrac{3}{5} = .60000$$

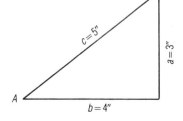

Fig. 1-5. Given three sides of a right triangle. Solve for missing angle A.

17

Using the sine column in the Table of Natural Trigonometric Functions, it is found that the angle nearest .60000 is 36° 52'.

$$\cos A = b/c = \tfrac{4}{5} = .80000$$

Using the cosine column in the Table of Natural Trigonometric Functions, it is found that the angle nearest .80000 is 36° 52'.

Formulas are also available for calculating missing linear dimensions. The formulas used when two sides of the triangle are known are given as follows:

$$c^2 = a^2 + b^2$$
$$a = \sqrt{(c-b)(c+b)}$$
$$b = \sqrt{(c-a)(c+a)}$$
$$c = \sqrt{a^2 + b^2}$$

As an example of how these formulas can be used, consider the following problem (Figure 1-6), where side b is 1.7″ and side c is 2.1″. To accurately construct this product, we must determine the length of side a. The problem can be solved with the following procedure:

$$a = \sqrt{(c-b)(c+b)}$$
$$= \sqrt{(2.1-1.7)(2.1+1.7)}$$
$$= \sqrt{(.4)(3.8)}$$
$$= \sqrt{1.52}$$
$$= 1.23″$$

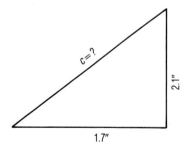

Fig. 1-6. Calculating missing side of right triangle when given two sides.

Formulas that can be used when one angle and one side are known are:

$$a = (\sin A)(c) = (\cos B)(c) = (\tan A)(b)$$
$$= (\cot B)(b) = b/\cot A = b/\tan B$$
$$b = (\cos A)(c) = (\sin B)(c) = (\cot A)(a)$$
$$= (\tan B)(a) = b/\tan A = b/\cot B$$
$$c = a/\sin A = a/\cos B = b/\cos A = b/\sin B$$

Consider the problem shown in Figure 1-7, for example, where side $c = 3''$ and angle A is 44°, and we must determine the length of side b. The solution to this problem could be as follows:

$$b = (\cos A)(c)$$
$$= (\cos 44°)(3)$$
$$= (.71934)(3)$$
$$= 2.15802''$$

Note that in this example problem the cosine of 44° was obtained from the Table of Natural Trigonometric Functions.

Oblique Triangles

An oblique triangle is any triangle where none of the angles are equal to 90° (i.e., not a right triangle). Figure 1-8 is an example of an oblique triangle and its elements. As with the right triangle, missing dimensions can be calculated by using a set of formulas based on three laws, presented as follows:

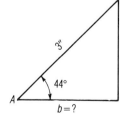

Fig. 1-7. Calculating missing side of right triangle when given one side and one angle.

19

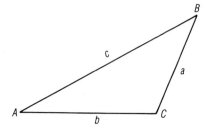

Fig. 1-8. An oblique triangle has no angle equal to 90°.

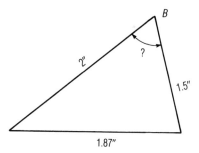

Fig. 1-9. Calculating angle *B* given three sides of an oblique triangle.

The Law of Cosines

$$a^2 = b^2 + c^2 - 2bc \cos A$$
$$b^2 = a^2 + c^2 - 2ac \cos B$$
$$c^2 = a^2 + b^2 - 2ab \cos C$$

To calculate missing angles, the Law of Cosines can be used to derive the following formulas:

$$\cos A = (b^2 + c^2 - a^2)/2bc$$
$$\cos B = (a^2 + c^2 - b^2)/2ac$$
$$\cos C = (a^2 + b^2 - c^2)/2ab$$

An example of how one would use these formulas is illustrated in Figure 1-9. Here, we know that side $a = 1.5''$, $b = 1.875''$, and $c = 2''$, and the unknown in this problem is the size of angle B. By using the derived law of cosines formula, this problem can be easily solved as follows:

$$
\begin{aligned}
\cos B &= (a^2 + c^2 - b^2)/2ac \\
&= (1.5^2 + 2^2 - 1.875^2)/(2)(1.5)(2) \\
&= (2.25 + 4 - 3.516)/6 \\
&= 2.734/6
\end{aligned}
$$

$$= .45567$$
$$\text{Angle } B = 62° \ 53' \ 30''$$

Note that the cosine of B (.45567) falls halfway between the cosine of 62° 53' (.45580) and 62° 54' (.45554). Therefore, it is possible to specify the 30'' (30 seconds) measure.

The Law of Sines

$$a/\sin A = b/\sin B = c/\sin C$$

When three of four values for a triangle are known, it is possible to select one of the following formulas derived from the Law of Sines:

$$a/b = \sin A/\sin B$$
$$a/c = \sin A/\sin C$$
$$b/c = \sin B/\sin C$$

An example of how these formulas can be used is illustrated in Figure 1-10, where $A = 54°$, $C = 48°$, and $c = 1.5''$, and side a is

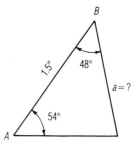

Fig. 1-10. Calculating dimensions of "side a" given two angles and one side.

unknown. To solve this problem, the following procedure was followed:

$$a/c = \sin A/\sin C$$
$$a/1.5 = \sin 54°/\sin 48°$$
$$a = (.80902/.74314)(1.5)$$
$$= (1.08865)(1.5)$$
$$= 1.6330''$$

The Law of Tangents

$$(a-b)/(a+b) = \tan .5(A-B)/\tan .5(A+B)$$
$$(a-c)/(a+c) = \tan .5(A-C)/\tan .5(A+C)$$
$$(b-c)/(b+c) = \tan .5(B-C)/\tan .5(B+C)$$

The Law of Tangents is not frequently used by sheet metal workers because of the relatively complicated procedures required to obtain the missing dimension. In most cases, it will be easier to use one of the formulas derived in the Law of Cosines or Law of Sines. If the Law of Tangents must be used, the same mathematical procedures should be implemented. Table 1-3 is a summary of problems and solutions.

Table 1-3
Trigonometric Problems and Solutions

Problems	Solution
1. Given two angles and one side	Solved by the Law of Sines
2. Given two sides and an opposite angle	Solved by the Law of Sines, but is an ambiguous problem
3. Given two sides and the included angle	A difficult problem that is solved by finding the angles by the Law of Tangents, followed by the Law of Sines to find the third side of the triangle
4. Given three sides	Solved by the Law of Cosines

Area of a Triangle

The area of a triangle is an important calculation for sheet metal workers, since many cost figures are based on the amount of sheet stock used, which is often priced per square foot. A triangle's area can also be found by using trigonometry. The basic requirement is that two sides and an included angle must be given. The basic formulas used to determine the area of a triangle are:

Area $= .5bc \sin A$
$= .5ab \sin C$
$= .5ac \sin B$

Based on the given formulas, consider the area problem for the triangle illustrated in Figure 1-11, where $a = 1.5''$, $c = 2.75''$, and $B = 75°$. The solution to this problem is as follows:

Area $= .5ac \sin B$
$= .5(1.5)(2.75)(\sin 75°)$
$= (2.0625)(.96593)$
$= 1.992 \text{ in}^2$

SHEET METAL FORMULAS

In the sheet metal industry, a number of formulas have been adapted to meet the needs of workers. These formulas represent a short-cut approach to figuring out dimensions, weights, and costs of jobs. Though some are specifically designed for sheet metal work, they are all based on sound mathematical theories and laws.

Basic Formulas

A mathematical formula is a rule that is expressed by signs, letters, symbols, and numbers. Symbols and letters are used in the place of words, so that problems can be solved more easily and quickly. Each individual symbol represents a value or number. Because some formulas are frequently used, sheet metal workers often memorize them, so that they will not have to look them up in a reference manual or table.

The procedure that should be used when working with formulas is the same in all cases. The first step is to determine what formula

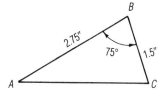

Fig. 1-11. Calculating area of a triangle given one angle and two sides.

is to be used; second, substitute the values or numbers for the letters and/or symbols; and, finally, perform the required calculations to obtain the correct answer. This section presents important formulas for a sheet metal worker.

Perimeter of a Square

The perimeter of a square, which is a right polygon with equal sides, is always defined in terms of linear measures: inches, feet, yards, millimeters, centimeters, meters, etc. In sheet metal work, the perimeter of a square is used to determine the size of a part's blank. The perimeter of a square is calculated by using the following formula:

$$P = 4s$$

where P = perimeter
s = length of one side

As an example of how this formula would be used, consider the product in Figure 1-12. To calculate its perimeter, we use the following procedure:

$$P = 4s$$
$$P = (4)(2.5)$$
$$P = 10''$$

Perimeter of a Rectangle

It is often necessary to calculate the perimeter of a rectangle. A rectangle is a right polygon where the two pairs of opposite sides

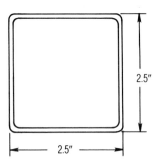

2.5″

2.5″

Fig. 1-12. Right polygon with four equal sides.

will be equal. The formula used to calculate the perimeter of a rectangle is:

$$P = 2l + 2w$$
where l = length, or longer dimension
w = width, or shorter dimension

Using Figure 1-13 as the product for which the perimeter must be determined, the following procedure should be used:

$$P = 2l + 2w$$
$$= (2)(4) + (2)(1.5)$$
$$= 8 + 3$$
$$= 11''$$

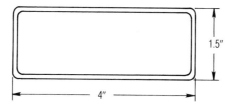

Fig. 1-13. Rectangle.

Circumference of a Circle

The circumference of a circle is the total length or distance around the circle. Two basic formulas that can be used to solve this problem:

1. $C = \pi d$
where C = circumference
d = diameter of the circle
$\pi = 3.1416$
2. $C = 2\pi r$
where r = radius of the circle

As an example problem that would employ the circumference formulas, consider the circumference of the circular part illustrated in Figure 1-14. To calculate its circumference, the following procedure should be used:

$$C = \pi d \qquad\qquad C = 2\pi r$$
$$= (3.1416)(3.75) \qquad = (2)(3.1416)(1.875)$$
$$= 11.781'' \qquad\qquad = (2)(5.8905)$$
$$\qquad\qquad\qquad = 11.781''$$

Perimeter of a Semicircular-Sided Object

An object or part that is semicircular-sided is made up of two half circles and a rectangle or square. The perimeter of such an object involves both circumference and perimeter (straight) measures. Figure 1-15 illustrates such an object. Note that the object's height is the same as the diameter of the half circles. To calculate the perimeter of this object requires calculations for both straight and circular surfaces. The basic formula used is:

$$P = \pi d + 2w$$

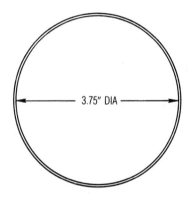

3.75" DIA

Fig. 1-14. Circle.

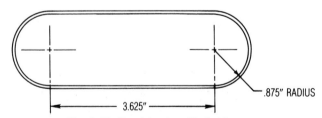

.875" RADIUS

3.625"

Fig. 1-15. Semicircular-sided object.

where

P = perimeter
d = diameter of the half circle
w = distance between the half circle

To find the perimeter of the object in Figure 1-15, the following procedures would be followed:

$$P = \pi d + 2w$$
$$= (3.1416)(1.75) + (2)(3.625)$$
$$= 5.4978 + 14.5$$
$$= 19.9978''$$

Special Sheet Metal Formulas

There are a number of formulas that have been derived specifically for use by sheet metal workers. These formulas are designed to help the worker design and make a better product or installation. Presented below is a review of several special sheet metal formulas.

Edge or Hem Allowance

Frequently, the sheet metal worker will be required to put a specific type of hem or edge onto a part or product, for reinforcement or appearance's sake. Simply, a hem is a fold at the edge of a product that not only provides a neat appearance, but also increases the total strength of the material. In all, there are three basic types of edges.

1. *Single Hem Edge.* A single hem edge is commonly referred to as a *Dutch hem* in the trade. As shown in Figure 1-16, the total

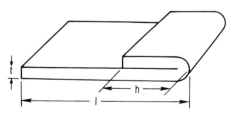

Fig. 1-16. Single hem allowance.

27

length (*TL*) of the stock is based on the outside measure (*l*) of the piece, plus the outside measure of the hem (*h*), minus half the metal thickness (*t*). This is represented in the formula:

$$TL = l + h - .5t$$

An example of how this formula would be used is a problem where the total length of the stock must be determined for a part where the outside length is 1.25," the hem is .25", and its thickness is .0625". The problem would be solved as follows:

$$
\begin{aligned}
TL = l + h - .5t \\
= 1.25 + .25 - (.5)(.0625) \\
= 1.50 - .03125 \\
= 1.46875'' \text{ or } 1.47'' \text{ (rounded to nearest hundredth)}
\end{aligned}
$$

2. *Wired Edge.*   The allowance for a wired edge (Figure 1-17) is two and a half times the diameter of the wire, and is represented by the formula:

$$\text{Allowance} = 2.5D$$

An example of how this formula would be employed would be to calculate the allowance for a wired edge that used a wire with a diameter of .125". The solution would be as follows:

$$
\begin{aligned}
\text{Allowance} = (2.5)(.125) \\
= .3125'' \text{ or } .31'' \text{ (rounded to nearest hundredth)}
\end{aligned}
$$

3. *Curling.*   A curling or *false wiring* edge is the same as for a wired edge, except that the wire is used inside the edge. Hence, the allowance is calculated the same as for the wired edge, where Allowance = 2.5D.

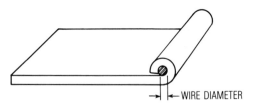

Fig. 1-17. Wire edge.

Seam Allowance

Numerous types of seams are used in sheet metal work to join two pieces of metal together. When used, an allowance is required for using additional metal for the seam. The amount of allowance required will equal the width of the seam. For example, if the seam is ¼″, then the allowance will also be ¼″. If a seam is offset, then the allowance will equal the width of the seam plus the addition of the two bends. Riveted seam allowances, by comparison, will be twice the seam width, since they must overlap for the rivet holes. Figure 1-18 is an example of four common seams.

USING CALCULATORS

One of the most significant technological developments made in the last half century is in the field of microelectronics. This field has spawned a number of products that only ten or twenty years ago seemed impossible. One of these products is the handheld calculator. The first calculators to hit the market in the middle to late 1960s cost $500 or more; today those same calculators can be purchased for less than $10.

Because of their relatively low cost, calculators are being used by everyone—including the sheet metal worker. A number of different types of calculators on the market, such as scientific and business calculators, have special functions that are commonly used in those fields. This section gives a brief discussion of the simple calculator.

Illustrated in Figure 1-19 is an example of a typical layout for

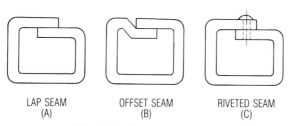

LAP SEAM   OFFSET SEAM   RIVETED SEAM
(A)   (B)   (C)

Fig. 1-18. Common seams.

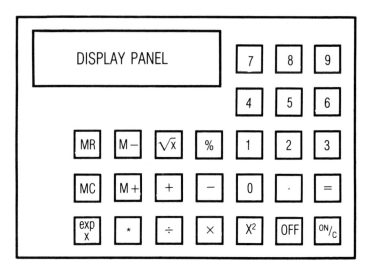

Fig. 1-19. Example of a pocket calculator configuration.

a calculator. As can be seen, there are three general groupings of keys or buttons. The first are the numerical keys, which are used to specify whole numbers and decimals. The second set of keys are function keys, which tell the calculator what mathematical function to perform (e.g., addition, subtraction, division, square root, percentage, etc). The last set of keys are memory keys, which will store information, such as commonly used numbers, or keep a running total after various calculations.

Simple Calculations

To make simple mathematical calculations on a calculator, one has to follow simple logic. To add $12 + 23 + 4$, press the numeric keys [1] and [2] for the twelve, then the addition sign [+], followed by [2] [3] [+] [4]; when all the numbers have been so entered, press the equal sign button [=] to obtain your answer (39), which will be displayed on the small display panel.

For subtraction, the procedure is similar. To subtract $45 - 5$, press the buttons in the following sequential order: [4] [5] [−] [4] [=], and the answer should read 41.

30

For a problem that calls for division, let's say $78 \div 22$, press the following buttons in sequential order: [7] [8] [÷] [2] [2] [=] to obtain the answer 3.5454545.
Obtain the square root of a number is extremely simple. For example, to find the square root of 2.5, press the buttons in the following sequential order: [2] [.] [5] [√] and obtain the answer 1.581388. Note that the equal sign will normally not have to be pressed.
Please be sure to *read the directions* for all calculators carefully, for there are slight differences in their operating procedure.

Complex Calculations

Calculators are extremely valuable tools, especially when complex calculations must be made. An example of this would be to use a formula that requires several mathematical calculations. In this situation, the memory keys would come into play. Consider the following problem:

> Right triangle ABC, where $a = 2.5''$
> and $b = 6''$. Find the length of side c.

Solution:

$$c = \sqrt{a^2 + b^2}$$
$$= \sqrt{2.5^2 + 6^2}$$

Use the following sequence with your calculator:

Step 1. [2] [.] [5] [×] [2] [.] [5] [=]
The answer will be 6.25. Place this number in memory by hitting the [M+] button. Now clear the display panel by hitting the [C] button—note that the 6.25 is safely stored in memory.

Step 2. [6] [×] [6] [=]
The answer will be 36. With the 36 still on the display panel, do step 3.

Step 3. [+] [MR] [=]
This adds 36 to the number in memory. The [MR]

31

stands for "memory release." The answer will be 42.25.
Leaving 42.25 on the display panel, do step 4.

Step 4. [√]
The final answer should read 6.5

Because of their ease of use, along with their accuracy, calculators are used by many sheet metal workers—especially in precision sheet metal work where calculations are sometime figured to the nearest thousandth of an inch.

SUMMARY

Central to accurate sheet metal work is the application of practical mathematical concepts and principles. Mathematics is used in the drawing of patterns, laying out of sheet metal stock, cutting and forming products, and in installation and assemblying work.

Basic arithmetic manipulation is the cornerstone of all mathematical work. With a complete mastery of the four basic types of calculations, one can solve all mathematical problems. These four calculations are addition, subtraction, multiplication, and division.

A number of different notations and abbreviations are used in sheet metal work. These are found to be helpful as a means of short-cut procedures for making statements about what type of calculation is to be executed. Examples of common types of notations are exponent and root expressions. Abbreviations, on the other hand, are letters or symbols used to represent specific values.

Trigonometry is important to the sheet metal worker, especially when missing dimensions must be determined for triangularly shaped objects. Trigonometry provides for calculations of both right and oblique triangles. Central to these calculations are ratios that are expressed as tangent, cotangent, sine, and cosine values. From these, specific formulas are derived in the form of the law of cosines, cosines, and tangents. In addition, the area of a triangle can also be determined by trigonometric functions.

Specific formulas have been developed for use by sheet metal workers. These formulas are based on sound mathematical laws and theories. Examples of these formulas are the calculation of the perimeter of a square, perimeter of a rectangle, circumference of a circle, perimeter of a semicircular-sided object, edge allowance, and seam allowances.

With the advent of small pocket calculators, many mathematical problems can be easily and quickly solved. The use of these calculators requires simple logic in the expression of numerical values and arithmetic manipulations. There are various types of calculators available, ranging from the standard basic calculator to those designed for specific use in business and science.

REVIEW QUESTIONS

1. Determine the sum totals of the following:
$$23 + 34 + 7 + 18 =$$
$$.766 + 1.25 + 18 + 5.75 =$$
$$2,345 + 14,457 + 1,000.05 =$$

2. Determine the difference between the following:
$$(12' - 11'') - (6' - 3'') =$$
$$(23' - 3'') - (18' - 10'') =$$

3. Multiply the following:
$$32 \times 23 =$$
$$14' - 6'' \times 5 =$$
$$23.2 \times 2.15 =$$

4. Divide the following:
$$23 - 4 =$$
$$12.224 - 6 =$$
$$134 - .25 =$$

5. What are the values of the following expressions:
$$4^3 =$$
$$34^2 =$$
$$\sqrt{36} =$$

6. What is the angular dimension of angle A, in a right triangle, if sides $a = 2''$ and $b = 5''$?

7. What is the length of side b, in a right triangle, if $a = 3.3''$ and $c = 6''$?

8. In oblique triangle ABC, what is angle A, if $a = 1.75''$, $b = 2''$, and $c = 2.25''$?

9. Calculate the edge allowance for a single hem, if the outside length is $11''$, the hem is $\frac{3}{8}''$, and the metal thickness is $\frac{1}{16}''$.

10. What is the seam allowance for a $\frac{1}{2}''$ seam that is to be riveted together?

CHAPTER 2

The Basic Principles of Drafting

Sheet metal workers are often required to read and interpret construction and mechanical drawings of various products, such as air-handling systems and architectural components. In some cases, these individuals are also required to design and draw accurate sheet metal patterns. To do this, it is important that one attain a sound basis and proficiency in the principles of basic drafting. Through the correct use of drawing instruments and tools, patterns and drawings can be generated that show proper line weights, view placement, and lettering techniques.

DRAFTING MATERIALS AND TOOLS

The appearance and accuracy of a drawing can be greatly affected by the quality and type of materials and tools used. The use of inferior quality or inappropriate drawing instruments and supplies often leads to inaccurate patterns and a poorly made product. To avoid this outcome, the sheet metal worker should take care in selecting the best materials and tools for the task at hand.

A wide variety of drawing materials and tools are available and this often creates a problem for the novice—what should be purchased and from whom? It is best for the beginning sheet metal worker to contact other individuals with more experience in the field and find out what they are using and who their suppliers are. They can give advice about acceptable quality levels and the best suppliers.

Specific Media

There is a vast array of drawing materials and media on the market today. All, however, are not appropriate or are of little value to the sheet metal worker. In most cases, sheet metal workers should only concern themselves with the basics and leave specialized drawings and instruments to designers and drafters.

All drawings should be made on a good grade of paper. The most common type of paper used is called *vellum*. Vellums are also referred to as *tracing vellums* and *tracing papers*. The primary advantage of vellum is its ability to make high-quality drawings and produce good prints. In practice, very little difference exists between vellum and tracing paper, since both come in varying degrees of strength and transparency. As a rule, the more transparent the paper, the more likely it will be called tracing paper. Another factor in determining a paper's name is its use. If the paper is to be used for preparing an original drawing, then it will probably be called vellum; if it is used for tracing, then it will be called tracing vellum or tracing paper.

Vellums were developed to combine transparency and strength. Hence, they tend to be thicker and stronger than traditional tracing papers, even though they may have the same degree of transparency. Vellum transparency is made possible by the inclusion of a synthetic resin that is added during manufacturing. As a result, the transparency, durability, and relative inexpensiveness of vellum make it a popular drawing material.

When a sheet metal pattern is being prepared, it may be first drawn on vellum, and then reproduced onto a thicker and more durable pattern material, or drawn directly on that material. Though some patterns are made out of sheet metal, wood, acrylic, and other materials, many are drawn or reproduced directly on more durable drawing materials. For customized, single-item products, the pattern is often developed and drawn directly onto the stock material itself, eliminating the need for a finished drawing.

One of the most durable materials used for pattern drawing is *polyester drawing film*. Polyester films provide an excellent surface for drawing, and can be easily cut by scissors. They have exceptional dimensional stability, strength, high transparency, and are heat and age resistant. In addition, these films are nonsoluble, waterproof, and offer a high-quality appearance. All these attributes are important for the typical workplace. If the pattern is first drawn on a vellum, it is possible to obtain polyester film with a special coating, so that a print or reproduction can be made directly onto the film. Another durable material that can be used as a pattern is cloth. Though more susceptible to moisture and dimensional changes, it can be used successfully for short-term situations. Drawing cloths are presently manufactured from cotton. Dimensional stability is obtained by use of a synthetic moisture-resistant sizing or starch. Compared to films and vellums, cloth materials do not receive pencil drawings readily, and are best suited for inking procedures.

A third material sometimes used for patterns is bond paper. These papers are often buff or yellowish in color, and are of heavier weight (comparable to the weight of paper used in manila folders). At one time, heavy bond papers were very popular, but with the advent of high-quality films, they are less frequently used.

All drawing materials are available in a variety of standard sizes of sheets or rolls, and are presented in Table 2-1. Sheet sizes of 8-½″ × 11″, 18″ × 24″, 24″ × 36″, and 36″ × 48″ are the most common because they can be easily filed and handled. In addition, pre-cut sheets can be ordered with printed borders, coordinates, and title blocks.

The vast majority of drawings will be done with lead, instead of ink. Because ink drawings are so seldom required of the sheet

Table 2-1
Standard Sizes of Drawing Materials

Sheets		Rolls	
Size in Inches	Size Designation	Width in Inches	Length in Yards
8-½ × 11	A	8.5	20 and 50
11 × 17	B	11	20 and 50
12 × 18	—	18	20 and 50
17 × 22	C	24	20 and 50
18 × 24	—	30	20 and 50
22 × 34	D	34	20 and 50
24 × 36	—	36	20 and 50
34 × 44	E	42	20 and 50
36 × 48	—	54	20 and 50

metal worker, they will not be covered in this book. Leads are usually categorized according to their hardness. In total, 18 degrees of hardness can be chosen for a given job. Presented in Table 2-2 is a listing of the lead hardness ratings.

The two softest leads are 6B and 5B, which are too soft for practical sheet metal drawings but acceptable for freehand sketching. 4B through HB leads are used for the drawing of certain types of renderings and sketches. Leads between F and 4H are normally used to produce sheet metal drawings and patterns. Very hard leads with a rating of 5H or higher are of value for layout work and drawing reference lines that are not to be reproduced.

The most common form of lead used in sheet metal work is the pencil, particularly in field work. On the drafting table, however, *stick lead holders* (Figure 2-1) are rapidly replacing pencils. The unique feature of these holders is that they can be purchased ac-

Table 2-2
Hardness Ratings of Leads

Rating	Degree of Hardness
6B	
5B	
4B	Soft
3B	
2B	
B	
HB	
F	Medium
H	
2H	
3H	Hard
4H	
5H	
6H	
7H	Very hard
8H	
9H	

Fig. 2-1. Stick lead holder.

cording to standard line widths, which vary in line thickness from 0.3 mm (millimeter) to 0.9 mm. Thus, lead sticks are available for each hardness rating per line thickness.

Stick lead holders are operated by either pushing down on the eraser end or by rotating the holder's barrel. The lead is stored in the barrel of the holder itself. As can be seen, the primary advantage of the lead stick holder is that it eliminates the need for all sharpening operations. Because of this, the holder is also starting to become a popular device in nondrafting settings.

Drafting Tools

It is not necessary for the sheet metal worker to go out and purchase an entire complement of drafting tools—all that is needed are the basics. Only if one is going to be a drafter, or become extensively involved with drafting procedures and the design and drawing of sheet metal developments, should serious consideration be given the purchase of a complete set of drafting tools.

One of the most basic items required is a drawing surface, such as a drawing board or table. A good size drawing surface would be about 31" × 42" (787.4mm × 1066.8mm) though sizes in excess of 42" × 84" (1066mm × 2133.6mm) are available. What should be questioned is the typical size of drawing required—if drawings hardly exceed 18" × 24" (457.2mm × 609.6mm), then the drawing surface should only be a few inches larger in both dimensions. Drawing boards are made of either white pine or basswood, are non-glaring, and less expensive than drawing tables.

Another item that should be considered is a parallel ruling unit, used to draw horizontal parallel lines. For most cases, a 36" T-square is best (see Figure 2-2). The T-square is composed of a fixed head and a blade. The blade should be made of hardwood, be perfectly

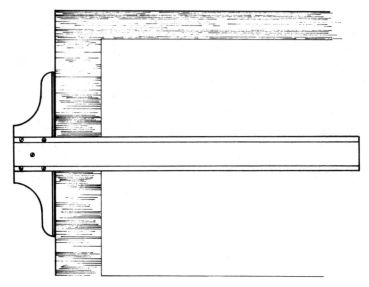

Fig. 2-2. A T-square as used on a drawing surface.

straight, and set exactly 90° to the head. A plastic transparent edge is often included along the length of the blade, to prevent excessive wear. Other materials that are used to make T-squares are plastic and metal.

Professional drafters will seldom use T-squares. Here, drafting *parallels* and *drafting machines* are more commonly used. Parallels are designed to move up and down the drawing surface along a set of wire guides that are fastened to the drawing surface. Drafting machines come with two blades, set at 90° to one another. The two blades are attached to a rotating protractor head, so that they can be set at various angles.

Triangles (Figure 2-3) are used as straightedges to draw vertical and standard angular lines. The two most common triangles are the 45° and 30°–60°. Triangles are available in standard heights of 2″ (50.8mm) increments, ranging from 4″ (101.6mm) to 18″ (457.2mm). When selecting these triangles, it is good practice to make sure that the 30°–60° triangle is 2″ taller than the 45° triangle.

Another triangle sometimes used is the *adjustable triangle*. This triangle combines the functions of a protractor and triangle; its

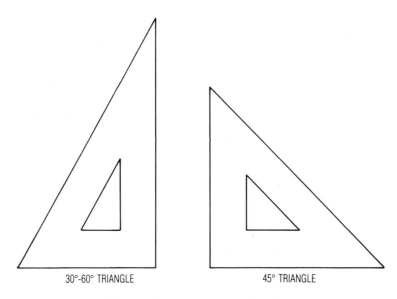

30°-60° TRIANGLE   45° TRIANGLE

Fig. 2-3. A common set of triangles.

hypotenuse can be set an any desired angle to within ½°. Because of its flexibility, some individuals prefer to use the adjustable triangle exclusively.

Curved rulers are known as irregular curves or French curves. They are used to draw curved lines other than circles (concentric curves). There are a variety of curves that can be purchased, but for most sheet metal work a general shaped curve will meet most requirements (Figure 2-4).

Scales are central to the accuracy of all drawings. A scale is a measuring device used to lay out and prepare drawings. There are four general types of scales available: mechanical, civil, architect's, and metric. As their names imply, each is classified according to its most common use. The scales of most importance to the sheet metal worker are the mechanical and architect's scales.

The mechanical scale is divided and numbered so that its scales are set at a fraction of an inch to an inch. In other words, the ¼″ scale would be used in drawings where ¼″ = 1″ (the drawing would be drawn one-fourth of actual size). The most common scales used here are ⅛, ¼, ½, and 1 inch to the inch. The architect's scale has similar fractional scales, but they are set to a fraction of an inch to a foot. Here, the ¼″ scale would represent ¼″ = 1′-0″. Common scales used in the architect's scale are ⅛, ¼, ⅜, ½, ¾, 1-½, and 3 inches to the foot.

The last category of basic drafting tools is *drafting instruments*. These tools are used to draw curved lines mechanically and/or transfer dimensions. Drafting instruments can be purchased as case instruments or independently.

Case instruments are a set of drafting instruments usually accompanied by various attachments. See Figure 2-5. Basically, a case instrument set would include various-size compasses and dividers. Compasses are used to draw circles and arcs, while dividers are used to transfer measurements. Some individuals, however, prefer to purchase their drawing instruments individually. They can then select the most appropriate instrument for their needs on an item-by-item basis.

PRINCIPLES OF ORTHOGRAPHIC PROJECTION

All drafting practices are based on the principles of orthographic projection, which is the method used to draw various views of an object. These views are what the object would appear as if viewed through imaginary planes (planes of projection) positioned about it. If these planes were drawn, they would appear as lines (edge views of planes) separating each view. Consequently, these lines are known as *cutting plane lines*.

Figure 2-6 is a comparison of perspective and orthographic

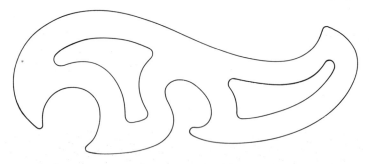

Fig. 2-4. A general shaped curve.

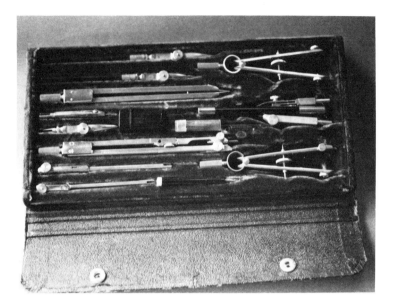

Fig. 2-5. Case instruments.

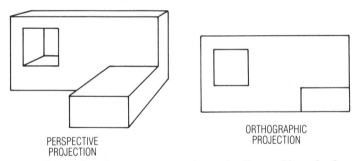

PERSPECTIVE
PROJECTION

ORTHOGRAPHIC
PROJECTION

Fig. 2-6. Comparison between perspective and orthographic projections
of the same object.

projection. In the first case, a transparent picture plane is placed
between the viewer's eye (station point) and the object. Where the
lines of sight intersect the picture plane, an image is formed. The
lines of sight are created by drawing lines from the station point to
the object.

In orthographic projection, the observer moves away from the
object until *infinity* is reached (a theoretical position). In this way,

the lines of sight do not meet at a station point, but are drawn parallel to one another. Furthermore, the lines of projection are drawn so that they are perpendicular to the plane of projection. The term "orthographic" is derived from the Greek term *orthos*, meaning straight or right, and *graphic* referring to drawings. Hence, orthographic projection is a projection method using straight and right (90°) drawn lines.

Using the projection plane as a basis, if we were to totally enclose an object by a set of picture planes that were 90° to one another, these planes would form a six-sided box. On each of these planes, projections can be used to show the front, top, right side, left side, bottom, and rear views of the object (Figure 2-7). These six views are known as the *six principal views* or projections.

In actual drafting practice, only three primary views are used: front, top, and right side. Only in rare instances are any of the other views incorporated into a drawing. When showing these primary views, it is critical that they be aligned as shown in the perpendicular projection planes. The top view should always be directly above the front view, and the right side view should always be to its right.

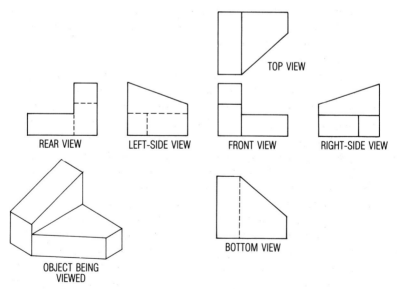

Fig. 2-7. Six principal views of orthographic projection.

One very important point should be brought out here: *true length lines*. These lines appear true size in views that they are parallel to. In other words, a line that is true length in the front view will be drawn parallel to that view's cutting plane line. When shown in its true length, however, it may not be parallel to any other views. This concept is very important in the development of many sheet metal patterns.

A basic consideration faced by the drawer is to decide which side of the object is the front view. This is left to the discretion of the individual, but should be selected on the basis that it is the view best describing the object. Hence, the front view is usually the most descriptive view of the object. An example of this is shown in Figure 2-8.

It is not always necessary to show three views of an object, especially in drawings of symmetrical objects. In Figure 2-9 only

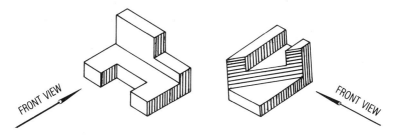

Fig. 2-8. Selecting the best frontal view.

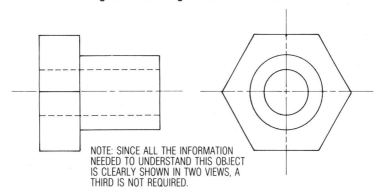

NOTE: SINCE ALL THE INFORMATION NEEDED TO UNDERSTAND THIS OBJECT IS CLEARLY SHOWN IN TWO VIEWS, A THIRD IS NOT REQUIRED.

Fig. 2-9. Object requiring only two views.

two views are needed. The top view would be the same as the front view. Since two views will adequately describe this object, then they are all that is required. Remember, never draw more or less than you need to present an object clearly.

DRAFTING CONVENTIONS AND PRACTICES

The use of established conventions and practices conveys information simply and clearly. Therefore, it becomes critical that sheet metal workers understand these procedures so that they will be able to produce, use, and interpret drawings that are necessary for their work. This section presents the basic conventions and practices frequently encountered in the sheet metal trade.

Lettering

An accurate and well-prepared drawing can be made difficult to interpret and understand with poor lettering techniques. Legible, clear, crisp lettering is essential if one is to read and understand dimensions, specifications, and notations that frequently accompany drawings. All letters should be Gothic capital letters (Figure 2-10). There are a few occasions when one will find lowercase lettering, but for those situations when sheet metal workers must prepare the drawing themselves, only capital letters should be used.

Each letter should have equal line density and weight, and be spaced evenly and neatly. The style of lettering may be either vertical or inclined. If inclined lettering is desired, it is recommended that the letters be slanted approximately 20° off perpendicular. The great majority of lettering will be done freehand. Mechanical lettering sets and typewriters are usually used only by professional drafters. It must be remembered that good lettering just does not happen—it requires hard work, practice, and patience.

Because lettering is used in various ways on a drawing, different

ABCDEFGHIJKLMNOPQRSTUVWXYZ
1234567890

Fig. 2-10. Simple Gothic lettering.

sized letters should be used for different purposes. Some recommended lettering sizes are as follows:

- Drawing titles, sections, and important notes should be lettered with a height of 3⁄16″ (4.762mm)
- All dimensions and general notes should have a height of 1⁄8″ (3.175mm)
- Dimensions and general notes that must be placed on crowded or small drawings should be made 3⁄32″ (2.381mm) high

Alphabet of Lines

As notations, specifications, and dimensions convey specific information, different types of lines are used for the same purpose. The *alphabet of lines* is an expression commonly used to describe the different types of lines used in drawings. Shown in Figure 2-11, these lines have varying thicknesses, are continuous, broken, or irregular. When used in a drawing, they each convey a specific message.

The application of these lines in a sheet metal drawing is shown and identified in Figure 2-12. A brief description of each follows:

1. *Construction lines* are drawn as light, thin, and continuous lines so that they can be easily erased. They are used for roughing in drawings, as guide lines for lettering, and for initial construction detailing. When drawn, a 4H lead, or harder, should be used.

2. *Visible lines* are thick, dark, continuous lines used to represent all edges of an object that are visible in the view.

3. *Hidden lines* are dashed lines of medium thickness, and are drawn about 1⁄8″ (3.175mm) long and evenly spaced approximately 1⁄16″ (1.588mm) apart. These lines are used to illustrate edges and other features that cannot be seen in a particular view—they are hidden from view. When seen in a drawing, the print reader should take note to look in another view for more information. It should be noted that if hidden lines confuse a view, then they will be omitted.

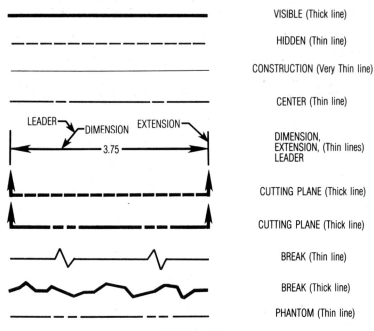

VISIBLE (Thick line)

HIDDEN (Thin line)

CONSTRUCTION (Very Thin line)

CENTER (Thin line)

LEADER
DIMENSION
EXTENSION
3.75

DIMENSION,
EXTENSION, (Thin lines)
LEADER

CUTTING PLANE (Thick line)

CUTTING PLANE (Thick line)

BREAK (Thin line)

BREAK (Thick line)

PHANTOM (Thin line)

Fig. 2-11. Alphabet of lines.

4. *Center lines* are dark thin lines drawn as broken lines composed of alternate long and short dashes. The long dashes are approximately ¾″ (19.05mm) to 1″ (25.4mm) long; the short ones are ⅛″ (3.175mm) long. These lines are evenly spaced, approximately ¹⁄₁₆″ (1.588mm) apart, and are used to indicate centers for holes, ducts, fans, casings, dampers, beams, columns, and openings.

5. *Dimension, extension, and leader lines* are used to provide dimensional specifications for an object. They are drawn as thin, dark, continuous lines that show the extent and direction of dimensions.

6. *Break lines* are used to show an object shorter than its true length. A short break is shown as a dark small wavy line, cylindrical breaks are illustrated by an "S" break line, and long breaks are drawn by a long line with a zig-zag line in the middle.

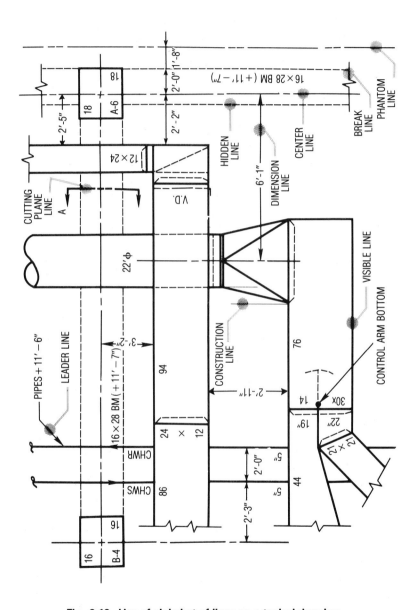

Fig. 2-12. Use of alphabet of lines on a typical drawing.

7. *Phantom lines* are drawn as dark, thin, broken lines where two short dashes follow a long line. The dashes are approximately ⅛" (3.175mm) long, while the long line is about ¾" to 1", separated by a ¹⁄₁₆" (1.588mm) space.

8. *Cutting plane lines* are used to view features of an object that are not clearly shown in conventional ways. By removing or cutting away a portion of the object, the features can be more clearly observed. Cutting plane lines are drawn as dark, thick broken lines. The broken lines may be shown as dashed lines, or one long and two short lines. At the end of the cutting plane line are two arrows, which are used to indicate the direction from which the cutaway section is being viewed.

Dimensioning

Two general types of dimensions are used in drawings: size and location. Size dimensions provide information relative to the characteristics and features of the object. By comparison, location dimensions tell the position of these characteristics and features. Figure 2-13 presents illustrations of both size and location dimensions.

The proper application and interpretation of dimensions are critical for accurate and precise work. To ensure that one interprets the exact meaning of dimensions, it is important to follow several

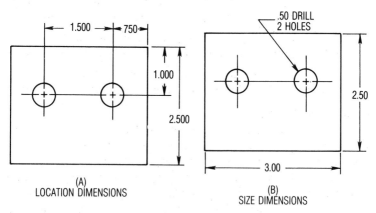

Fig. 2-13. Two basic types of dimensions.

basic dimensioning rules. Dimensioning rules that can simplify the process of dimensioning and interpreting dimensions are illustrated in Figure 2-14 and presented as follows:

1. The dimensioning of smaller features should always be kept closest to the object, after which the next largest dimensions are given.

2. The overall or largest dimension should be placed furthest from the object (the last dimension shown along a feature).

3. Size and location features will frequently require at least two dimensions.

4. Dimensions should be kept off the objects's surface and placed between views as often as possible.

5. Dimensions should not be shown from hidden lines.

6. In most situations, dimensions are shown from center lines, base lines, and/or finished surfaces.

7. All circles and holes should be dimensioned according to their diameter, while all arcs are dimensioned by radii.

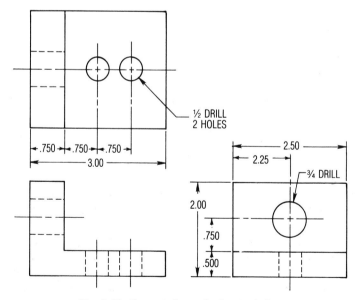

Fig. 2-14. Correct dimensioning techniques.

8. The position of all circular and symmetrical features should be located to their center line.

In addition to the general dimensioning practices just presented, several dimensioning practices are unique to the sheet metal industry (see Figure 2-12). One of these is the size dimensioning of ducts. These dimensions should always be placed at the points of connection, and given in inches. If the duct is square or rectangular, no inch designation is needed. On the other hand, if the duct is round, the inch symbol (″) must be shown. Spiral conduits, however, are dimensioned in terms of feet and inches.

The first dimension given for a rectangular duct is for the surface shown in that particular view, and is shown vertically. Round ducts should always use the diameter symbol (ϕ). If the size of the duct is the same throughout its run, then it does not need to be dimensioned at each connection.

Portions of a sheet metal drawing that are not drawn to scale should be noted with the abbreviation NTS, which stands for *not to scale*. Dimensions that show lineal duct measures do not use dimension lines or arrowheads. These dimensions are lettered directly onto the duct along the side of the running length. Angular dimensions for elbows and bevel-leg lengths are indicated in degrees at the vertex (degrees exceeding the straight line direction).

Abbreviations

An important factor in the preparation of any drawing is minimizing the amount of actual drawing time. One commonly used technique is the substitution of abbreviations for fully spelled-out words. As might be expected, a number of different terms are used in sheet metal drawings, many with their own particular abbreviations. Table 2-3 is a list of abbreviations frequently used in sheet metal drawings.

GEOMETRIC CONSTRUCTIONS

The preparation of sheet metal drawings often requires geometric construction procedures. Geometric construction consists of graphical procedures that are used to create certain shapes and forms for the purpose of solving problems. All geometric constructions are

Table 2-3
Common Abbreviations

Abbreviation	Meaning
AA	All around
ABV	Above
AC or A/C	Air conditioning
ACN	Asbestos-cloth neck
AD	Access door
ADJ	Adjustable
AF	Air filter or angle frame
AFF	Above finished floor
AHU	Air-handling unit
ALD	Automatic louver damper
AMBD	Automatic multiple-blade damper
ARCH	Architecture
ATC	Acoustical tile ceiling
AUTO	Automatic
B	Bottom
BD	Bottom down
BG	Bottom grille
BJ	Bar joist
BL	Building line
BLDG	Building
BM	Beam
BOD	Bottom of duct
BR	Bottom register
BS	Below slab
BTM	Bottom
BTU	British thermal units
BU	Bottom up
CCW	Counterclockwise
CCWBAD	Counterclockwise bottom angular down
CCWBAU	Counterclockwise bottom angular up
CCWBH	Counterclockwise bottom horizontal
CCWDB	Counterclockwise down blast
CCWTAD	Counterclockwise top angular down
CCWTAU	Counterclockwise top angular up
CCWTH	Counterclockwise top horizontal
CCWUB	Counterclockwise up blast
CD	Ceiling diffuser
CFM	Cubic feet per minute
CG	Ceiling grille
CH	Ceiling height
CIR	Circular or circle

Table 2-3
Common Abbreviations (Cont'd)

Abbreviation	Meaning
CIRC	Circumference
CL COLL	Clinch collar
COD	Clean out door
COL	Column
COMM	Commercial
CONN	Connection
CR	Ceiling register
CT	Cooling tower
CW	Clockwise
CWBAD	Clockwise bottom angular down
CWBAU	Clockwise bottom angular up
CWBH	Clockwise bottom horizontal
CWDB	Clockwise down blast
CWTAD	Clockwise top angular down
CWTAU	Clockwise top angular up
CWTH	Clockwise top horizontal
CWUB	Clockwise up blast
DEFL	Deflector
DEG	Degree
DET or DETL	Detail
DIA	Diameter
DMPR	Damper
DN	Down
DT	Duct turn or drop top
DWDI	Double width, double inlet
DWG	Drawing
EA	Exhaust air or each
EB	Equal brake
EL	Elbow
ELEC	Electric or electrical
ELEV or EL	Elevation
ENG or ENGR	Engineer
EQUIP	Equipment
EQUIV	Equivalent
ESH	Electric strip heater
ET	Equal taper
EXH	Exhaust
FA	Free area or fresh air
FAI	Fresh air intake
FB	Flat bottom
FC	Flexible connection or full corner

Table 2-3
Common Abbreviations (Cont'd)

Abbreviation	Meaning
FD	Fire damper
FIN FL or F Fl	Finished floor
FIN	Finished
FLBR	Fusible link bottom register
FLEX	Flexible
FLG	Flange
FLTR	Filter or fusible link top register
FP	Fireproof
FPM	Feet per minute
FS	Flat slip or full size
FSAA	Flat slips all around
FSB	Flat slip on bottom
FS&S	Full size and shape
FST	Flat slip on top
FT	Flat top
FTG	Fitting or footing
FVD	Friction volume damper
GA	Gage
GAL	Gallon
GALV	Galvanized
GC	General contractor
GI	Galvanized iron
GPM	Gallons per minute
HC	Heating coil or hanging ceiling
HD	Head
HGR	Hanger
HOR	Horizontal
HP	High pressure
HU	Humidifier
HV	Heating and ventilation
HVAC	Heating, ventilation, and air conditioning
ID	Inside dimension
INCL	Inclusive
IND or INDUST	Industrial
INT	Interior or internal
J	Joggle
JT	Joint
KD	Knock down
KE	Kitchen exhaust
KIT	Kitchen
LCC	Lead coated copper

Table 2-3
Common Abbreviations (Cont'd)

Abbreviation	Meaning
LDR	Leader
LE	Large end
LG	Long
LH	Left hand
LNG	Lining
LP	Low pressure
LVG	Leaving
MA	Matched angles
MAX	Maximum
MB	Mixing box
MD	Manual damper
MIN	Minimum or minute
MISC	Miscellaneous
MO	Masonry opening
NC	Normally closed
NEOP	Neopreme
NIC	Not in contact
NK	Neck
NO	Normally opened or number
NOM	Nominal
NORM	Normal
NR	Near
NTS	Not to scale
OA	Outside air or overall
OAI	Outside air intake
OAL	Overall length
OBD	Opposed-blade damper
OC	On center
OD	Outside diameter
OH	Opposite hand
OPNG	Opening
OPP	Opposite
OS	Outside
PBD	Parallel-blade damper
PT	Point or pint
PVC	Poly vinyl chloride
R	Radius or raw
RA	Return air
RE	Raw end
REQ or REQ'D	Required
RF	Roof fan
RH	Right hand or reheat

Table 2-3
Common Abbreviations (Cont'd)

Abbreviation	Meaning
RHC	Reheat coil
ROVD	Remotely operated volume damper
RPM	Revolutions per minute
RT	Raise top or right
SA	Supply air
SD	Splitter damper
SE	Small end
SECT	Section or sectional
SK	Sketch
SL	Slab
SLD	Slim line diffuser
SPL	Splitter
SQ	Square
SS	Stainless steel
ST or STD	Standard
STL	Steel
STR	Straight
SWSI	Single width single inlet
T	Top
TC	Telescoping collar
TD	Top down
TEMP	Temperature
TG	Top grille
THK	Thick
THR	Throat
TOD	Top of duct
TOIL	Toilet
TOS	Top of steel
TR	Top register
TU	Top up
TX	Toilet exhaust
TYP	Typical
UON	Unless otherwise noted
US	Underside of slab
VD	Volume damper
VE	Vibration eliminator
VERT	Vertical
VOL	Volume
VOLFD	Volume adjustable fire damper
WMS	Wire mesh screen
WT	Watertight or weight

based on the basic laws of geometry. In fact, most geometric procedures that are solved by mathematical methods were first derived
and solved by drawing procedures.

As might be expected, literally hundreds of geometric constructions are used in the drafting field. Since sheet metal workers are
not drafters, it is not necessary for them to know all, or even a great
number of, geometric constructions. There are, however, several
basic geometric construction procedures often found in sheet metal
work. The purpose of this section is to present those procedures
that are frequently used for solving common sheet metal problems.

Bisecting a Straight Line

The bisecting of a line consists of dividing it into two equal parts.
This simple procedure has many different applications to the sheet
metal trade. A common example of how this procedure is used is
in the location of the center line of a duct (Figure 2-15b).

Presented in Figure 2-15a is an illustration of the bisecting of
a straight line. Here, the given is line AB, and we must be able to
divide it into two equal parts. The solution to this problem is as
follows:

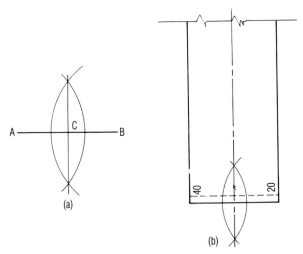

Fig. 2-15. Bisecting a line.

Step 1. With a compass, draw two arcs with a radius greater than one-half the length of line AB from points A and B.

Step 2. From where the two arcs intersect one another, draw a straight line.

Step 3. The point of bisection, point C, is where the connecting line intersects line AB.

Dividing a Line into a Number of Equal Divisions

Another common construction technique is to divide a given line into a number of equal parts. This construction technique is used, for example, when four supply ducts must be equally spaced along a central duct (Figure 2-16b).

Figure 2-16a shows the theoretical procedures used to divide a line into four equal parts. In our basic construction procedure, we are given line EF that must be divided into four equal parts. The procedure used is as follows:

Step 1. Draw a line from any end of line EF at any convenient angle.

Step 2. Along the drawn line, mark off four equal units and number them.

Step 3. From point 4, draw a line to point F.

Step 4. Draw lines from points 1, 2, and 3 that are parallel to line 4F, until they intersect line EF. These points of intersection will show the equal division of line EF.

Drawing a Perpendicular from a Point on a Line

A third geometric construction procedure that has practical use in sheet metal work is the construction of a perpendicular line that originates from a given point on a line. An example is the drawing of a perpendicular center line for a duct that intersects another at a 90° angle (Figure 2-17b).

Figure 2-17a is an illustration of the basic procedures used in the drawing of a perpendicular from a point on a line. In this illustration, we are given line MN and point P. From point P, we

are required to construct a perpendicular to line MN. The procedure
consists of the following steps:

Step 1. From point P, draw an arc so that it will intersect line
MN at two locations.

Step 2. With the two intersection points as a center, draw two
more arcs of greater radii, so that they intersect.

Step 3. Draw a straight line from point P to where the two
arcs intersect. This line will be the constructed
perpendicular.

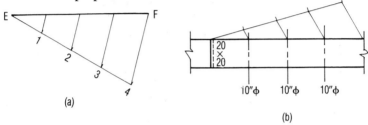

(a)

(b)

Fig. 2-16. Dividing a line into an equal number of parts.

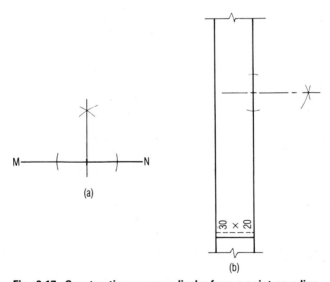

(a)

(b)

Fig. 2-17. Constructing a perpendicular from a point on a line.

Drawing a Perpendicular to a Line from a Point Off the Line

Similar to the previous construction problem is the drawing of a perpendicular line from a point in space to a given line. A practical application of this procedure would be to locate the perpendicular path of a line to another line from some outside location (Figure 2-18b).

In Figure 2-18a, we are given line CD and point K located somewhere in space. To construct a perpendicular from point K to line CD, the following procedure was used:

Step 1. From point K, draw an arc that will intersect line CD at two locations.

Step 2. Using these two intersecting points as centers, draw additional arcs of greater distance than the mid-point of line CD, so that they will intersect.

Step 3. Draw a straight line from point K to where the two arcs intersected. The perpendicular will be the intersecting line drawn between point K and the intersecting arcs.

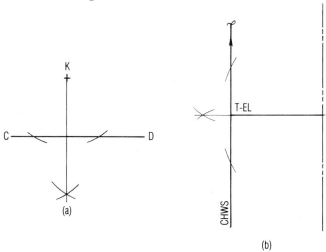

Fig. 2-18. Constructing a perpendicular from a point in space to a line.

Drawing Parallel Lines

The drawing of a parallel line to an existing line is another geometric construction technique with wide application. One of the more common applications for this procedure is to locate the center line of a duct that is to be constructed parallel to an existing wall (Figure 2-19b).

Presented in Figure 2-19a is line FG, to which another line must be drawn parallel at a given distance. The geometric construction procedure used is as follows:

Step 1. Select any two points on line FG and draw two arcs at a radius equal to the desired distance that the lines are to be separated.

Step 2. Draw a line tangent to the two arcs. The drawn tangent will be the constructed parallel.

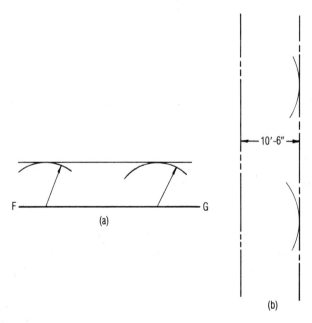

Fig. 2-19. Constructing a parallel.

Bisecting an Angle

As the name implies, the bisecting of an angle is its division into two equal angles. An example of how angle bisections are used in sheet metal work is the determination of the center of two bisecting ducts that intersect at a given angle (Figure 2-20b).

The standard procedure used to bisect a given angle is illustrated in Figure 2-20a. The following steps were used in the bisecting of angle BAC:

Step 1. Using A as the center point, strike an arc so that it will intersect sides AB and AC of angle BAC.

Step 2. From the two intersection points, strike two additional arcs so that they will intersect one another.

Step 3. Draw a straight line from point A to the point where the arcs intersected. This line will be the line of bisection for angle BAC.

SUMMARY

There are times when sheet metal workers must be able to prepare—as well as interpret—construction and mechanical drawings. It is therefore important that they have a clear understanding of the basic principles of drafting.

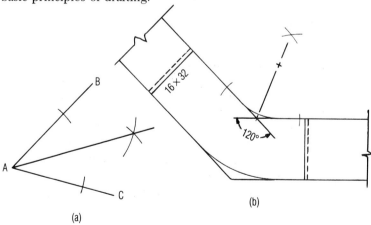

Fig. 2-20. Bisecting an angle.

One of the most important factors necessary for preparing clear and accurate drawings is using appropriate drafting materials and tools. There is a wide variety of drafting materials and media available on the market today, so one should take care in their selection. The most common type of drafting paper used is called vellum; others are cloth and polyester film. The vast majority of drawings prepared will have been done using leads, which come in various degrees of hardness, ranging from very soft to very hard.

The drafting tools selected should include only the most basic ones. The first is a drawing board, or simple drafting table, that will provide a drawing surface of about 31″ × 42″ (787.4mm × 1066.8mm). Next, is a T-square, for drawing horizontal lines. In a few cases, parallels or a drafting machine may be required. For drawing vertical and standard angular lines, a set of triangles is recommended. A set of case instruments or individual compasses and dividers would be used to round out a well-equipped set of drafting tools.

All drawings are based on the concepts of orthographic projection. This drawing procedure provides for six views of an object. Only three of these are commonly used: front, top, and right side views. To clarify a drawing, clear lettering should be used for all dimensions, notations, specifications, and directions. There is also a series of standard lines, known as the alphabet of lines, that are used for showing different features of an object. The lines most often found in sheet metal drawings are construction lines, visible lines, hidden lines, center lines, dimension, extension, and leader lines, break lines, phantom lines, and cutting plane lines.

To minimize the amount of time spent on drawings, especially when noting specifications and procedures, common abbreviations are used. These abbreviations are standardized throughout the industry. To prepare sheet metal drawings accurately requires knowledge of how to graphically produce various geometrical forms. The procedure used for drawing these forms is known as geometric construction.

REVIEW QUESTIONS

1. What is the most common type of drawing media used for the preparation of sheet metal drawings?

2. What lead hardness ratings should be used when preparing a drawing? Explain the advantage of stick lead holders over pencils.

3. Make a list of the basic drafting supplies, tools, and equipment that would be needed by a sheet metal worker.

4. Briefly explain application of the following categories of lines: visible, hidden, center, extension, cutting plane, and phantom lines.

5. List the basic guidelines that should be followed when dimensioning a drawing.

6. Explain the meaning of the following abbreviations: AFF, BJ, CCWBH, DIA, EL, FLBR, GPM, LP, OA, SLD, TOD, VOL, and WMS.

7. Draw a line 2.5″ in length and bisect it.

8. Draw a line 5″ in length, and locate a point 2″ above that line, anywhere along its length. Construct a perpendicular from that point to the line.

9. Divide a 7″ (177.8mm) line into five equal divisions.

10. Draw a 145° angle and bisect it.

PART II

LAYOUT AND PATTERN
DEVELOPMENT

CHAPTER 3

Basic Concepts of Sheet Metal Drawing

Unlike many trade areas, sheet metal work often involves the use of two basic types of drawings. The first is known as a *layout drawing*, where a sheet metal part, unit, or system is drawn and fully dimensioned. Examples of sheet metal products that incorporate this type of drawing are duct systems, brackets, blanks, and chassis. The second type of sheet metal drawing is known as the *development*. Developments are "stretch-outs" or patterns of the product itself, and are directly used in making the part. This chapter describes both layout and development drawings.

LAYOUT DRAWINGS

Layout drawings are very important, especially when one needs information about dimensional sizes, product materials, and installation. Generally speaking, there are two categories of layout drawings. The first is used for a specific part, such as a sheet metal bracket or brace. Here, the item is shown in traditional orthographic views. The second is primarily used in showing HVAC (Heating-Ventilation/Air Conditioning) systems for residential and commercial structures. As can be surmised, the first type of layout drawing has primary applications in the manufacturing industry, while the second is commonly found in the construction industry.

Precision Sheet Metal Drawings

There is a significant difference in the type of sheet metal drawing used in the construction and manufacturing industries. This difference is primarily attributed to the need for more precise dimensions and tolerances required for manufacturing. Two manufacturing industries that employ close tolerance sheet metal work are electronics and instrumentation.

Sheet metal work in the electronics and instrumentation industries often requires tolerances to be kept to within .001″ (.0254mm) or .0005″ (.0127mm). For this reason such work is referred to as *precision sheet metal work*. For the purpose of discussion, precision work will be defined as working with thin-gauged sheet metal to within machine-shop tolerances.

Products that are made from precision sheet metal processes are first machined in the flat. They are then folded and/or formed into shape while holding specified tolerances. Drawings that are used to show these products must also provide for bend allowances, which are either calculated by formula or derived from charts. Figure 3-1 shows a drawing for a precision sheet metal housing.

When working with precision sheet metal drawings, several

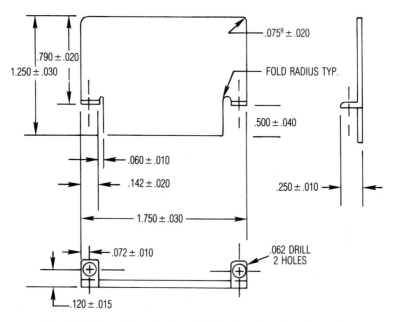

Fig. 3-1. A precision sheet metal drawing for a housing unit.

terms must be understood. Some of these terms are illustrated in Figure 3-2. Definitions of commonly used terms follow:

- *Bend allowance.* The amount of linear material that is required for a bend from bend line to the other bend line.
- *Bend angle.* The entire angle through which the sheet metal is bent.
- *Bend line.* A line that is the tangent between the bend and the flat surface. All bends have two bend lines.
- *Blank.* The flat piece of sheet metal that is pre-cut to approximate finished size. Once the blank is cut, it is then machined, folded, and/or formed into the finished product.
- *Center line of bend.* The radial line that passes through the bend radius. It is the bisector of the angle between the bend lines.
- *Developed length.* The total length of a flat pattern.
- *Flat pattern.* The pattern used to lay out on a blank.
- *Mold line.* An imaginary point formed by the intersection of the extended projections of the two flat surfaces.

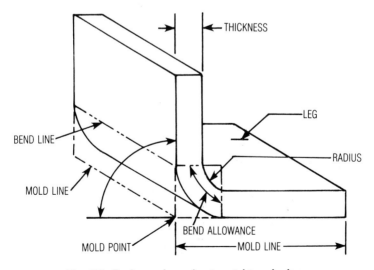

Fig. 3-2. Basic precison sheet metal terminology.

- *Set-back.* The amount of length reduction that occurs from a bend.

When sheet metal is bent, the length of the bend will be affected by the type of metal used. As shown in Figure 3-3, in the bend area there are three behaviors exhibited by the metal. The first is metal compression, which is exhibited along the inside radius of the bend. The second is metal stretching, which occurs along the outside radius of the bend. The third is a modification of the first two. The area, or line, where metal compression and stretching meet is called the *median line.*

The use of the median line is important for calculating bend allowances. Since various metals perform differently from one another, many manufacturers will run test bends on their stock to determine the median line. This normally requires the bending of at least two blanks. Any adjustments needed for bending can then be made on the subsequent blank.

Good manufacturing practice dictates that some form of relief be provided in the material for bending. This is normally made by a *relief notch.* The use of notches eliminates any wrinkling or buckling in the part and minimizes internal stresses in the metal itself.

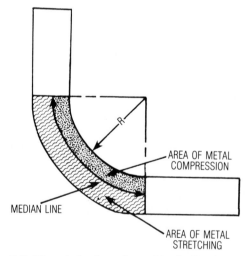

Fig. 3-3. Three behaviors of metal in the bend area.

There are two general types of notches: straight and radius (Figure 3-4). The first, a straight corner cut, is made at 45° and allows for easy folding of the flanges. The second, a radius notch, offers the same advantage as the straight notch, but is more common where appearance is important.

A good percentage of sheet metal work is presently being machined on numerically controlled (N/C) equipment. As a result, many drawings are prepared that use a system of dimensioning known as *datum dimensions*. This is based on a datum point or line from which all dimensions are referenced. In terms of the N/C machine, the datum is the reference (or beginning) point from which all machine movements and operations are based. Figure 3-5 gives an example of a precision sheet metal drawing that uses datum dimensioning.

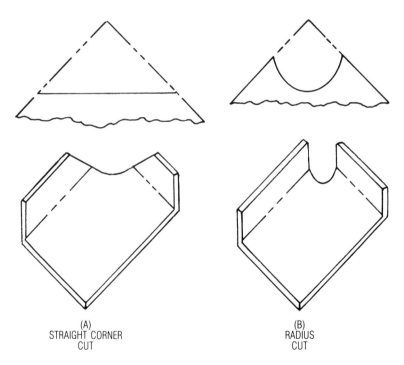

(A)
STRAIGHT CORNER
CUT

(B)
RADIUS
CUT

Fig. 3-4. Two basic types of notches.

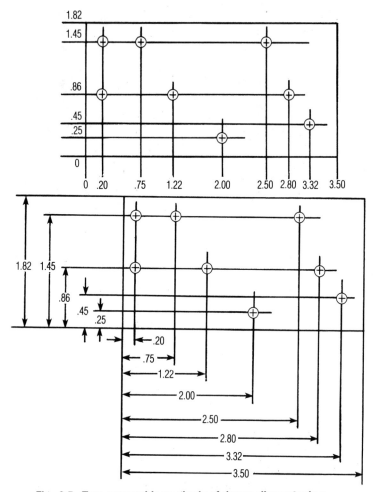

Fig. 3-5. Two acceptable methods of datum dimensioning.

HVAC Plans

One of the most frequent applications of sheet metal layout drawings in the construction industry involves HVAC plans. These drawings are employed to show how ambient (existing), cooled, and heated air can be circulated through a building. The drawings give all specifications for the heating and cooling system within residential and commercial buildings.

74

Normally, the HVAC drawing will be superimposed onto an existing floor plan layout (see Figure 3-6). In some situations, it is necessary to show how the ductwork will be viewed through a sectional view. HVAC drawings will include drawings for each floor serviced by the system, and give dimensions and specifications for devices such as dampers, thermostats, ductwork, distributors, diffusers, furnaces, and air-conditioning units.

A well-developed HVAC drawing will incorporate the following characteristics:

1. There will be a floor plan layout for every level serviced by the HVAC system.

2. System units, such as furnaces and air-conditioning, will be dimensionally located.

3. The size, location, and capacity of all outlets will be given.

4. All ducts will be laid out for each room and meet minimum system requirements.

5. Rectangular ducts are drawn as viewed and dimensioned. Circular ducts may be drawn with single-line symbols and accompanying sizes.

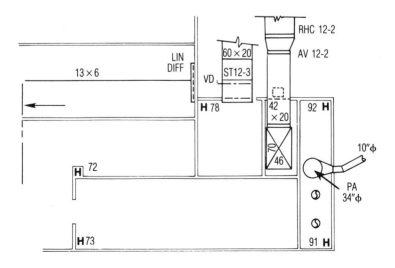

Fig. 3-6. HVAC drawing incorporated into a floor plan.

6. Gaseous and liquid pipes are drawn as single-line schematics.

7. The HVAC system will be drawn in a heavier line weight than the floor plan layout.

8. When necessary, structural details may be given.

DEVELOPMENT DRAWINGS

The development drawing is perhaps the most important type of drawing encountered in the sheet metal field. A development is a drafting term that refers to the actual layout of a sheet stock's pattern. The pattern is what makes it possible to produce a box, carton, duct, or chassis. Without a pattern, it would be extremely difficult to execute sheet metal work. Within the scheme of sheet metal drawings, the development is made after the layout drawing has been prepared. Most specifications are obtained from the layout drawing.

Generally, two types of patterns can be developed: ruled and double-curved surfaces. Ruled surface patterns can be developed into a single surface pattern, while double-curved surfaces require multiple surface patterns. An example of a double-curved surface would be a sphere or ellipsoid. Since these patterns are rarely found in most sheet metal pattern requirements, this section will only deal with ruled surface patterns.

Ruled surface patterns can be further divided into two subcategories. The first, plane surface patterns, are for objects that only have flat surfaces, such as a box or pyramid. The second subcategory, warped surface patterns, is for objects that have one or more planes that are curved (warped). Accurate and precise patterns can only be developed for the plane surface pattern, while close *approximations* are developed for warped surface patterns.

Rectangular Prism Development

The development of a rectangular prism is one of the most basic types of patterns used in sheet metal work. Rectangular prisms are found in ductwork, housings, chassis, and other common sheet metal products. Figure 3-7 presents an example of the development of such a prism, where the pattern is laid out in line with the front

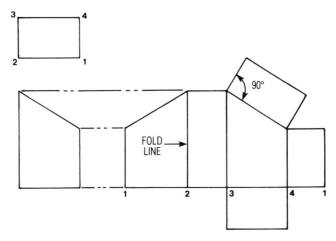

Fig. 3-7. Development of a rectangular prism.

view of the object. The following procedure is used in this development:

Step 1. Draw the top and front view of the prism and number all corners appropriately.

Step 2. Project construction lines away from the front view so that all height dimensions will be carried over to the stretch-out.

Step 3. In a clockwise manner, start with corner 1 in the top view, and transfer the measurement of each side of the prism to the stretch-out.

Step 4. Join the points of each plane of the stretch-out.

Step 5. Project 90° lines to form bevel surfaces and bottom, and lay off their widths with a compass.

Step 6. Join the remaining points, and add material needed for seams as required.

Cylinder Development

A number of cylindrically shaped objects are made of sheet metal, including containers, ducts, and supports. Figure 3-8 is an illustra-

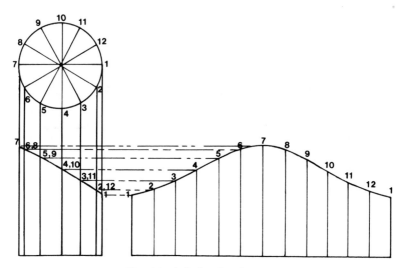

Fig. 3-8. Cylinder development.

tion of the development of a cylinder that has an inclined bevel. The procedures used for its development are as follows:

Step 1. Draw the top and front view of the cylinder, and divide the top view into a given number of equal parts and number them.

Step 2. Project the equal divisions about the cylinder's circumference to the front view, and number accordingly.

Step 3. Project into the stretch-out all height dimensions given in the front view.

Step 4. Determine the length of the stretch-out by either (a) transferring measurements between the equal spaces in the top view, or (b) mathematically calculating the circumference of the circle. If the second method is used, you must then divide the line into the same number of equal divisions as shown in the top view.

Step 5. Mark off the height for each appropriate division and connect with a curve.

Step 6. Allow material for required seam.

Pyramid Development

The development of a pyramid, especially one that is truncated (cut off at the top), is commonly used in duct systems. Truncated pyramid parts are used to join two rectangular ducts of different dimensions (smaller to larger). Figure 3-9 is an illustration of the development of a truncated pyramid. Note that this process involves finding the true length of lines, since they are not shown in either the top or front view. The procedures used here are as follows:

Step 1. Draw the front and top view of the pyramid and number all corners.

Step 2. Since the edges of the corner appear foreshortened in both views, their true length must be found. This is accomplished by revolving edges in the top view, so that they will be parallel to the front view (frontal plane of projection), and transferring the new position to the front view. The front view position will show the edges in true length. Note that the true length lines are labeled "TL."

Step 3. With the true length of the edge, draw an arc whose radius will equal the distance from the vertex of the pyramid to the base.

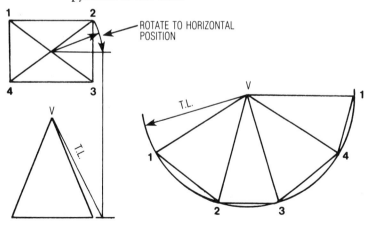

Fig. 3-9. Pyramid development.

Step 4. Along the arc, measure off the base of the pyramid by transferring measurements from the top view, and draw a line from these base points to the vertex.

Step 5. For each edge of the pyramid, measure off the true length of each edge onto the stretch-out.

Step 6. Allow sufficient materials for a seam.

Cone Development

Similar in application to truncated pyramids, truncated cones are used to connect round ducts of varying sizes. In addition, their development also involves the use of radial lines (radiating from a vertex) and the determination of true length lines. Figure 3-10 illustrates how a truncated right cone is developed. The procedures used are as follows:

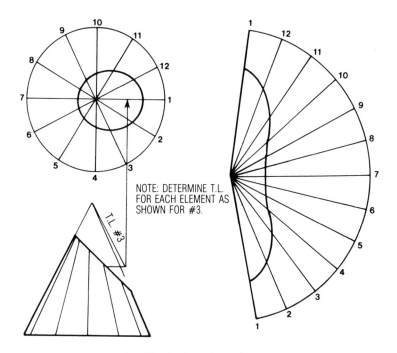

NOTE: DETERMINE T.L. FOR EACH ELEMENT AS SHOWN FOR #3.

Fig. 3-10. Cone development.

Step 1. Draw the front and top views of the truncated cone.

Step 2. Divide the top view into a given number of equal parts; number and transfer the divisions to the front view. Note that all divisions will radiate to the vertex of the cone.

Step 3. With V-1 as true length, strike an arc for the development of the cone.

Step 4. Transfer the lengths of each cord (division lines) from the top view to the stretch-out.

Step 5. Provide for additional material for a seam.

Transition Piece Development

A transition section is a part of a duct system that can accommodate two differently shaped ducts—usually round and rectangular. These transition pieces are used in either gaseous or liquid systems, where pipes or ducts of different shapes must be joined. A typical development for a transition piece is presented in Figure 3-11. The following procedures are used:

Step 1. Draw the front and top view of the transition piece.

Step 2. Divide the circular section into equal parts and project the divisions to the corners. These lines will represent the different bend lines of the transition piece.

Step 3. Determine the true lengths for each bend line.

Step 4. Make a seam midway through one of the flat planes, and begin stretch-out at that point.

Step 5. Strike true length arcs to form the stretch-out for the flat section.

Step 6. Continue successive stretch-outs for each adjacent triangle. Note that the radiating lines that form the circular opening are a series of triangles.

Step 7. Allow for additional material for the seam.

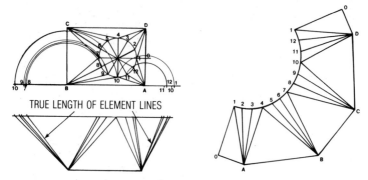

Fig. 3-11. Transition piece development.

DESIGN DRAWINGS AND SPECIFICATIONS

The most common type of design drawings encountered by sheet metal workers are known as mechanicals. These are schematic drawings designed to show the arrangement of equipment and system devices, as well as size requirements for pipes and ducts. Many times, location dimensions are left to the discretion of the sheet metal worker, though these dimensions are often given. If location dimensions are not given, a reason will normally be noted on the drawing.

HVAC Drawings

Of major importance to sheet metal workers are heating-ventilation and air-conditioning drawings. These drawings will consist of floor plans, layouts for mechanical equipment rooms (MER), plan and sectional views, details, schedules (listing of specific equipment), flow control diagrams, and riser diagrams. Depending on the size of the project, the drawing will be titled with a prefaced HVAC, AC (air-conditioning), M (mechanical), or H (heating).

Though most sheet metal work will involve ductwork for the HVAC system, drawings will also include information about pipes for heating and cooling, fuel lines, and pneumatic tube systems. Most drawings will use double-line layouts, though single-line schematics are favored by many drafters. Thus, the sheet metal worker should become familiar with both types of symbols. Figure 3-12 shows duct drafting symbols.

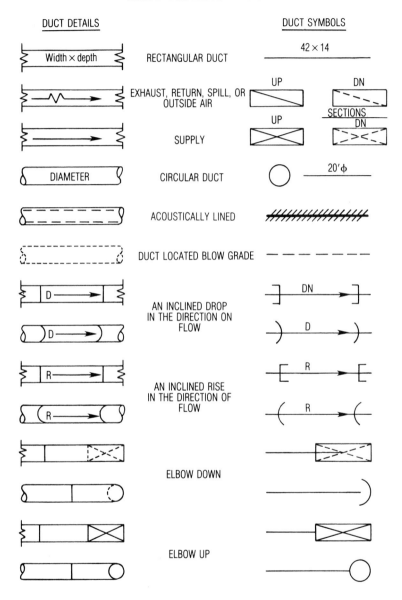

Fig. 3-12a. Duct drafting symbols.

DETAILS   SYMBOLS

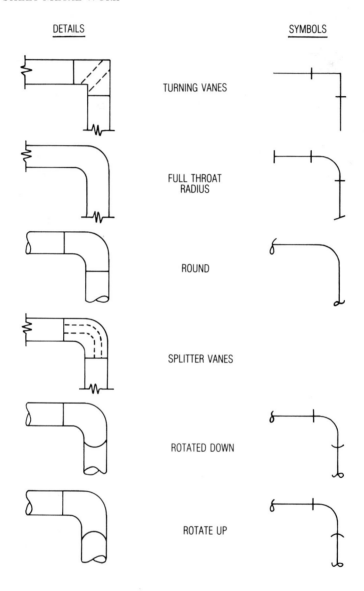

TURNING VANES

FULL THROAT
RADIUS

ROUND

SPLITTER VANES

ROTATED DOWN

ROTATE UP

Fig. 3-12b. Duct elbow symbols.

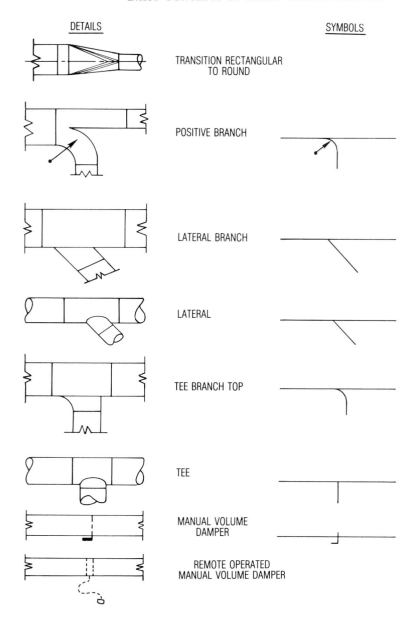

DETAILS

SYMBOLS

TRANSITION RECTANGULAR
TO ROUND

POSITIVE BRANCH

LATERAL BRANCH

LATERAL

TEE BRANCH TOP

TEE

MANUAL VOLUME
DAMPER

REMOTE OPERATED
MANUAL VOLUME DAMPER

Fig. 3-12c. Duct branch symbols.

DETAILS   SYMBOLS

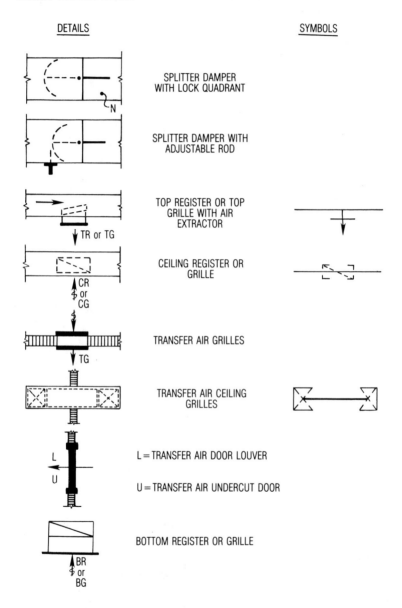

SPLITTER DAMPER
WITH LOCK QUADRANT

SPLITTER DAMPER WITH
ADJUSTABLE ROD

TOP REGISTER OR TOP
GRILLE WITH AIR
EXTRACTOR

CEILING REGISTER OR
GRILLE

TRANSFER AIR GRILLES

TRANSFER AIR CEILING
GRILLES

L = TRANSFER AIR DOOR LOUVER

U = TRANSFER AIR UNDERCUT DOOR

BOTTOM REGISTER OR GRILLE

Fig. 3-12d. Other duct drafting symbols.

Floor Plans

Individual working drawings are usually adequate to show an entire floor plan HVAC system. Some buildings, however, are very large and require two or more drawings to adequately show the details for a single floor. When this occurs, *match lines* are used. Match lines are individual lines that are terminated and labeled (e.g., continued on drawing AC-2) so that one will know exactly where the plan continues on subsequent drawings.

As already mentioned, HVAC floor plans are used to show the general arrangement of the system's duct distribution, inlets, and outlets. By using these drawings, and structural and architectural specifications, the sheet metal worker is responsible for constructing and installing air-system components so that they will conform to the engineering plan. Because floor plans do vary, it is important that the sheet metal worker visually analyze the plan to become aware of any special type of construction and/or material needed for the job.

Materials used for underground or below-grade duct systems will often require special coatings and construction. These sheet materials need to be special ordered and consequently require additional lead time. Single and double duct systems that run to terminal units or pressure reducing valve controls are commonly referred to as high-pressure ducts. Such duct systems require special considerations that are usually noted on the plan itself. An example is the requiring of an acoustical lining for ductwork that is located downstream from a pressure reducing box.

Grilles, registers, and diffusers come in various styles, designs, and types. For this reason, the drawing must be carefully checked to see if a specific type has been noted. If not, the specific type may be left to the discretion of the individual worker. Most drawings, however, will make note not only of where the grilles and devices are to be located, but also their size and type.

Mechanical Equipment Room

Drawings that are not often considered in the area of sheet metal work are for the mechanical equipment room (MER). More commonly referred to as fan rooms, these areas provide for the storage and operation of large equipment, ducts, and pipes. MERs are primarily used where floor space is at a premium, or where special platforms must be constructed to support HVAC equipment.

Of primary concern to the sheet metal worker is the type of duct and material required for each fan, drive, and inlet box arrangement. In most situations, a notation system will be used to indicate the arrangement design. The basic abbreviations used are SW for single width, DW for double width, SI for single inlet, and DI for double inlet. The basic designs (Figure 3-13) for fan arrangements are as follows:

- **No. 1, SW, SI**. Belt drive or direct connection where the wheel is overhung, with bearings on the base.

- **No. 2, SW, SI**. Belt drive or direct connection where the wheel is overhung, and the bearings are in a bracket supported by a fan housing.

- **No. 3, SW, SI**. Belt drive or direct connection where one bearing is on each side and supported by the fan housing.

- **No. 4, SW, SI**. Direct drive only, where the wheel is overhung on a prime mover shaft. There are no bearings on the fan, and the base is mounted on integrally direct connected prime mover.

- **No. 7, SW, SI**. Belt drive only on direct connection, with a No. 3 arrangement, plus the base as the prime mover.

- **No. 8, SW, SI**. Belt drive or direct connection with a No. 1 arrangement, plus a base for prime mover.

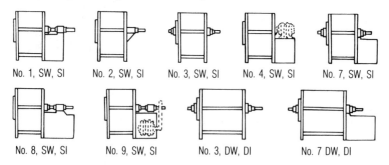

Fig. 3-13. Fan, drive, and inlet box designs.

- **No. 9, SW, SI**. Belt drive only with a No. 1 arrangement for mounting the prime mover on the side of the base.

- **No. 3, DW, DI**. Belt drive or direct connection, with one bearing on each side and supported by a fan housing.

- **No. 7, DW, DI**. Belt drive or direct connection with a No. 3 arrangement, plus a base for prime mover.

HVAC Equipment

As might be expected, several different types of equipment are used in HVAC systems, many with primary application in commercial settings. Because it would be extremely difficult to list every type of equipment and device used in these systems, this overview presents the more common product types.

Air Moving Device.

Also referred to as an AMD, this device is a power-driven piece of equipment used to provide for the continuous movement of a given volume of air.

Central Station Units.

This is a factory-produced product specifically designed to carry out certain functions, such as air circulation, cleaning, heating, cooling, and humidifying or dehumidifying. Not included in this category are refrigeration units, self-contained air-conditioners, and other units designed for room installation.

There are several categories of central station units found in HVAC systems. These include draw-through central station units designed with heat exchangers upstream of the fan, blow-though central station units with heat exchangers downstream of the fan, air-conditioning units for cooling, and heating and ventilating units.

Industrial, Axial, and Propeller-Type Fans.

Fans are used to promote airflow through a given system, and are considered to be AMDs. Examples of different types of fan AMDs are axial fans that provide for airflow through an impeller that is aligned parallel to a rotating axial, tubeaxial fans that have no guide vanes through which the air is blown, vaneaxial fans that have a set of inlet and/or discharge vanes, and propeller fans that have a propeller type disc mounted on a ring or plate.

Power Roof Ventilators.

Another type of AMD is the power roof ventilator. This unit is specifically designed to move air out of a building, through the roof. The unit should always be weather resistant, and fitted to the shape and pitch of the roof. The impeller, which can be centrifugal, axial, or an integral drive, is supported by a specially designed base that allows for rotation.

DUCT DESIGN CONSIDERATIONS

The majority of duct designing will be accomplished by engineers or engineering consulting firms. It is important, however, for sheet metal workers to become familiar with those factors influencing the design and layout of duct systems. An understanding of duct design makes the interpretation of drawings requiring rerouting of ducts, calculating tap sizes, resizing ducts, and incorporating other similar changes in duct systems easier to interpret.

Central to duct design are calculations that measure the amount of air flow through the systems. The *British Thermal Unit* (Btu) is the base unit of measure for heat transfer. One Btu is the amount of energy (heat) that is needed to increase the temperature of one unit of water one unit degree Fahrenheit at atmospheric pressure. The heating and cooling *loads* of a duct system are given in terms of Btuh, or British Thermal Unit Hour.

Heating and Cooling Quantities

Heating and cooling quantities are commonly referred to as *loads*. Heat load is calculated as the sum of losses of the heat transmission through an enclosed area, plus the amount of heat needed for ventilation and infiltration, minus any heat increases caused by internal heat gains. This load is expressed in terms of the supply-air volume (Q) in cubic feet per minute (CFM). The basic formula used is

$$Q = H/(1.085)(\Delta T)$$

where H = Btuh or heat load in space

$\Delta T =$ the difference in temperature between the supplied air and the temperature desired in the space

This formula would be used, for example, if we were required to find the amount of heat needed to heat a small building having a heat loss of 150,000 Btuh, when the building temperature is to be maintained at 72°F and the supplied air temperature is 112°F. The solution to this problem is as follows:

$$Q = 150,000/(1.085)(112 - 72)$$
$$= 150,000/(1.085)(40)$$
$$= 150,000/(43.4)$$
$$= 3,456 \text{ cfm}$$

Cooling loads are calculated as the sum of the external and internal gain in heat and moisture. The basic formula used to calculate the Q through a series of cooling coils is

$$Q = H/(4.5)(iwb - fwb)$$

where $iwb =$ the initial wet-bulb temperature (total heat content)
$fwb =$ the final wet-bulb temperature (total heat content)

A table that shows the amount of heat removed per pound of dry air Btu at specific wet-bulb temperatures is critical in the use of this formula. Table 3-1 is a partial presentation of this data.

This formula and table would be used when we must calculate the amount of air needed for a room with a total heat gain of 80,000 Btu. The initial wet-bulb temperature feeding into the cooling coils is 72°F, and the final wet-bulb temperature (of the air leaving the cooling coils) is 64°F. The solution to this problem would be as follows:

$$Q = 80,000/(4.5)(6.50)$$
$$= 80,000/29.25$$
$$= 2,698 \text{ cfm}$$

Air Pressure

The architectural design of modern buildings often requires construction techniques that employ minimum usage of windows, or windows with a movable sash. In these cases, the physical comfort

Table 3-1
Heat Removed per Pound of Dry Air

Final Wet-Bulb Temp. (°F)	Initial Wet-Bulb Temperature (°F)						
	66	67	68	69	70	71	72
60	4.36	5.14	5.94	6.76	7.60	8.46	9.34
61	3.67	4.45	5.25	6.07	6.91	7.77	8.65
62	2.97	3.75	4.55	5.37	6.21	7.07	7.95
63	2.25	3.03	3.83	4.65	5.49	6.35	7.23
64	1.52	2.30	3.10	3.92	4.76	5.62	6.50
65	.77	1.55	2.35	3.17	4.01	4.87	5.75
66		.78	1.58	2.40	3.24	4.10	4.98
67			.80	1.62	2.46	3.32	4.20
68				.82	1.66	2.52	3.40
69					.84	1.70	2.58
70						.86	1.74
71							.88

of the building's occupants is primarily handled by the mechanical ventilation system. Because of the relatively high airtight characteristics of these buildings, consideration must be given to the amount of air pressure provided for a given area of space.

Designs that call for the introduction of outside air relief vents must be used to prevent a positive pressure build-up. If no outside air is available, negative pressure can build, requiring the use of exhaust systems for air recirculation and reclamation. As might be expected, such designs often require extensive ductwork systems.

The ventilation of air for personal comfort may take various forms, such as outside air treatment through a conditioning unit, or recirculation of air through a charcoal filter system. The specific amount of air needed for each individual will vary. Standard rules of thumb call for a minimum of 5 cfm per person for nonsmoking areas, to a maximum of 30 cfm in heavy smoking areas.

SUMMARY

There are two general types of drawings encountered in the sheet metal field. The first are layout drawings that are used for specific parts and total systems. Layout drawings used for parts are usually production-oriented drawings where products must be held to close tolerances, and are known as precision sheet metal drawings. The second category of layout drawing is commonly found in HVAC drawings, where an entire duct system is shown for a building or structure.

The second general type of sheet metal drawing is known as the development. This drawing is used to produce a sheet metal pattern for a particular unit or part. To develop a pattern requires a basic knowledge of drafting procedures. Several basic types of developments can be found in most sheet metal work: rectangular prism, cylinder, pyramid, cone, and transition developments.

Mechanicals are the most common design drawings that sheet metal workers use. Basically, these are schematic drawings that illustrate the arrangement of equipment, system devices, ducts, and pipes within a building. In these drawings, dimensions may or may not be given, and are dependent on the design of the system and skill of the tradesman. Elements of these mechanicals include HVAC systems drawn onto floor plans, mechanical equipment room construction and arrangement, and details for specific HVAC equipment.

Because engineers make a majority of the design and drawing of ductwork systems, the sheet metal worker should become aware of the elements involved in the design function. In all, there are three important factors considered: heating quantities, cooling quantities, and air pressure.

REVIEW QUESTIONS

1. Briefly explain what a precision sheet metal drawing is and where it is primarily used.
2. Define the following terms:

    bend allowance   bend angle
    bend line   blank

center line of bend   developed length
flat pattern   mold line
set-back

3. What are HVAC drawings?

4. What are developments? Explain their importance to sheet metal workers.

5. What is the relationship between floor plans and HVAC drawings?

6. Explain the function of MERs.

7. Identify common types of HVAC equipment.

8. Explain the meaning of the following notations:

Btu   Btuh
iwb   fwb
H ΔT
cfm

9. Briefly explain how heating and cooling quantities are calculated.

10. Of what importance is building air pressure?

CHAPTER 4

Sheet Metal Standards and Specifications

Sheet metal materials and procedures are commonly found in many different industries. As already discussed, the levels of accuracy and means of production will vary greatly from one industry to another. Two sheet metal fields considered to be highly specialized, requiring unique standards and specifications, are the aircraft and the precision sheet metal industries. Such specialized fields, however, are beyond the scope of this book.

The industry that employs perhaps the most significant number of sheet metal workers (in terms of all-around skill requirements) is the construction industry. This industry encompasses both structural and architectural fields. Examples of sheet metal products used in these fields are rectangular and round ducts, casings, gutters, downspouts, screens, siding, and roofs. As a result, a number of standards and specifications have been developed within the construction industry for these products. This chapter presents the standards and specifications for sheet metal products used in the construction industry.

DUCT SYSTEMS

The design of modern buildings and structures has necessitated varying sizes of ducts. Duct systems have therefore been designed to carry varying amounts of air at different velocities. Within the industry, duct systems are broken down into two major categories: *low velocity* and *high velocity* duct systems. It should be noted that as air velocity increases, so does the loss of duct friction. As duct friction increases, so does the amount of pressure needed to force the air through the system. For this reason, the terms "velocity" and "pressure" are used together. Hence, high or low velocity describes high or low pressure/velocity systems.

In the construction industry, low velocity ducts are usually found in conjunction with single duct systems, while high velocity ducts are normally associated with dual duct systems. A more precise difference, however, is the air velocity, in feet per minute (fpm), within the system. All standards define high velocity duct standards in terms of velocities that exceed 2,000 fpm. Those under 2,000 fpm are considered low velocity.

Duct System Construction Materials

Many different types of sheet metal materials are available on the market. Their selection, however, should be made according to acceptable usage. Because of the potential problems associated with the proper selection of materials, the Sheet Metal and Air Conditioning Contractors National Association (SMACNA) has identified the recommended usage for common construction materials. These guidelines are presented as follows:

- *Galvanized sheet steel.* This is the most commonly used sheet metal material found in the construction industry. It is relatively low in cost, easy to work with, and has sufficient structural strength. It is recommended that the following items be constructed with galvanized sheet steel:

    a. Air ducts not exposed to extreme acid, fume, or humidity

    b. Casings or housings used for coils, fans, filters, or air washers

    c. Roof ventilators and cowls

    d. Volume control dampers

    e. Duct hangers

    f. Hoods

    g. Intake and exhaust louvers

- *Black steel sheets.* These iron sheet materials may be either hot or cold rolled, and are recommended for the construction of:

a. Hoods

b. Smoke pipes

c. Belt guards

d. Fire dampers

e. High temperature air or gas ducts and hoods

• *Aluminum and aluminum alloys.* When aluminum sheet material is used, it is recommended that allowances be made for greater expansion and contraction caused by temperature changes. These materials are not recommended where temperatures may exceed 800°F, or where there is contact with chlorinated water or wet lime. Typical construction applications of aluminum sheet materials are:

a. Exterior ducts

b. Ventilators

c. Louvers

• *Stainless steel.* This sheet metal material is more expensive than other types, and should be carefully considered where excessive corrosion is a problem. Examples of where these metals are used include:

a. Intake and exhaust louvers

b. Unpainted and exposed ducts

c. Shower and pool ducts

d. Kitchen range hoods

e. Fume exhaust hoods

Low Velocity Duct Standards

Low velocity duct systems are commonly found in houses and small commercial buildings. An example of a typical duct arrangement is presented in Figure 4-1. As one can see, the system is fairly simple, and does not require the construction of added structural supports.

Before discussing specific standards, it is necessary to present typical duct connections. Figures 4-2 and 4-3 illustrate the configurations found in common cross joints and longitudinal seams. Their letter codes (A, B, C, etc.) should be noted, for they will be used throughout this section of the book. The recommended usage of these connections is as follows:

Cross Joints

A. Drive slip—recommended for ends of ducts that are inserted under cleats, for ducts with sides that are less than 18″. If the sides exceed 18″, a reinforced angle ($1″ \times 1″ \times \frac{1}{8}″$) is recommended.

B. Plain "S" slip—used on the wide sides or at the ends of small ducts. Inserted into the open ends of the "S."

C. Hemmed "S" slip—same as B, except used where added stiffness is required.

E. Bar slip—same as B, except that the standing edge is used for reinforcement.

F. Alternate bar slip (standing "S" slip)— same as E, except added strength is provided at standing edge.

G. Reinforced bar slip (cleat)—similar to E, except that an inserted bar is used to reinforce the standing edge.

H. Angle slip—same as G, except an inserted reinforcing angle is used.

I. Standing seam—this seam is used to join the ends of adjoining ducts. The buttons illustrated are punched at intervals of six inches.

J. Angle reinforced standing seam—same as I, except an angle is fastened to the duct for reinforcement.

K. Pocket lock—typically used on four sides of ducts. The break is a clip punch made near the corners and then spaced approximately every six inches.

L. Angle reinforced pocket lock—same as K, with the addition of an angle for added stiffness.

M. Companion angles (caulk or gasket)—this cross joint is used where the duct must be removed periodically.

Longitudinal Seams

N. Pittsburgh lock—the most common type of longitudinal

seam. Usually roll-formed on machines, but can be made in a brake or press brake.

O. Acme lock-grooved seam—used primarily to join two flat sheets for increasing their width.

T. Double seam—this standing seam is most often used on the inside of ducts.

Z. Button punch snap lock—not recommended for aluminum ducts; this seam makes it possible to "snap" the button flange into place.

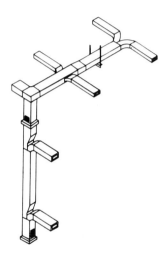

Fig. 4-1. Typical arrangement for a low velocity duct system.

The construction of low velocity metal ducts will vary considerably from one area of the country to the next. Table 4-1 gives recommended sheet metal gauges and construction for low velocity rectangular ducts.

Several standard items are found in every duct system. What varies is their size and construction. Because there are literally thousands of different duct designs, it is impossible to present specifications for every condition. This section describes several common and representative items found in low velocity duct systems. (For a more complete discussion and coverage of these standards, see the SMACNA reference: *Low Velocity Duct Construction Standards.*)

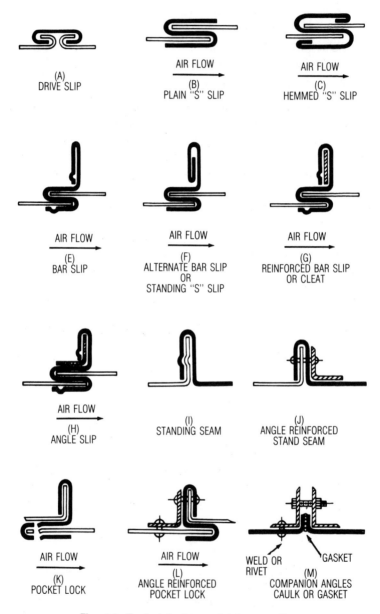

Fig. 4-2. Typical duct cross joint connections.

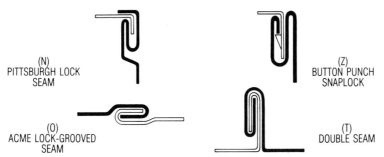

(N)
PITTSBURGH LOCK
SEAM

(Z)
BUTTON PUNCH
SNAPLOCK

(O)
ACME LOCK-GROOVED
SEAM

(T)
DOUBLE SEAM

Fig. 4-3. Common longitudinal seams.

Table 4-1
Recommended Construction of Low Velocity Rectangular Ducts

Dimension of Longest Duct Side	Steel Metal Gauges		Joints
	Steel	Aluminum	
to 12″	26	24 (.020)	A,B,K
13″ thru 18″	24	22 (.025)	A,B,K
19″ thru 30″	24	22 (.025)	C,E,K
31″ thru 42″	22	20 (.032)	E,G,K
43″ thru 54″	22	20 (.032)	E,G,K
55″ thru 60″	20	18 (.040)	E,G,K
61″ thru 84″	20	18 (.040)	G,H,J
85″ thru 96″	18	16 (.051)	H,J,L,M
over 96″	18	16 (.051)	H,J,L,M

Rectangular Ducts.

The basic design for smaller ducts is shown in Figure 4-4. It is recommended that a 26 gauge steel, or aluminum thickness of .020″ (.508mm), be used for sizes under 13″ (330.2mm). For ducts that have dimensions 13″ (330.2mm) through 18″ (457.2mm), a 24 gauge

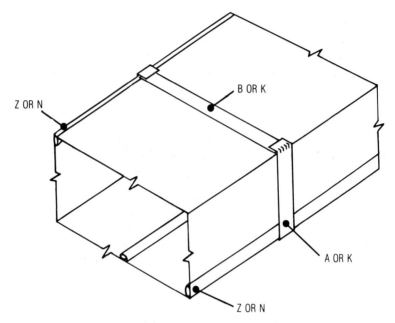

B OR K

Z OR N

A OR K

Z OR N

Fig. 4-4. Duct construction to 18."

steel or .025 (.635mm) aluminum should be specified. See Table 4-1 for a more detailed presentation.

The primary difference between this duct and larger dimensioned ducts is construction. Shown in Figure 4-5 is another duct design, but for a larger system. In each instance, note that the joints and seams are identified by letter coding.

Round Ducts.

When a strong duct system is required for air distribution, a round duct is recommended. The design of the duct will again vary according to system design. Figure 4-6 presents the standards for round duct construction. Table 4-2 lists recommended steel gauge sizes for round duct construction.

Duct Hangers.

The function of duct hangers is to hold the duct in place and position. How the duct is arranged will greatly influence the design, place-

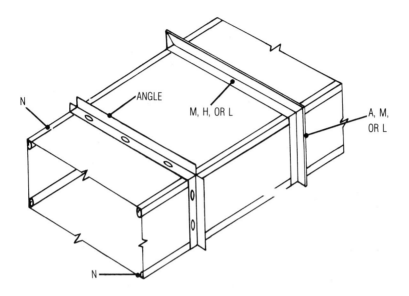

Fig. 4-5. Duct construction for ducts over 96″ long.

ment, and specification for the hangers. Figure 4-7 illustrates several hanger designs.

Elbows.

One of the most basic elements of a duct system is the elbow, used to change the direction of air flow. Basic design dictates that the radius of the throat should always be equal to the width of the elbow. This is maintained to minimize the amount of air turbulence and static pressure loss. If physical constraints make it impossible to maintain this relationship, a vane spacing should be included. Figure 4-8 illustrates common elbow standards.

Tapers and Offsets.

One of the most common construction problems found in duct systems involves tapers and offsets. Tapers are used to feed air from a larger to smaller duct, (or vice versa), while offsets change the direction of air flow. Figure 4-9 shows common construction standards and considerations for duct system tapers and offsets.

103

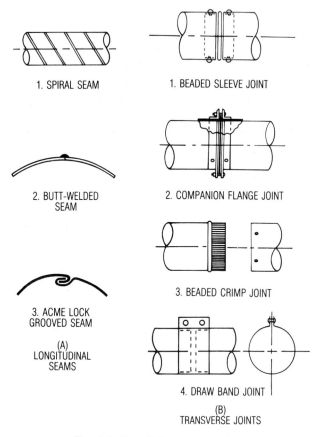

1. SPIRAL SEAM

1. BEADED SLEEVE JOINT

2. BUTT-WELDED SEAM

2. COMPANION FLANGE JOINT

3. BEADED CRIMP JOINT

3. ACME LOCK GROOVED SEAM

(A) LONGITUDINAL SEAMS

4. DRAW BAND JOINT

(B) TRANSVERSE JOINTS

Fig. 4-6. Round duct construction.

Duct Branch from Main.

A duct branch is a tap into the main duct that is used to distribute air to other locations of the building. All branches are composed of three basic parts: the main duct head, the main duct after the branch, and the branch duct. Figure 4-10 is an illustration of a duct branch from main.

Tee Connections.

A tee connection is a type of branch, but is not necessarily connected to a main. As might be expected, a tee can connect to a duct at

Table 4-2
Gauge Sizes for Round Duct Construction

Duct Diameter (inches)	Spiral Seam Duct	Longitudinal Seam Duct	Duct Fittings
to 12	28	26	26
13 thru 18	26	24	24
19 thru 28	24	22	22
29 thru 36	22	20	20
37 thru 52	20	18	18

various angles. Figure 4-11 contains various illustrations for tee connection standards.

High Velocity Duct Standards

High velocity duct systems are made of round, rectangular, and flat oval shapes. Unlike a low velocity system, this system is primarily limited to large commercial or industrial buildings, where high pressures are required for feeding air. The most common types of ducts used in these systems are round ducts. They are considered the most economical type of duct to construct and erect.

Rectangular high velocity ducts are limited to those cases where a round duct cannot be installed, but is significantly more expensive to construct. Flat oval ducts (Figure 4-12) are a combination of the round and rectangular duct.

The primary difference between a high velocity and low velocity duct system is the significant strength requirement for the latter. (For a complete discussion on this, see the SMACNA reference: *High Velocity Duct Construction Standards.*) High velocity ducts and components will require heavier gauge metals and more rigid joint and seam construction. In fact, it is not unusual to find many joints welded, bolted, or riveted together. Figure 4-13 illustrates the common types of joints used in high velocity duct systems.

Because of the size and high pressure requirements of high

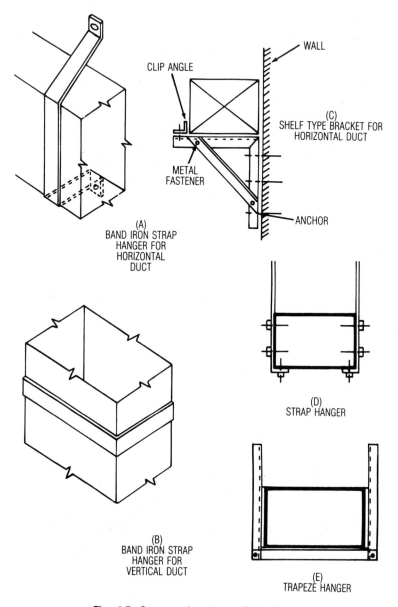

Fig. 4-7. Common hanger configurations.

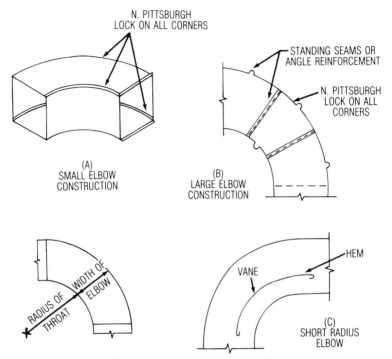

Fig. 4-8. Basic elbow construction.

velocity ducts, it becomes critical to minimize the number of leaks within the system. Thus, all joints and seams must be made airtight with a sealant. The only exceptions to this are welded joints and spiral lock seams that are machine-made. There are four general types of sealants used for this purpose:

1. *Liquid sealants.* Recommended for slip-type joints, liquid sealants can be applied by brush or pump. Having a consistency of a thick syrup, the sealant will flow into the joint and harden as it dries.

2. *Mastic sealants.* Most mastic sealants are used for fillet or groove connections. These sealants, though, must be applied by a pressure gun to the inside surface of an assembled joint. The internal air pressure will force the mastic sealant against the joint.

3. *Gasket sealants.*   Gaskets are usually made of soft neoprene. Some are available in extruded forms of curtain wall sealants. To make their installation easier, many manufacturers provide gaskets with an adhesive backing that will adhere to the metal during the assembling process.

4. *Tape sealants.*   The most recognizable sealants are tapes. They are made of either cloth, plastic, or foil with an adhesive backing. Note that tapes should *never be used as the primary sealer for high velocity connections.* Tapes should always be used in conjunction with other sealants.

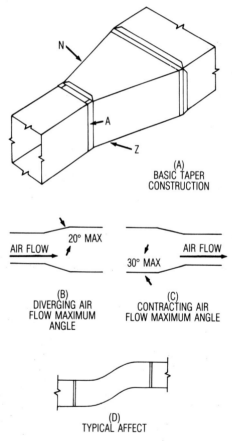

Fig. 4-9. Tapers and offset.

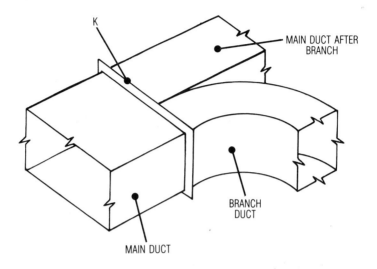

Fig. 4-10. Branch from main.

ARCHITECTURAL SHEET METAL STANDARDS

One of the most active areas for work in the sheet metal field is in the architectural field. Based on architectural plans, sheet metal contractors prepare a complete set of drawings and details that must be submitted to the architect for review and approval. In general, sheet metal workers are used to fabricate and install sheet metal products that are made of Number 10 U.S. gauge or lighter. Heavier gauge metals are usually pre-manufactured and shipped to the building site.

The variety of units, products, and devices encountered in building projects is enormous. To get an idea of the type of work sheet metal workers are involved in, refer to Table 4-3 for a representative (but not complete) listing of sheet metal items.

In addition to the fabricating and installation of sheet metal products, the sheet metal worker is also responsible for examining all surfaces that are to be covered by sheet metal and reporting any improper or defective surfaces. The workmanship should always conform to the standards of practice—either the *Architectural Sheet Metal Manual* or *SMACNA Manual*.

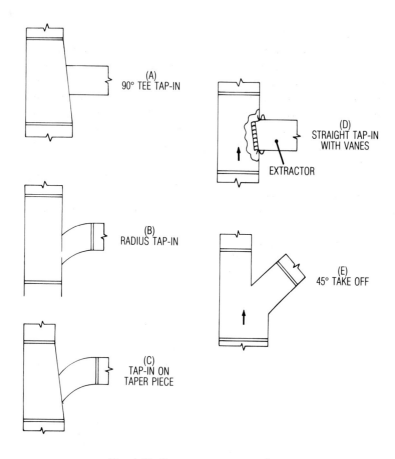

(A)
90° TEE TAP-IN

(B)
RADIUS TAP-IN

(C)
TAP-IN ON
TAPER PIECE

(D)
STRAIGHT TAP-IN
WITH VANES

EXTRACTOR

(E)
45° TAKE OFF

Fig. 4-11. Common tee connections.

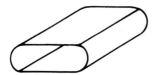

Fig. 4-12. Flat oval duct.

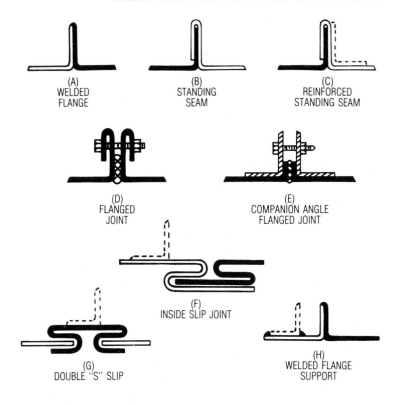

(A)
WELDED
FLANGE

(B)
STANDING
SEAM

(C)
REINFORCED
STANDING SEAM

(D)
FLANGED
JOINT

(E)
COMPANION ANGLE
FLANGED JOINT

(F)
INSIDE SLIP JOINT

(G)
DOUBLE "S" SLIP

(H)
WELDED FLANGE
SUPPORT

Fig. 4-13. Types of joint configurations used in high velocity ducts.

Gutters

The most basic and common sheet metal products used in buildings are gutters. The most critical element here is the selection of the proper size gutter. When determining this, the following factors should be considered:

- The spacing and size of the outlet opening
- The angle or slope of the roof from where the run-off will drain
- The desired style of gutters
- The location and type of expansion joint

111

Table 4-3
Fabricated and Installed Sheet Metal Work

Access doors	Louvered screens and penthouses
Bins	Metal letters
Cabinets for fire extinguishers	Metal form decks
Cabinets for waste disposal	Mullion covers
Chutes for linen and rubbish	Pans for showers and kitchen
Closures	Parapet wall covering
Column covers	Partitions
Conductor heads	Pass windows
Corner guards	Planter box liners
Cornerstone boxes	Roofing
Copings	Scuppers
Cornices	Scuttles
Corrugated roofing and siding	Scuttle covering
Crosses	Shelving
Doors	Smoke hatches
Downspouts	Snow guards
Draft curtains	Spires
Drapery pockets	Splash pans
Enclosures that are louvered	Spray booths
Expansion joints for roofs, walls,	Stacks
and slabs	Sunshades
Flashings	Ventilators
Gravel stop	Wall panels
Gutters	Water diverts
Hoods	
Lighting troughs	

There are three general types of pre-formed gutters available: rectangular, half round, and ogee. Rectangular gutters come in a variety of sizes as well as in 12 different designs (Figure 4-14). Half round and ogee gutters, by comparison, only come in different sizes (Figure 4-15). In addition to style and size, gutters are also available in different types of metals, which are specified by thickness in the following units:

- Galvanized steel: Gauge Number
- Copper: Ounces
- Aluminum: Inches
- Stainless steel: Gauge Number

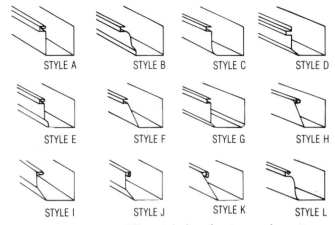

Fig. 4-14. Twelve different designs for rectangular gutters.

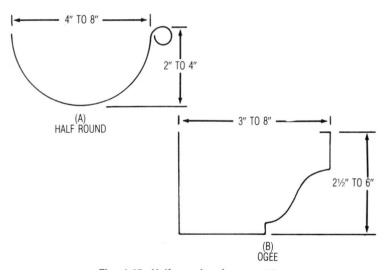

Fig. 4-15. Half round and ogee gutters.

As might be expected, there are several methods for the hanging of gutters (for installation). The most common installation methods shown are in Figure 4-16.

In addition to installing pre-formed gutters, the sheet metal worker will sometimes be required to fabricate a built-in gutter (see

113

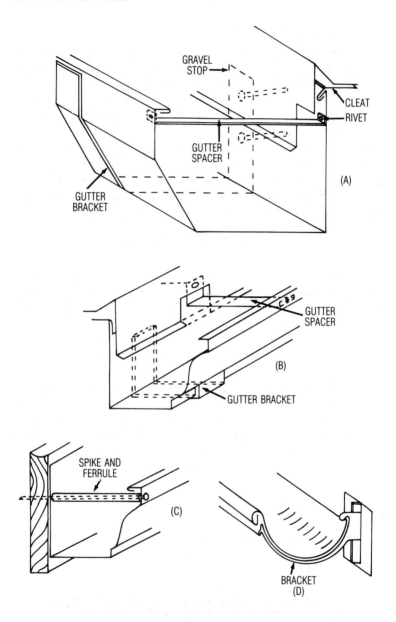

Fig. 4-16. Common hanging gutter installations.

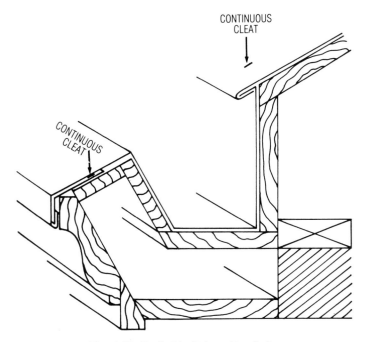

Fig. 4-17. Typical built-in gutter design.

Figure 4-17). These gutters are used when it is more desirable not to view the gutter itself (from a design perspective). If these gutters are specified in architectural plans, special care must be taken to prevent leakage, which is a major problem with built-in gutters. Some considerations that must be given to these type of gutters are:

- The sheet metal material should be corrosion resistant.
- Since all joints must be seamed and soldered, the material selected should be suitable for soldering operations.
- The gutter should be completely supported by a wood box frame.
- Expansion joints must be built into the gutter system.

Scuppers

A technique frequently used in commercial buildings to allow water to run off the roof involves construction of a scupper. Basically, a scupper is a passageway or opening in the roof's wall that enables run-off to flow into the gutter system. Figure 4-18 is a typical scupper design. To minimize leakage, a number of seams may require soldering. In cases where aluminum is used, the seam must be either sealed or welded.

Downspouts

Once the water leaves the gutter, it usually enters the downspout, which carries the overflow away. Downspouts are of two types: manufactured and shop fabricated. Manufactured downspouts are are made so that the top section will fit into the lower one. When the direction of the flow of water must be changed, an elbow (either style "A" or "B") may be used. Manufactured downspouts are also available in three basic shapes: plain round, corrugated round, and rectangular corrugated. See Figure 4-19.

At times, it may be more advantageous to use shop fabricated downspouts. These are usually made by sheet metal workers, rather than by forming millings in a manufacturing plant. Illustrated in Figure 4-20 are common shop fabricated downspout designs.

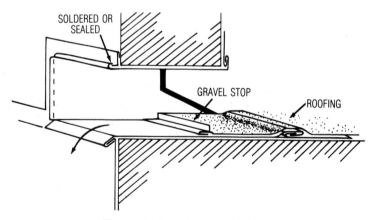

Fig. 4-18. Typical scupper design.

Metal Roofs

There is a wide variety of metal roofs that are used primarily within the commercial construction industry. It should be noted, however, that architectural treatment sometimes calls for the use of metal roofs on residential structures (houses). As a result, it becomes important for the sheet metal worker to gain competence in the construction and installation of sheet metal roofs. This section is a review of the specifications for common metal roofs.

Flat Seam Metal Roofs.

The flat seam metal roof is most frequently used as roofing material where the pitch or incline of the roof is slight. This roof is also used for covering domes and towers. When the pitch of the roof is less than 3:12, the seams must be sealed, usually with a soldered seam.

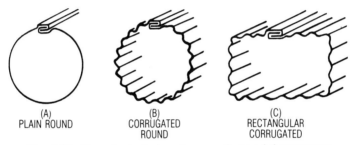

(A)
PLAIN ROUND

(B)
CORRUGATED
ROUND

(C)
RECTANGULAR
CORRUGATED

Fig. 4-19. Three basic designs for manufactured downspouts.

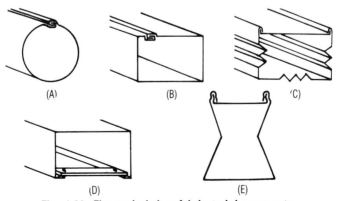

(A)

(B)

'C)

(D)

(E)

Fig. 4-20. Five typical shop-fabricated downspouts.

Prior to installation, the roof's surface (usually wood) must be smooth, dry, and covered with some type of building paper. Where the roof pitch is slight, 30-square-foot (maximum) divisions should be made by using expansion battens. Presented in Figure 4-21 are illustrations of specifications for the use of flat seam metal roofs.

Standing Seam Roofs.

Roofs that have a pitch greater than 3:12 are usually of the standing seam type. If a non-wood roof base is used, then a nailing strip must be installed for receiving the roofing cleats. Again, the surface must be smooth and dry. Prior to the laying of a smooth building paper, a saturated roofing felt should be laid.

There are two basic methods used for installing standing seam roofs. The first is known as the *pan method*, where the sides of the metal are formed as shown in Figure 4-22a. Pans are installed by nailing cleats onto 12″ (305mm) centers (see Figure 4-22b). Each pan is then "locked" into position to a lower positioned pan (Figure 4-22d), the next row of pans is then installed, and the standing seams appear as shown in Figure 4-22c.

The second way of installing a standing seam roof is by the *roll method*. Here, the seams of the metal sheets are pre-joined by a double flat lock seam, rolled, and shipped to the construction site. Once at the site the standing seam is formed (Figure 4-22e). The roofing material is then installed in eave-to-ridge lengths and cleated onto 12″ centers.

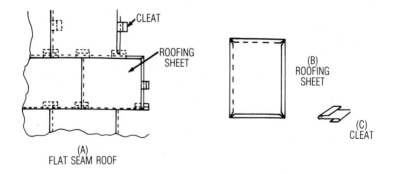

Fig. 4-21. Flat seam metal roof.

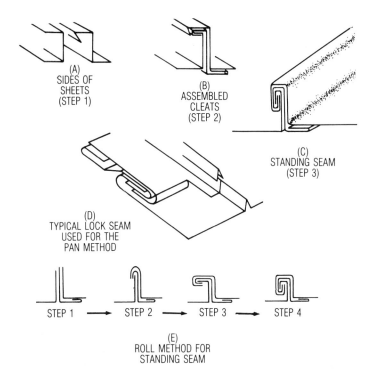

Fig. 4-22. Standing seam metal roof.

Batten Seam Roofs.

The batten roof is applicable when the roof's pitch exceeds 3:12. Similar to the standing seam roof, if a non-wood roof base is used, nailing strips must be installed. The surface should be smooth, dry, and covered with some type of saturated roofing felt. The felt is then covered by a building paper.

Depending on the architectural design of the building, the battens may be spaced at any distance to a maximum of 20″ (510mm). Common batten details are presented in Figure 4-23a. The sheet metal is formed into pans at the site as shown in Figure 4-23b. The pans are then installed in a sequence, starting at the eaves, and are cleated into position.

119

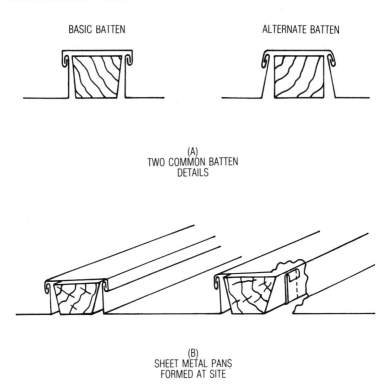

BASIC BATTEN ALTERNATE BATTEN

(A)
TWO COMMON BATTEN
DETAILS

(B)
SHEET METAL PANS
FORMED AT SITE

Fig. 4-23. Batten seam roofs.

Metal Siding

In many parts of the country, metal siding is widely used and has become a popular method for minimizing the amount of building maintenance. The most common types of metal siding used in the industry, for both commercial and residential structures, are presented in Figure 4-24a. In addition to various configurations, siding metal is also available in a variety of gauges, finishes (e.g., galvanized, painted, dip-coated), and metals (e.g., steel and aluminum). Figure 4-24b has illustrations of common types of locks and seams used for the installation of metal siding.

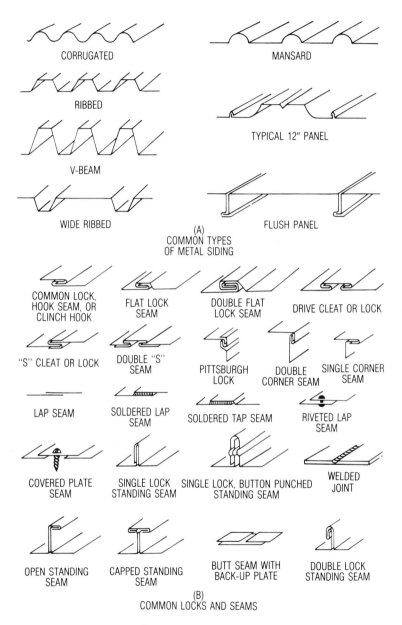

CORRUGATED

MANSARD

RIBBED

TYPICAL 12" PANEL

V-BEAM

WIDE RIBBED

FLUSH PANEL

(A)
COMMON TYPES
OF METAL SIDING

COMMON LOCK,
HOOK SEAM, OR
CLINCH HOOK

FLAT LOCK
SEAM

DOUBLE FLAT
LOCK SEAM

DRIVE CLEAT OR LOCK

"S" CLEAT OR LOCK

DOUBLE "S"
SEAM

PITTSBURGH
LOCK

DOUBLE
CORNER SEAM

SINGLE CORNER
SEAM

LAP SEAM

SOLDERED LAP
SEAM

SOLDERED TAP SEAM

RIVETED LAP
SEAM

COVERED PLATE
SEAM

SINGLE LOCK
STANDING SEAM

SINGLE LOCK, BUTTON PUNCHED
STANDING SEAM

WELDED
JOINT

OPEN STANDING
SEAM

CAPPED STANDING
SEAM

BUTT SEAM WITH
BACK-UP PLATE

DOUBLE LOCK
STANDING SEAM

(B)
COMMON LOCKS AND SEAMS

Fig. 4-24. Metal siding.

121

SUMMARY

Because of the wide use of sheet metal products throughout the economy, specific standards and specifications have been developed to ensure consistency of products and their installation. The majority of individuals employed in the sheet metal trades are found in the construction industry, though most of the products are manufactured. Thus, it is extremely important that sheet metal workers become familiar with the standards and specifications of sheet metal work in the construction industry.

One of the most common usages of sheet metal products is in duct systems. Duct systems are divided into two major groups: low and high velocity systems. High velocity systems are those where the air velocity exceeds 2,000 fpm, while low velocity are less than 2,000 fpm.

Common materials used in duct work are galvanized sheet metal, black steel sheets, aluminum and aluminum alloys, and stainless steel. Specific standards for low velocity systems include cross joints, longitudinal seams, rectangular ducts, round ducts, duct hangers, elbows, tapers and offsets, duct branch from main, and tee connections. High velocity duct system specifications not only include the same types of considerations, but also use sealants. A complete set of standards and specifications should be checked with the SMACNA.

Another major area of the construction industry includes the architectural field. Sheet metal products used in architectural projects are varied, and include such items as doors, bins, drains, decks, siding, and roofs. Specific standards for these items can be found in either the *SMACNA Manual* or the *Architectural Sheet Metal Manual*.

REVIEW QUESTIONS

1. Briefly explain the difference between a low velocity and high velocity duct system.

2. Give examples of products made from the following types of sheet metal materials: galvanized sheet steel, black steel, aluminum, and stainless steel.

3. Sketch the cross-sectional appearance of the following:

drive slip	"S" slip	angle slip
standing seam	pocket lock	companion angle
Pittsburgh lock	acme lock	dutton punch snap lock

4. Briefly identify and describe the different types of ducts used in low velocity systems.

5. What are tees and duct branches?

6. Why are sealants important in high velocity duct systems?

7. Identify the units used to specify (order) the following types of sheet metal materials: galvanized steel, copper, and aluminum.

8. What are scuppers and how are they used?

9. Explain the differences between the following sheet metal roofs: flat seam, standing seam, and batten seam.

10. Identify the common types of pre-formed sheet metal sidings used for buildings.

Part III

SHEET METAL PRACTICES

CHAPTER 5

Sheet Metal Materials

The term "sheet metal" pertains to a family of specific materials. By chemical definition, a metal is an element that when exposed to an acid will have a positive (+) charge and is, therefore, attracted to a negative (−) pole. In all, metals are divided into four major groups: light metals, brittle metals, ductile metals, and low melting metals. Table 5-1 is a listing of elements that are considered to be chemically metal.

Sheet metal refers to the physical form in which the metal appears. It is material produced in various thicknesses and compositions—as pure metals and alloys. Because of the variety of sheet metal materials available on the market, it is the intent of this chapter to briefly review the properties or metals, types of sheet metals, and industrial standards associated with this group of materials.

METAL PROPERTIES

The properties and behavior of metals are extremely important in the making of products. A great number of properties are considered by product designers and engineers, such as density, vapor pressure, thermal expansion, chemical resistance, thermal conductivity, and electrical and magnetic properties. Each will differ in importance, depending on the use of that metal product.

Those properties most often associated with sheet metal materials, however, are known as *engineering properties*. Examples of these properties include tensile strength, compression strength, torsion strength, modulus of elasticity, and hardness. Of the five engineering properties, the two most important are tensile strength and hardness.

Table 5-1
Metallic Elements

Group	Element	Symbol
Light metals		
	Lithium	Li
	Beryllium	Be
	Sodium	Na
	Magnesium	Mg
	Potassium	K
	Calcium	Ca
	Rubidium	Rd
	Strontium	Sr
	Cesium	Cs
	Barium	Ca
	Francium	Fr
	Radium	Ra
Brittle Metals		
	Scandium	Sc
	Titanium	Ti
	Vanadium	V
	Chromium	Cr
	Manganese	Mn
	Yttrium	Y
	Zirconium	Zr
	Niobium	Nb
Ductile Metals		
	Iron	Fe
	Cobalt	Co
	Nickel	Ni
	Copper	Cu
	Molybdenum	Mo
	Technetium	Tc
	Ruthenium	Ru
	Rhodium	Rh
	Palladium	Pd
	Silver	Ag
	Hafnium	Hf
	Tantalum	Ta
	Tungsten	W
	Rhenium	Re
	Osmium	Os
	Iridium	Ir
	Platinum	Pt
	Gold	Au

Table 5-1
Metallic Elements (Cont'd)

Group	Element	Symbol
Low Melting Metals		
	Aluminum	Al
	Zinc	Zn
	Gallium	Ga
	Germanium	Ge
	Cadmium	Cd
	Indium	In
	Tin	Sn
	Antimony	Sb
	Mercury	Hg
	Thallium	Tl
	Lead	Pb
	Bismuth	Bi
	Polonium	Po

Tensile Strength

Tensile strength refers to the capability of the metal material to be stretched. More technically, it is the resistance to a lengthwise stress that is measured in terms of greatest load of weight per unit area. This weight is a pulling force, in the direction of the length, that results in the eventual stretching of metal below the break point.

In test laboratories, tensile strength is calculated by pulling on two ends of a test specimen (see Figure 5-1). The standard test specimen will be about 8 in. (205mm) in length, and machined from ¾ in. (19mm) stock. Two gauge marks are made on the specimen, and it is then subjected to a pulling force. From this force, two properties can be calculated: stress and strain. Stress is assessed by dividing the applied force by the finished area of the test specimen (stress $= F/A$), and strain is calculated by dividing the difference in specimen length by its original length (strain $= (L_1 - L)/L$).

Compression Strength

The use of compression strength is usually limited to fairly brittle material that will fracture under an applied load. For ductile metals,

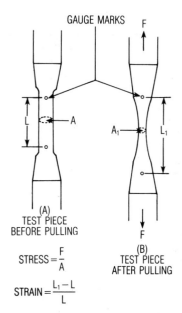

GAUGE MARKS

F

L — A

A₁ — L₁

(A)
TEST PIECE
BEFORE PULLING

F

(B)
TEST PIECE
AFTER PULLING

$$STRESS = \frac{F}{A}$$

$$STRAIN = \frac{L_1 - L}{L}$$

Fig. 5-1. Tensile test on specimen.

however, it is more difficult to determine compression strength since they will normally not fracture but only deform. Consequently, compression strength for ductile metals is only calculated in terms of the amount of deformity that has occurred in the metal.

Ductility

One of the most important properties for sheet metal materials is ductility. Ductility is the ability of a metal to bend, draw, stretch, form, or become permanently deformed without breaking. Metals that are very ductile will not be brittle or very hard. By comparison, hard metals that are brittle will usually lack ductility. Ductility is often calculated by the tensile test. Here, ductility is calculated as the percent of elongation of the test specimen at the break point. The formula used for calculating elongation is $\%e = [(L_F - L)/L] \times 100$, where L is the original gauge length, and L_F is the distance between the gauge marks as measured on the reassemble test specimen after fracture.

Hardness

The metallic property of hardness is determined in terms of its resistance to penetration by a small hardened sphere, cone, or pyramid. The degree of hardness can be specified in several ways, depending on the type of test used. The most common metal tests used are the Rockwell, Brinell, and Shore Scleroscope methods. Under each method a specific scale is used to specify metal hardness.

One of the oldest hardness scales used is the Moh's scale; it ranges in hardness rating from 1 to 10. Materials that fall in each category are as follows:

1 talc	6 feldspar
2 gypsum	7 quartz
3 calcite	8 topaz
4 fluorite	9 titanium nitride
5 apotite	10 diamond

Another common scale used is the Knoop Scale. This scale is considered more descriptive, since it offers a wider range of hardness ratings. Comparative examples of Knoop ratings are:

30 gypsum	820 quartz
135 calcite	1350 topaz
160 fluorite	2500 titanium nitride
400 apatite	6500 diamond
550 feldspar	

SHEET METALS

The most common metals used for sheet material are steel, aluminum, and copper. Of these, the most widely used are sheet steel materials. This section discusses the common types of metals used by sheet metal workers.

Sheet Steel

Steel is a product made by adding carbon to iron, along with a substantial quantity of manganese. Since steel is not a "pure" metal, but a combination of several elements, it is considered an *alloy*. Common steel is alloyed in a furnacing operation, usually a basic oxygen furnace (BOF) or electric furnace. The open hearth furnace was a traditional method for production, but is seldom employed in manufacturing settings.

Types of Steels.

During the molten state of this alloy, various types of elements are added to create certain material properties and they give steels a wide range of behaviors. Examples of how elements can change the properties of steel are given as follows:

Carbon. When the carbon content of steel increases, so will the metal's strength and hardness.

Manganese. Added to all steels, this element is used to improve the hot working qualities of steel and contributes to its heat treating strength.

Chromium. Widely used in low alloy steels, this element contributes to the corrosive and oxidation resistance of steels.

Nickel. This element is used to increase steel toughness and hardenability.

Vanadium. Increases hardenability.

Niobium. Reduces hardenability and increases the strength of low carbon steels.

Zirconium. Increases steel toughness.

Cerium. Increases steel toughness.

To specify and identify specific types of steels, a coding or numbering systems has been devised. The basic system used in the steel industry is the American Iron and Steel Institute (AISI) number system. The usual notation is given in terms of an AISI number. A more common system is the Society of Automotive Engineers (SAE) system, which is usually followed for ordering steels. It should be noted that the two systems are almost identical for all steels, except for stainless steels where the AISI only uses the last three digits of the SAE number. Table 5-2 lists some of the common classifications of steels and their first two digits.

Table 5-2
Steel Classifications

AISI/SAE Number	Classification
1xxx	Carbon steel
10xx	plain carbon
11xx	free machining
12xx	resulphurized
13xx	Manganese 1.5% to 2.0%
2xxx	Nickel
23xx	3.5% nickel
25xx	5.0% nickel
3xxx	Nickel-chromium (Ni-Cr)
31xx	1.25% Ni, 0.65% Cr
32xx	1.75% Ni, 1.00% Cr
33xx	3.50% Ni, 1.55% Cr
4xxx	Molybdenum (Mo)
40xx	carbon-molybdenum (0.25% Mo)
41xx	chromium-molybdenum
43xx	nickel (1.8% Ni)-chromium (0.65% Cr)-molybdenum
46xx	nickel (1.75% Ni)-molybdenum
47xx	nickel-chromium (0.45 Cr)-molybdenum (0.2% Mo)
5xxx	Chromium
50xx	0.5% Cr
51xx	1.0% Cr
52xxx	1.5% Cr
6xxx	Chromium-vanadium
61xx	1% Cr-0.12% V
92xx	Silicon (Si 2%)-manganese (0.85% Mn)

Sheet and Wire Gauges.

All sheet metal workers must become familiar with the meaning and use of sheet and wire gauge sizes. Basically, gauge size is a method used to specify and order a particular thickness of sheet metal and diameter of wire.

133

In the metals industry, the term "gauge" is used to describe various systems or scales for the identification of thickness or weight per unit area of thin sheets, strips, plates, or diameters of wire or rods. Gauge sizes are specified as a numeral followed by the word gauge, such as 14 gauge. Gauge sizes for flat rolled material are only used where the thickness is ¼ in. or less, or the weight per square foot is under 10 lbs. Thicker and heavier products are always designated by weight per unit area or length, or in terms of thickness.

There are a number of different gauge systems or scales encountered in the sheet metal industry. Thin black and galvanized sheet metal and wire can be specified in various gauges. Most steel wire, however, is usually manufactured to the *Washburn and Moen* (W&M) or *Roebling* gauge. The *Stubs* gauge is used for both steel wire and for numbered twist drill sizes. The *Birmingham* wire gauge is widely used in the United States for specifying brass wire size. A common gauge system used in the industry is the *Brown & Sharpe* gauge, which is based on a uniform geometrical progression, where each gauge size is equal to 0.89053 times the preceding size. Table 5-3 is a comparison of standard gauge systems.

Table 5-4 presents the data for the Galvanized Sheet Metal Gauge system. Note that the information not only gives the thickness of the metal, but also provides gauge weights.

Zinc and Tin Finishes.

The term "sheet steel" refers to a wide range of steel products that are manufactured into sheet form. Many of these products not only have different compositions and properties, but also different finishes, depending on the type of coating applied to the metal itself. These coatings usually act to protect the base metal (steel) from corrosion and oxidation. Naturally, there are many situations where such coatings are not required.

Zinc-coated sheets are said to be *galvanized*. Here, the steel is rolled through a bath of molten zinc, which adheres to the metal's surface. As the sheet steel is pulled from the bath, the molten zinc hardens and crystallizes so that a frost-like pattern forms on the surface. This type of finish is most commonly used for sheet steel products. A less common method of zinc coating is by an electrical process known as electrolysis.

Table 5-3
A Comparison of Standard Gauge Systems (Thicknesses and Diameters in Inch Decimals)

Gauge No.	BWG, Stubs Iron Wire	AWG, B&S	US Steel Wire, Amer. Steel & Wire, Washburn & Moen, Steel Wire	SWG	Manufacturer's Standard
0000000	...	...	0.4900	0.500	
000000	...	0.580000	0.4615	0.464	
00000	...	0.516500	0.4305	0.432	
0000	0.454	0.460000	0.3938	0.400	
000	0.425	0.409642	0.3625	0.372	
00	0.380	0.364796	0.3310	0.348	
0	0.340	0.324861	0.3065	0.324	
1	0.300	0.289297	0.2830	0.300	
2	0.284	0.257627	0.2625	0.276	
3	0.259	0.229423	0.2437	0.252	0.2391
4	0.238	0.204307	0.2253	0.232	0.2242
5	0.220	0.181940	0.2070	0.212	0.2092
6	0.203	0.162023	0.1920	0.192	0.1943
7	0.180	0.144285	0.1770	0.176	0.1793
8	0.165	0.128490	0.1620	0.160	0.1644
9	0.148	0.114423	0.1483	0.144	0.1496
10	0.134	0.101897	0.1350	0.128	0.1345
11	0.120	0.090742	0.1205	0.116	0.1196
12	0.109	0.080808	0.1055	0.104	0.1046
13	0.095	0.071962	0.0915	0.092	0.0897
14	0.083	0.064084	0.0800	0.080	0.0747
15	0.072	0.057068	0.0720	0.072	0.0673
16	0.065	0.050821	0.0625	0.064	0.0598
17	0.058	0.045257	0.0540	0.056	0.0538
18	0.049	0.040303	0.0475	0.048	0.0478
19	0.042	0.035890	0.0410	0.040	0.0418
20	0.035	0.031961	0.0348	0.036	0.0359
21	0.032	0.028462	0.03175	0.032	0.0329
22	0.028	0.025346	0.0286	0.028	0.0299
23	0.025	0.022572	0.0258	0.024	0.0269

Table 5-3
A Comparison of Standard Gauge Systems (Thicknesses and Diameters in Inch Decimals) (Cont'd)

Gauge No.	BWG, Stubs Iron Wire	AWG, B&S	US Steel Wire, Amer. Steel & Wire, Washburn & Moen, Steel Wire	SWG	Manufacturer's Standard
24	0.022	0.020101	0.0230	0.022	0.0239
25	0.020	0.017900	0.0204	0.020	0.0209
26	0.018	0.015941	0.0181	0.018	0.0179
27	0.016	0.014195	0.0173	0.0164	0.0164
28	0.014	0.012641	0.0162	0.0148	0.0149
29	0.013	0.011257	0.0150	0.0136	0.0135
30	0.012	0.010025	0.0140	0.0124	0.0120
31	0.010	0.008928	0.0132	0.0116	0.0105
32	0.009	0.007950	0.0128	0.0108	0.0097
33	0.008	0.007080	0.0118	0.0100	0.0090
34	0.007	0.006305	0.0104	0.0092	0.0082
35	0.005	0.005615	0.0095	0.0084	0.0075
36	0.004	0.005000	0.0090	0.0076	0.0067
37	· · ·	0.004453	0.0085	0.0068	0.0064
38	· · ·	0.003965	0.0080	0.0060	0.0060
39	· · ·	0.003531	0.0075	0.0052	
40	· · ·	0.003144	0.0070	0.0048	

Another type of coating used on sheet steel is tin. Commonly referred to as *tin plate*, this sheet material is produced by coating thin sheets of steel with tin by either hot dipping or electrolysis. The brightness of the tin plate will depend on the grade of tin used (i.e., A, AA, or AAA, with AAA the highest). Unlike zinc coatings, the electrolysis process is rapidly replacing the hot dip process.

Briefly, electrolysis, or electrolytic process, is a procedure by which metal is dipped in a chemical solution. While in the solution, the metal is attached to one electrode, and the other electrode is a solid piece of tin. When an electrical charge is sent through the electrodes, the tin ions flow and attach onto the steel sheet, depositing a thin coating. Because tin plate is made of thin metal, it

Table 5-4
Galvanized Sheet Metal Gauge System

Galvanized Sheet Gauge Number	Gauge Weights		Thickness
	lb/sq.ft.	lb/sq.in.	(inch)
8	7.0312	0.048828	0.01681
9	6.4062	0.044488	0.1532
10	5.7812	0.040148	0.1382
11	5.1562	0.035807	0.1233
12	4.5312	0.031467	0.1084
13	3.9062	0.027127	0.0934
14	3.2812	0.022786	0.0785
15	2.9688	0.020616	0.0710
16	2.6562	0.018446	0.0635
17	2.4062	0.016710	0.0575
18	2.1562	0.014974	0.0516
19	1.9062	0.013238	0.0456
20	1.6562	0.011502	0.0396
21	1.5362	0.010634	0.0366
22	1.4062	0.0097656	0.0336
23	1.2812	0.0088976	0.0306
24	1.1562	0.0080295	0.0276
25	1.0312	0.0071615	0.0247
26	0.90625	0.0062934	0.0217
27	0.84375	0.0058594	0.0202
28	0.78125	0.0054253	0.0187
29	0.71875	0.0049913	0.0172
30	0.65625	0.0045573	0.0157
31	0.59375	0.0041233	0.0142
32	0.56250	0.0039062	0.0134

is normally specified in terms of weight per base box. Table 5-5 gives the data for tin plate base weights.

Sheet Aluminum and Its Alloys

Aluminum is widely used because of its low density, high strength, resistance to corrosion, and good working properties. Pure aluminum,

Table 5-5
Tin Plate Base Weights

Weight per Base Box (lbs)	Weight per sq. ft. (lbs)	Thickness (inch)
55	0.2526	0.0061
60	0.2755	0.0066
65	0.2985	0.0072
70	0.3214	0.0077
75	0.3444	0.0083
80	0.3673	0.0088
85	0.3903	0.0094
90	0.4133	0.0099
95	0.4362	0.0105
100	0.4592	0.0110
107	0.4913	0.0118
112	0.5143	0.0123
118	0.5418	0.0130
128	0 5878	0.0141
135	0.6199	0.0149
139	0.6383	0.0153
148	0.6796	0.0163
155	0.7117	0.0171
168	0.7714	0.0185
175	0.8036	0.0193
180	0.8265	0.0198
188	0.8633	0.0207
195	0.8954	0.0215
208	0.9551	0.0229
210	0.9643	0.0231
215	0.9872	0.0237
228	1.0469	0.0251
235	1.0791	0.0259
240	1.1020	0.0264
248	1.1388	0.0273
255	1.1709	0.0281
268	1.2306	0.0295
270	1.2398	0.0297
275	1.2628	0.0303

however, is not generally used in sheet metal work. Like steel, most commercial aluminum metals are alloys made up of various types of elements.

Aluminum metals are categorized according to a *series* number, which consists of a four-digit number. The major series categories are as follows:

1xxx Series is a designation for aluminum metals that are at least 99 percent pure. This series of metals is primarily used for conducting electricity.

2xxx Series is used to designate the alloying of copper and aluminum. They can be heat treated, and are utilized where high strength is required.

3xxx Series involves manganese as the major alloying element. These metals are considered good general purpose metals that are used for a variety of applications.

4xxx Series is used to note all aluminum-silicon alloys, and is best suited for situations where the metal must be welded or brazed.

5xxx Series is an alloy with the primary alloying element being magnesium. These metals are resistant to corrosion by sea water, and are easily welded.

6xxx Series uses silicon and magnesium in approximately the same proportions in the alloy. These aluminum alloys are heat treatable, and are used for machining and where corrosion resistance is important.

7xxx Series makes use of zinc as the primary alloying element to give added strength, and is typically employed in the aircraft and construction industries.

8xxx Series includes all other alloying elements, other than those used in series 1xxx through 7xxx, and comprises usually special-purpose alloys.

9xxx Series is presently an unused series.

A wide variety of aluminum materials is available for use by sheet metal workers. In ready supply are sheets, plates, wire, rods, bars, tubing, pipe, and structural shape items. Sheet aluminum is available in widths of 1, 2, 3, 4, 6, and 8 feet. Lengths will vary from several hundred feet for large coils to standard lengths of 4, 8, 12, and 20 feet. Plate thickness will be specified as either fractional or decimal measures, and will range in thickness from .250 in. (¼") (6.35mm) to 4 in. (101.6mm). Table 5-6 gives the standard thicknesses and weight for aluminum sheet metals.

Copper and Its Alloys

Copper is a natural element that is soft and ductile. This metal is known for its high electrical and thermal conductivity, as well as its resistance to atmospheric and water corrosion. Several copper alloys, such as brasses and bronzes, also exhibit similar properties.

Coppers.

Practically all commercial coppers can be obtained in sheet, rod, and wire forms. Many are also available as tubing. Examples of common commercial coppers include electrolytic tough-pitch copper, oxygen-free copper, phosphorus deoxidized copper, tellurium copper, sulfur copper, zirconium copper, beryllium copper, and chromium copper.

Copper can be hot-worked between 1400 and 1600°F, and is very easy to work with cold because of its excellent ductility. Sheet copper is usually cold formed because of the increased strength and hardness that results. Copper wire, on the other hand, is formed by hot rolling.

The more copper is cold-worked (e.g., bent and folded), the harder it becomes. For this reason, many copper products must be *annealed* to relieve internal stresses. The common annealing process used for coppers involves heating it to about 900 to 1000°F, and quenching (cooling) it immediately in water.

Sheet copper is usually ordered and specified by thickness and weight. Thickness is noted in either fractional or decimal measures, and weight is in either ounces or pounds per square foot. In some instances, gauge thicknesses of sheet copper are measured by Birmingham or Stubs gauge, or B&S gauge. Table 5-7 presents the thickness and weights of copper sheet metals. It should be noted,

Table 5-6
Thickness and Weight for Aluminum Sheet Metals

Thickness Fractional Decimal (inch)		B&S Gauge	Weight (lbs/sq.ft.)
1/8	0.1250	· · ·	1.762
	0.1144	9	1.605
7/64	0.1094	· · ·	1.542
	0.1019	10	1.436
3/32	0.0938	· · ·	1.322
	0.0907	11	1.282
	0.0808	12	1.141
5/64	0.0781	· · ·	1.101
	0.0720	13	1.014
	0.0641	14	0.901
1/16	0.0625	· · ·	0.881
	0.0571	15	0.803
	0.0508	16	0.718
3/64	0.0469	· · ·	0.661
	0.0453	17	0.634
	0.0403	18	0.563
	0.0359	19	0.507
	0.0320	20	0.451
1/32	0.0313	· · ·	0.441
	0.0285	21	0.394
	0.0253	22	0.352
	0.0226	23	0.324
	0.0201	24	0.282
	0.0179	25	0.253
	0.0159	26	0.224
1/64	0.0156	—	0.220
	0.0142	27	0.200
	0.0126	28	0.177
	0.0113	29	0.159
	0.0100	30	0.141

Table 5-7
Thickness and Weights of Copper Sheet Metals

| oz./sq.ft. | Thickness | | Weight |
	Fractional	Decimal	lbs/sq.ft.
96	⅛	0.1290	6.000
88		0.1190	5.500
80	⁷⁄₆₄	0.1080	5.000
72	³⁄₃₂	0.0972	4.500
64		0.0863	4.000
56	⁵⁄₆₄	0.0755	3.500
48	¹⁄₁₆	0.0647	3.000
44		0.0593	2.750
40		0.0539	2.500
36	³⁄₆₄	0.0485	2.250
32		0.0431	2.000
28		0.0377	1.750
24	¹⁄₃₂	0.0323	1.500
20		0.0270	1.250
18		0.0243	1.125
16		0.0216	1.000
15		0.0202	0.938
14		0.0189	0.875
13		0.0175	0.813
12	¹⁄₆₄	0.0162	0.750
11	¹⁄₆₄	0.0148	0.688
10		0.0135	0.625
9		0.0121	0.563
8		0.0108	0.500
7		0.0094	0.438
6		0.0081	0.375
4		0.0054	0.250
2		0.0027	0.125

however, that all thicknesses and weights are *averages* and are subject to the tolerances set by individual mills.

Brass and Bronze.

Both brass and bronze are available in either sheet or wire form. Brass is a general term used to describe an entire family of copper alloys where zinc is the primary alloying element. Examples of common commercial brasses are red brass, yellow brass, low brass, cartridge brass, and muntz metal. Their hardness will range from soft to hard (red brass to yellow brass and muntz metal, respectively).

Bronze is a form of brass to which traceable amounts of tin are added. Bronzes are considered very hard metals, but have limited use in the sheet metal industry. Primary applications for bronzes are found in the metal machining and manufacturing industries.

Other Sheet Metals

The sheet metal materials just covered by no means describe every type of material used by sheet metal workers. They are, however, representative of the majority of materials encountered. Examples of other sheet metals used are nickel and nickel alloys (Monel), lead, zinc, and tin (terne). Presented in Tables 5-8 to 5-10 are specifications for some of these metals.

Table 5-8
Monel Thicknesses and Weights

B&S Gauge	Thickness (inch)	Weight lbs/sq.ft.
14	0.0641	2.94
15	0.0571	2.62
16	0.0508	2.33
17	0.0453	2.08
18	0.0403	1.84
19	0.0359	1.64
20	0.0320	1.47
21	0.0285	1.31
22	0.0253	1.16
23	0.0226	1.04
24	0.0201	0.923
25	0.0179	0.822
26	0.0159	0.730
27	0.0142	0.652
28	0.0126	0.579
29	0.0113	0.519
30	0.0100	0.459

Table 5-9
Thickness and Weight of Lead Sheets

Thickness Fractional Decimal (inches)		Weight (lbs/sq.ft.)
1/80	0.0117	0.750
1/64	0.0156	1.000
3/128	0.0234	1.500
1/32	0.0312	2.000
5/128	0.0391	2.500
3/64	0.0468	3.000
7/128	0.0547	3.500
1/16	0.0625	4
5/64	0.0781	5
3/32	0.0937	6
1/8	0.1250	8
5/32	0.1563	10
3/16	0.1875	12
7/32	0.2188	14
1/4	0.2500	16
1/3	0.3333	20
2/5	0.4000	24
1/2	0.5000	32
2/3	0.6667	40
1	1.0000	64

SUMMARY

Sheet metals are a group of metal materials manufactured into a flat sheet stock. Other materials used by sheet metal workers include plate and wire metal products. Metals are elements that are divided into four major groups: light metals, brittle metals, ductile metals, and low melting metals.

Though there are a great variety of metals available today, not all are suited for sheet metal work. Thus, the properties and behavior of metals are extremely important. Those properties usually associated with sheet metal work are known as engineering properties. Examples of properties important in this area are tensile strength, compression strength, ductility, and hardness.

Table 5-10
Thickness and Weights of Rolled Sheet Zinc

Zinc Gauge	Thickness (Inch)	Weight (lbs/sq.ft.)
4	0.008	0.30
5	0.010	0.37
6	0.012	0.45
7	0.014	0.52
8	0.016	0.60
9	0.018	0.67
10	0.020	0.75
11	0.024	0.90
12	0.028	1.05
13	0.032	1.20
14	0.036	1.35
15	0.040	1.50
16	0.045	1.68
17	0.050	1.87
18	0.055	2.06
19	0.060	2.25
20	0.070	2.62

The most common metals used in sheet metal work are steel, aluminum, and copper. Of these, sheet steel is the most important and widely used. Steel is an iron alloy composed of carbon and manganese. Other elements, such as chromium and nickel are added to change the physical properties of metal. To note the specific type of steel, and its properties, numbering systems have been developed. The most common systems used are known as the AISI and SAE numbers.

Sheet metal specifications are made by either material thickness and/or weight. A method for identifying these specifications involves sheet and wire gauges. Gauges used to describe various scales for the identification of thickness or weight per unit are of thin strips, sheets, plates, or diameters of wire or rods. Examples of common gauges used are Brown & Sharpe, Stubs', Birmingham, and Washburn and Moen.

Sheet aluminum products usually are aluminum alloys, rather

than pure aluminum. To specify the type of aluminum desired, a special aluminum series has been developed for different groups of alloys. These range in numbers from1xxx series through 9xxx series. Aluminum products are available in different formats, ranging from sheets and plates to wire and rods.

Copper sheets, like aluminum, are seldom found in the pure state. Commercial coppers always include some form of alloying element. Sheet copper is usually ordered by thickness and weight, though the B&S gauge is sometimes employed.

Brass is a copper based alloy with zinc as the primary alloying element. Brass is a general term used to describe a vast array of alloys. Bronze is a form of brass where traceable amounts of tin are added. Other sheet metal materials encountered by sheet metal workers include nickel, lead, zinc, and tin.

REVIEW QUESTIONS

1. What is a metal? What are sheet metals?
2. Briefly describe the characteristics of metals that fall into the four major groups of metals.
3. Explain what engineering properties pertain to.
4. Briefly explain the importance that the following properties have for the sheet metal worker: tensile strength, compression strength, ductility, and hardness.
5. What is steel? Give examples of the different types of commercial steels. Give examples of the common finishes applied to sheet steel products.
6. Explain what AISI and SAE stand for, and how they are used in specifying steel products.
7. What are sheet and wire gauges, and how are they used in the sheet metal industry?
8. Explain the series system used to categorize aluminum metals.
9. What advantages does copper offer the sheet metal worker in terms of its workability?
10. Explain the makeup of brass and bronze.

CHAPTER 6

Safety Practices for Sheet Metal Work

Safety within the sheet metal industry is based on common sense, good judgment, and correct work procedures. Though many pieces of equipment come with protective guards and devices, safety statistics show that they provide only 15 to 20 percent of worker protection. The remaining 80 to 85 percent requires other factors, such as individual work habits and the work environment.

Individual workers are the primary factor contributing to a safe work environment. This chapter gives a general overview of safe work habits and procedures that are not only important in the sheet metal industry, but for a majority of industries.

WORKPLACE SAFETY

Within the workplace, a formal safety program should be developed and maintained. To help in this process, the Occupational Safety and Health Administration (OSHA) and the National Institute for Occupational Safety and Health (NIOSH) have published a number of booklets, pamphlets, and evaluation devices that can make significant contributions to such a program. All safety programs must incorporate several major elements. The most important are: leadership by management, identified responsibility, hazard control and identification, safety training, recordkeeping, first aid and medical assistance, and worker awareness.

Leadership by Management

Sheet metal business owners and managers must develop a concerned attitude toward job safety and health. If one is serious about preventing accidents, it will be reflected in the safety record of one's employees, and how they conduct themselves at the work site.

Management must always exhibit a keen interest in work safety and health by attending to these matters as required. There should be no doubts in the minds of workers as to a manager's or supervisor's personal concern for employee safety and health, as well as the priority placed on them at the workplace.

Leadership in the safety and health area can be exhibited by manangement's demonstrated actions. Some of the practices that should be followed by management are:

1. Post safety posters where all employees can see them. The OSHA poster entitled "Job Safety and Health Protection" is a requirement under the law.

2. Hold meetings with employees to discuss job safety and health matters.

3. Familiarize all employees with OSHA and trade standards that apply to the sheet metal industry, and make them available.

4. Establish a safety policy that will be carried out. Don't let your safety plan become just a paper and poster program— make it work!

5. Establish a code of safety practices and procedures that will provide specific instructions to all employees.

6. Carefully review and examine all inspection and accident reports, so that they can be followed up and any unsafe condition corrected.

7. Make sure you react to good safety habits as well as poor ones.

8. Set an example; be a model all employees can copy.

Identified Responsibility

The key question here is: "Who has responsibility for safety on the job?" Safety supervision should be assigned to one person at each job site, in all operations.

SAFETY PRACTICES FOR SHEET METAL WORK

Once the basic safety and health policies have been developed, they should be carried out by all workers. Assignment of safety responsibility is usually given to supervisors, foremen, or group leaders. Thus, if anything goes wrong, there is always one person you can go to. A common assignment practice followed here is to allocate the safety and health responsibility in the same manner as assigning job or production responsibilities.

In many sheet metal businesses, the owner serves as the direct supervisor on all jobs, and therefore assumes responsibility for all health and safety activities. This may seem a difficult responsibility to carry out, but it isn't. Remember that the owner is probably the individual most familiar with the problems of the business, and is closer to all employees than in a larger organization.

In addition to management responsibility, there must also be responsibility assignments to individual workers. Each person on the job has the responsibility to follow the company's safety and health procedures and instructions. In addition, employees should also be able to recognize hazards within the work area, and take corrective action. If an unsafe practice is being observed, efforts should be made by everyone to correct it.

Hazard Control and Identification

A safe and healthful workplace is maintained where developing or existing workplace hazards can be identified and eliminated. This process sometimes appears easier than it really is. As already mentioned, the first step is to establish a safety and health program. This requires a thorough knowledge of all tools, equipment, materials, and supplies used on the job. The second step is to actively maintain your safety and health program.

Though there are a number of specific items and procedures that should be followed, two major items are essential for identifying and controlling hazards. The first is to require specific tests and check-ups that are to be made at certain times over the work year. Sometimes an OSHA inspector will make an official inspection of your job site, which requires immediate corrections and actions as dictated. To prevent any surprises, you should periodically conduct your own inspection.

The second procedure is to change safety requirements as

needed. Remember, safety and health programs are not static—
they are dynamic and ever changing. The development and use of
new materials and procedures should be accomplished by changes
in safety and health programs. As a sheet metal worker, you must
keep abreast of process, material, and safety changes that affect your
job.

Safety Training

A good, effective safety program requires the correct job performance from everyone in the workplace. Employees, therefore, must
know about the materials and equipment they are working with, as
well as their accompanying hazards and how to minimize or eliminate them. As a result, it is recommended that a code of safe
practices be followed by everyone. An example of such a code is as
follows:

- Employees are not required to take on jobs that they did not
  receive appropriate instructions in and have not been
  authorized to execute.

- Employees should not take on a job that appears to be
  unsafe.

- Mechanical safeguards should always be installed and
  maintained where applicable.

- All employees should be required to report unsafe work
  conditions encountered at the work site.

- All injuries and illness suffered by employees must be
  reported at once—regardless of how minor they may appear.

- Once the safety program has been implemented, changes
  and adaptations must be made according to the use of new
  materials and procedures.

In addition to these points, employees should explain to workers any safety rules and conditions required for employment. For
example, many sheet metal workers are required to use foot and
eye protection on the job. This is usually explained and carefully
enforced. Some firms and union organizations require workers to
get additional safety training in first aid and certain types of power
tools and equipment.

Particular attention is often given to new employees. Immediately beginning employment, these individuals will learn to develop safety and health attitudes from other workers and supervisors. In addition, time must also be spent with experienced workers who have developed poor work habits.

Identifying whether or not additional training is needed is difficult. However, some indicators show a need for training or retraining: excessive material waste and scrap, high employee turnover, an increase in the number of near misses that almost result in an accident, an increase in actual accidents, high injury and illness rates, business expansion, new employment, and change in equipment or proceses.

Recordkeeping

All successful businesses keep records of profits, losses, job bids, and expenses. They should also keep records of accidents, related injuries, illnesses, and property losses. In fact, these records are required by law and are specified by OSHA. The major aspects of a safety and health recordkeeping program are as follows:

- *Injury and illness records.* These records are used to provide a business with data necessary to measure the effectiveness of its safety and health practices. A successful program would be indicated by a decrease in or lack of injury and illness reports.

- *Exposure records.* The use of exposure records is recommended wherever employees are exposed to toxic substances and hazardous materials. It should be noted that these records are not required for all cases, but only for those where the workplace and job come in contact with such hazards and materials.

- *Activity documentation.* The documentation of all health and safety activities is legally required for workers' compensation, insurance programs, and OSHA inspections. They are also a sign of sound business management, proof of a serious safety program, and a means of evaluating current safety and health standards.

First Aid and Medical Assistance

Most sheet metal businesses do not have an organized first aid and medical system as are commonly found in large manufacturing settings. They are, however, required by law to have the following:

1. Employers must ensure that at least one person on the job has received first aid training and is available to administer it. Furthermore, first aid supplies must be readily available for emergency use.

2. Whenever workers may be exposed to corrosive or injurious materials, adequate equipment for drenching or flushing must be provided in the work area for immediate use. Employees are also required to be trained in the use of this equipment.

3. If health problems begin to develop in the workplace, the employer is expected to get medical help and advice to resolve or eliminate them and the cause.

Worker Awareness

Part of a worker awareness program is the employees' acceptance and participation in a health and safety program. As already discussed, there are a number of ways that the employer and other employees can help to create a safe work environment. Because most sheet metal businesses are small, there is an inherent advantage in promoting property safety and health practices. Several recommendations can help employees to accept their roles in promoting good work safety and health practices. These are:

1. Employees and employers must act with conviction. If there is no positive attitude toward safety and health consciousness, then there will be no effective program.

2. Everyone must realize that accidents may occur, but it is possible to prevent almost all of them.

3. Make sure that all policies and standards are reasonable, and understood by all.

4. If there is no safety program, begin some type of activity now.

5. Make sure that safety posters, pamphlets, and information are readily displayed and available.

6. Involve all workers in inspecting, detecting, and correcting.

7. Reward good safe work habits.

RECOMMENDED SAFETY AND HEALTH GUIDELINES

Because the work environment for sheet metal workers varies greatly, it is beyond the scope of this book to list technical guidelines for every conceivable situation. This section is an overview of OSHA regulations that apply to general working conditions and operations.

Walking and Working Surfaces

All work areas, including walkways, storage, service, and maintenance areas, must be clean, orderly, and sanitary. Floor surfaces must be kept free from spills, scraps, and other debris so as to minimize worker slippage. In areas constantly exposed to wet conditions, a nonslip surface or mat should be installed.

Work areas that often come in contact with nails, splinters, holes, loose boards, screws, and other similar items must be continually cleaned and maintained. If mechanical handling equipment is used, such as lift trucks, sufficient clearances must be made to ensure easy foot and vehicular traffic. Where aisles exist, no obstruction can be placed in it that would create a hazardous condition. All permanent aisles must be easily recognizable.

Portable Ladders

Portable ladders must be properly maintained in good condition at all times. This includes tight rung joints, securely attached hardware and fittings, and freely operating movable parts. In addition, ladders should be coated with a suitable protective material.

Ladders must be inspected frequently. Any defective ladders found must be tagged "Dangerous—Do Not Use" and removed from service for repair or destruction. Examples of defective ladders include those with broken or missing steps, rungs, or cleats, and cracked or broken side rails.

Ladders should not be used near energized electrical equipment. Metal ladders, in turn, should never be brought in contact with a conducting electrical wire. When used, all ladders should have secure footings, and should never be placed on boxes, barrels, boards, bricks, or other unstable bases to obtain additional height. If a base must be used for stability, it should be made of a nonslip material.

Scaffolds

All scaffolding must have a sound, solid footing and/or anchoring. It must also be capable of holding the intended load without settling, shifting, or moving. Unstable items, such as boxes or blocks, must not be used as supports for scaffolds and planks.

Guardrails and toeboards must be used on all open sides and ends of platforms that are more than 10 feet above ground level. In addition, scaffolds 4 to 10 feet in height and less than 45 inches wide must also have guardrails (see Figure 6-1).

When selecting scaffolds and components, one must be sure that they can support at least four times the maximum load expected. Wire or fiber rope used for scaffold suspension must be capable of supporting at least six times the maximum intended load.

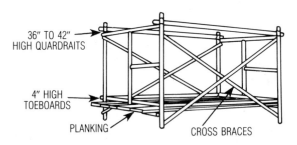

36" TO 42" HIGH QUARDRAITS

4" HIGH TOEBOARDS

PLANKING

CROSS BRACES

Fig. 6-1. Typical scaffolding arrangement.

Planking used on scaffolds must overlap at least 12 inches, or be secured to eliminate any movement. Planks must extend over the end supports of the scaffolding a minimum of 6 inches and maximum of 18 inches. If used at a construction site, the maximum extension should be 12 inches. Never place planks onto guardrails to obtain greater heights. Planking must be scaffold grade for the type of wood used. The maximum permissible spans for 2 x 10s or wider are presented in Table 6-1.

Table 6-1
Maximum Spans for 2 × 10 (inch) and Wider Planks

Specifications	Full Thickness Undressed Lumber			Nominal Thickness Lumber	
Working load (lbs/sq.ft.)	25	50	75	25	50
Permissible span (feet)	10	8	6	8	6

Rolling Scaffolds

The height of rolling scaffolds, also known as free-standing mobile scaffolds, must never exceed four times the minimum base dimension. These scaffolds must be properly braced by cross bracing and horizontal bracing. At least two of the four casters or wheels on the scaffold must be secured in place when used. At no time should anyone ride on a scaffold that is being pushed or pulled.

Environmental and Health Controls

Several industrial materials produce a certain amount of health risks to workers. To identify which ones have potentials as hazards, employers and employees should carefully examine information sheets supplied by manufacturers. In many cases, Material Safety Data Sheets are given with each procurement.

To ascertain occupational hazards, a health analysis should be conducted that identifies materials and substances used, the number or workers exposed to risk, the products made, and any other factors associated with these conditions. The physical form of the substances should be noted, such as duct, liquid, vapor, or fume. The most probable form of exposure—such as eye, skin, or inhalation—should also be noted. Finally, as part of the analysis, methods for controlling exposure should be noted.

Various methods can be employed to reduce or prevent exposure to hazardous materials. Some of these methods include:

- Substitute less toxic materials.
- Change the process or procedure used on the job.
- Improve ventilation.
- Initiate administrative controls, such as minimizing the amount of time that individuals are exposed to these materials.
- Implement an on-going training and education program for all workers.
- Put an emphasis on personal hygiene.
- Secure and use personal protective equipment.

One of the primary methods used to control air contaminants is by mechanical exhaust ventilation. In most cases, this will be used in shop-type situations. A properly designed system should either remove air contaminants or, at least, lower their concentration. Local ventilation units are to be used to remove hazardous materials at or near their point of origin. By comparison, general dilution ventilation will reduce, but not eliminate, the level of contaminants to a nonhazardous level.

There are many harmful materials that sheet metal workers can come in contact with. Examples are: acetic acid, adhesives, ammonia, asbestos, beryllium, body fillers, cadmium, carbon dioxide, carbon monoxide, caustics and other corrosive chemicals, chlorine, chromium, cutting fluids, drain cleaners, dusts, epoxy resins, fibrous materials, formaldehyde, formic acid, fumigants, hydrochloric acid, hydrogen sulfide, insecticides, insulating foam, lactic acid, lead fumes and dusts, lime, mercury, methane, oxalic acid, solvents, perchloroethylene, phenol, polyvinyl chloride, refrigerants, soda ash, sodium hydroxide, sodium sulfide, sulfuric acid, and zinc oxide fumes. If one comes in contact with any one of these materials, care should be taken to know how to handle and work with them in a safe and unhazardous manner.

Flammable and Combustible Liquids

A wide range of flammable and combustible liquids is used for commerical and industrial application. These materials are usually categorized according to their ease of ignition. Generally, there are two groups of liquids: flammable and combustible. Flammable liquids are considered more volatile than combustible liquids. Flammable liquids include gasoline, acetone, lacquer, and thinners; combustible liquids are kerosene, fuel oil, and Stoddard solvent. Table 6-2 gives the classifications of some common types of flammable and combustible products.

Often, flammable liquids must be transferred from one container to another (e.g., from a large drum to a smaller portable container). To make such an operation safe, both containers should be bonded and grounded (see Figure 6-2.). This eliminates any sparks or electrical charges that might occur as a result of static electricity. In addition, all spills of either flammable or combustible liquids must be cleaned immediately.

Supplies of flammable and combustible liquids are to be stored in fire-resistant, and rated, safety containers. All flammable liquids should be stored in closed containers when not in use. Finally, all combustible waste materials must be disposed of at least once a day.

Flammable and combustible liquids that are stored inside must be kept in a location where there is no open flame or smoking allowed. Openings to other areas of the building must be protected by self-closing fire doors. In addition, a general exhaust ventilation system must be installed for a complete change of air, within the storeroom, at a rate of six times each hour. Explosion-proof lights are also required for flammable liquid storage areas.

Flammable and combustible liquids that are stored outdoors should be kept in an area that is properly graded so that spills will flow away from any building. This area should be properly maintained and kept free of combustible materials and waste; open flames and smoking must be prohibited.

Table 6-2
Classification of Flammable and Combustible Materials

Category	Class	Material	Flash Point
Flammables	A	Gasoline Pentane	Less than 73°F
I	B	Acetone Denatured alcohol	Less than 73°F
		Naphtha, VM and P Toluene	
	C	Xylene	Equal to or greater than 73°F
Combustibles	II	Kerosene	Equal to or greater than 100°F
		Mineral spirits Naphtha Stoddard solvent	
	III	Asphalt	Equal to or greater than 140°F
		Brake fluid Fuel oil #4, #5, and #6	

Personal Protective Equipment

An important factor in the protection of sheet metal workers is their personal protective equipment. Such equipment is not designed to be the first line of defense, but to act as a back-up system. The main items that fall into this category are eye and face protection, hearing protection, head protection, foot protection, and protective clothing.

Eye and Face Protection.

One of the most important types of personal protective equipment includes those items used to guard the eyes and face from flying

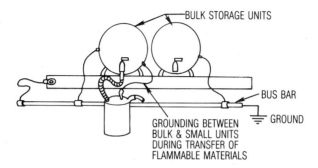

Fig. 6-2. Example of electrically interconnected storage drums and small cannister for transferring flammable liquids.

objects, glare, injurious radiation, or splashes from hazardous liquids. Examples of some of these protective items are:

- *Goggles.* Goggles are contour-shaped eyecups that are made with either plastic or safety glass lenses. In all, four types of goggles are found in the industrial setting: eyecup goggles, flexible fitting goggles, plastic eyeshield goggles, and foundrymen's goggles.

- *Spectacles.* Safety spectacles resemble conventional eyeglasses, but are more substantial in their construction and can come with or without side shields. The lenses themselves must be made with impact-resistant glass or plastic.

- *Helmet and hand shields.* Protection against strong radiant energy is often offered by shields. Not only do shields protect the eyes, but they are also designed to protect the face, ears, and neck area. There are two common types of shields. The first is the helmet type that protects the entire head area and the second is the hand shield typically used in welding operations.

Hearing Protection.

Work areas where the noise level exceeds 90 dBA are a physical hazard to workers unless some type of hearing protection is provided. Most common forms of protection are ear plugs and ear muffs that are designed to filter out and absorb harmful noise.

Head Protection.

Hard hats are required in many areas where the sheet metal worker operates. Legal standards require the wearing of head protection wherever a person may be struck in the head by falling or flying objects. Six categories of head protection gear are given as follows:

Type	1	Helmet with full brim
Type	2	Brimless helmet with peak
Class	A	Limited voltage protection
Class	B	High voltage protection
Class	C	No voltage protection
Class	D	Limited voltage protection, fire fighters' service (Type 1 only)

Foot Protection.

Safety shoes are recommended for most construction and industrial situations. They are designed to protect the foot from injury from falling objects and other hazards, and should be worn wherever heavy stock material is used. Safety shoes are grouped into three classes, and are presented in Table 6-3.

Table 6-3
Protective Footwear

Classification	Compression Resistance (lbs)	Impact Resistance (lbs)
75	2,500	75
50	1,750	50
30	1,000	30

Protective Clothing.

There is a wide range of protective clothing that is used in construction and industrial settings. Four general types of protective clothing are common. The first includes gloves and hand leathers used to prevent lacerations that result from handling sharp-edged objects and to avoid contact with chemicals. The second type, aprons, protects against sparks, hot metals, and splashing liquids. The third group includes coveralls and overalls that are used for body protection and are recommended for most building construction jobs. Finally, shop coats are used for general body protection.

SAFETY GUIDELINES FOR RELATED OPERATIONS

Several related operations sometimes encountered in the sheet metal trade require special safety attention—in particular, the use of compressed air equipment, spray painting, mechanical machinery, and welding equipment. This section is an overview of the general safety guidelines recommended for each area.

Compressed Air Equipment

As with any tool, machine, or piece of equipment, the individual must first be familiar with the air compressor's operation and maintenance instructions. All air tanks must be constructed according to standards set by the American Society of Mechanical Engineers (ASME) Boiler and Pressure Vessel Code (Section VIII). This can be easily checked by observing the ASME standard permanently stamped directly onto the tank itself.

To prevent the excessive accumulation of liquid within the air tank, the drain valve should be opened frequently. Air tanks must also be equipped with an adequate set of safety-relief valves, which should be regularly checked and tested. All pressure controllers and gauges must be properly maintained and there must be absolutely no valves between the air tank and the safety valve.

Though it is common practice to use compressed air for cleaning areas and equipment, it is an unsafe practice. If compressed air must be used for this purpose, then the pressure should be reduced to below 30 psi whenever the nozzle is dead-ended.

Spray Painting

There are times when sheet metal products must be spray painted. The procedures followed will depend on where and how this finishing operation is conducted. General spray painting requirements dictate that portable lamps should be removed from the area. A "No Smoking" sign should be posted, and a fire control sprinkler system should be installed and kept clean and free from paint buildup at all times. Low flash point thinners may be used for cleaning only if the area is well ventilated. There should never be more than a one day's supply of paint in the area at one time. Finally, protective devices and clothing such as respirators, gloves, apron, and cap should be worn by the spray paint operator.

Spray areas must be positioned so that they are a mininum of 20 feet (6.1m) from flames, sparks, non-explosion-proof electric motors, or any other type of ignition source. Lights in the area must be covered and protected from breakage, and must not be heat lamps. Some form of ventilation system must be provided to remove vapors during the spraying operation.

Mechanical Machinery

The most important safety aspect for using mechanical machinery involves proper guarding techniques. In some sectors of the safety community, it is said that the degree to which machinery is guarded is directly related to the management's interest in safety. Guards are used because individuals cannot be relied on to act safely around moving machines.

There are a number of different ways in which machines can be guarded. The most common are:

- Enclosing the entire operation
- Interlocking devices
- Moving barriers
- Removing devices

- Remote control
- Two hand tripping devices
- Electronic safety devices

Though there are many different guarding systems, established general requirements for machine guarding do exist. The first is that there should be at *minimum* one guarding method per machine that protects the operator and the general area from hazards. The guard is best functional if it is attached to the machine itself, and should be designed not to create its own hazard.

Next, all fixed or stationary machines must be secured so that there is no movement. All guarding devices should conform to appropriate standards. If no standard exists, the design should meet the general criteria of keeping the operator away from the danger zone during the machine's operating cycle.

All belts, pulleys, chains, gears, and similar moving parts must be guarded. Finally, all chain drives, shafting, coupling, keys, collars, and clutches that are positioned less than 7 feet (2.1m) above the ground must be guarded. Here, chain and V-belts must be completely enclosed by the guarding device.

Welding Equipment

The most common operations performed in both shop and field sheet metal work are in the areas of welding, cutting, brazing, and soldering. All welding-related considerations must be based on the fire potentials to the facility and area. Attempts should be made to do all welding and related operations in areas with no combustible materials. If this is impossible, steps must be taken to guard against fire. Appropriate fire extinguishers and other fire fighting equipment must be handy at all times.

No welding, cutting, brazing, or soldering are to be done on drums, barrels, tanks, or other containers unless they have been thoroughly cleaned. Avoid welding operations where the surface is covered with flammable materials or substances such as greases, acids, or tars. It is extremely important to make sure that the surrounding atmosphere is totally free of any flammable gases, liquids, and vapors.

163

Gas Welding, Brazing, and Soldering.

All cylinders must be kept and stored away from sources of heat. If stored indoors, cylinders should be located in a protected, ventilated, and dry location that is a minimum of 20 feet (6.1m) from any highly combustible materials. Cylinders must also be kept away from elevators, stairs, and gangways.

Oxygen and fuel gas cylinders must be stored separate from each other at a minimum distance of 20 feet (6.1m). If this is not possible, a noncombustible barrier of at least 5 feet (1.5m) must be erected between them. In addition, this barrier must have a fire resistance rating of at least ½ hour.

When work is completed, all cylinder valves must be closed. All fuel tank valve wrenches must be located in such a position that they can be easily reached in case of emergency. All cylinders must be clearly and legibly marked as to their contents.

It is unsafe to have a cylinder standing alone and unsecured. If acetylene gas is the fuel gas, the pressure level on the gauge must not exceed 15 psi (.967 N/m^2) (30 psi absolute) (1.934 N/m^2). Gas storage fuel tanks, located indoors, are to have a limited total capacity of 2000 cu.ft. or 300 lbs of liquefied petroleum gas.

Electric Arc Welding.

Less common in the sheet metal area is electric arc welding. However, because several forms of arc welding (TIG and MIG) are sometimes used with sheet material, it is important that sheet metal workers become familiar with safety procedures when using such equipment.

Before welding, the welding machine must be checked to make sure that it is thoroughly dry. Coiled welding cable must be spread out and the ground lead attached securely to the work. All cables must be checked for damage and repaired before use. If a cable has a splice in it that is within 10 feet (3m) of the welder, it may not be used.

Welders must be prohibited from coiling cables around their body. Welders and individuals near the welding operation must wear appropriate eye protection. Finally, arc welders should wear protective clothing to guard against flying sparks, splashing metal, and arc welding rays.

SUMMARY

The primary responsibility for a safe work environment rests with the individual worker. Since a majority of accidents are caused by human carelessness, it is important to develop safe work habits.

All safety programs must incorporate several major elements. The most important are leadership by management, identified responsibility, hazard control and identification, safety training, recordkeeping, first aid and medical assistance, and worker awareness. Only if employer and employees are serious about job safety and health will there be a reduction in job related accidents.

The sheet metal field involves a wide range of work environments. To become acquainted with every one would be a difficult task. The priority for every individual is to become knowledgeable about his own environment, working conditions, and materials, and determine what conditions and behaviors are conducive to good safety and health. Good sources of information in this area are the Occupational Safety and Health Administration and the National Institute for Occupational Safety and Health.

Recommended safety and health guidelines for the sheet metal industry cut across many different areas. These include walking and working surfaces, portable ladders, scaffolds, rolling scaffolds, environmental and health controls, handling of flammable and combustible liquids, and personal protective equipment. Specific operations that are of a general nature in the sheet metal area include the use of compressed air equipment, spray painting, mechanical machinery guarding, and related welding operations. In each case, general safety procedures are common to all industries.

REVIEW QUESTIONS

1. Identify the major elements of any good safety program.
2. Briefly give examples of the major elements for the following aspects of a safety program: identified responsibility, hazard control and identification, recordkeeping, safety training, and worker awareness.
3. Explain the first aid requirements for every workplace.

4. What are safe conditions associated with walkways and work surface areas?

5. Explain the characteristics of a safe ladder and scaffolding system.

6. Why is it important to establish certain procedures in handling materials and substances used in the workplace? Give examples of hazardous materials and their potential effect on human health.

7. Explain the difference between flammable and combustible liquids, and give examples of each.

8. Identify several items of personal protective equipment and describe where and how they are most appropriately used.

9. Describe the safe operational guidelines for working with compressed air.

10. List the conditions needed to have a safe spray painting operation.

11. Why are mechanical guards so important?

12. List the major safety considerations when working with gas welding, brazing, and soldering equipment.

CHAPTER 7

Sheet Metal Layout

The actual process of laying out and producing sheet metal forms is the responsibility of the sheet metal worker. The information needed for the process will come from sheet metal drawings or a prototype. In either case, the individual must be able to execute the task with competence in both tools and techniques.

When using a prototype, the sheet metal worker can take all dimensions and metal specifications directly from the model itself. However, if a sheet metal drawing is the source of information, it then becomes necessary for the individual to have an understanding of sheet metal and mechanical drawings and drafting methods. To review, a well-prepared sheet metal drawing will contain the following information:

1. Type and thickness of sheet material(s)
2. The total number of pieces required
3. Required tolerances for the piece
4. All location and size dimensions
5. Any and all hardware that must be installed, such as nuts, bolts, studs, and washers
6. The final treatment or finish, if any, that is needed

The layout of sheet metal parts is a responsible and important operation. The accuracy, quality, and success of a job often depends on how competent the individual is in layout work. This chapter presents information that deals with proper layout tools and procedures employed in the field.

THE PURPOSE OF LAYOUT WORK

The process of laying out sheet metal is a sequence of operations where a blank piece of metal is "drawn" on to identify all cut and bend lines. It is the operation of *scribing*, or scratching, lines and points onto the metal's surface. Points, however, are usually indicated by prick punches for identifying the centers of holes. The layout itself is then used for further processing such as cutting, filing, bending, and folding.

The accuracy that is required for layout work will vary, though most work will be accomplished to within 1/64". To attain such accuracy, the sheet metal worker must carefully and thoroughly examine the drawing of the part. From the drawing, the type of material used and sequence of operations should be determined. Next a layout plan is identified for the most appropriate method and order of scribing and prick punching. This plan is normally accomplished by mental note. For the beginner, however, it is recommended that this sequence be noted on paper.

The sheet and related materials to be laid out are then closely inspected. Their sizes are re-measured and the material is checked for any defects such as cracks, scratches, and pits. The material is cleaned so that there is no dirt, oil, or other foreign material on the layout surface. Once this is accomplished, sheet metal workers will check over their tools to see that they are in proper working condition. The layout operation can then begin.

It cannot be overly stressed that the layout process requires careful attention, since the slightest error can cause a defective and rejected product. In some cases, even if the error is found prior to full fabrication, it may still be necessary to discard the product. For these reasons, sheet metal workers must take their time and check every detail in the layout before actual work begins.

LAYOUT TABLES AND TOOLS

A number of layout tools and equipment are available to the sheet metal worker. Some are more appropriate to the shop situation, while others tend to have more application to field settings. With either, the individual should not only become familiar with these tools, but also competent in their use.

Layout Tables

It is important that layout work be done on a hard, flat, sturdy surface. In the shop, tables are usually metal to prevent the formation of dents and holes that would be caused by the prick punching, and sometimes the scribing, of thin sheet stock. Where this is not a problem, a table with a wood surface can be used.

A typically designed layout table will have a large bench plate mounted onto a base. The surface size of these tables will vary greatly up to 118×196 in. ($3m \times 5m$) and larger, with heights between 28 (711mm) and 40 in (1016mm). If the layout work is performed in the field, the layout table is typically constructed at the site and will be made out of construction lumber. The hardness of the surfaces (as required for shop metal tabletops) are not as critical here. What is important is for the layout surface to be flat, smooth, and sturdy.

Layout Tools

Various tools are used in layout work for scribing lines and prick punching marks. Basic layout tools, however, should not be thought strictly in terms of scribing and marking, but also for measuring and checking. This section is an overview of layout tools that are used in mensuration, checking, and scribing.

Measuring Tools.

One of the most basic tools used in layout work is the steel rule. Its typical length will range between 6 and 24 in., with shorter rules used for short distance checks and longer ones primarily at the layout table itself. Scale graduations should be $1/4$, $1/8$, $1/16$, $1/32$, and $1/64$ in.

Another measuring tool that is often employed to scribe lines that are parallel to the blank's edges is the *beam divider* (see Figure 7-1). The beam divider is equipped with two movable mounts that are fastened onto a scale. One mount is known as the working section; the other is the reference section. The scale is used to provide the measurement between the reference and working sections. The working section will usually have a scribing tool or edge on it, though some come with a lead pencil (e.g., scribing lines on

Fig. 7-1. A beam divider.

duralumin parts), while the reference section will have a simple straight edge.

Using the beam divider is quite simple. First, the working section is set at the desired distance from the the reference section and securely fastened by a small screw. The reference end is placed in direct contact with the edge of the sheet metal blank. The working edge is then placed in the appropriate direction from the edge. At this time, the beam divider is moved along the edge so that the working section scribes the line into the metal's surface.

A measuring tool that is used to indicate angle measures is the protractor. The protractor can come in various forms (see Figure 7-2), from a simple protractor with an accompanying straightedge to

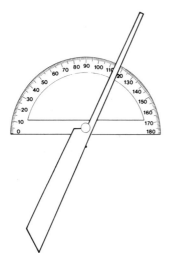

Fig. 7-2. Protractor.

a universal bevel protractor that can accurately lay off angles to within 5' (.5°).

Checking Tools.

A basic checking tool is the *square*. Squares in sheet metal layout work can serve as checking or measuring tools. They have two edges that are at right angles (90°) to each other, and one is usually equipped with a measuring scale. Generally, squares are used for one of the following applications:

- To test the accuracy of two surfaces or lines that must be at 90° to each other
- To lay out lines that are to be parallel to each other
- To set up or install sheet metal pieces

The square itself is usually made of hardened steel. Each blade of the square can be ordered in different lengths, from as short as 6 in. (15cm) for a steel square to over 18 in. (46cm) for a carpenter's square.

A variation of the square is known as the *combination set*. This tool is made up of four separate tools in one. These tools are:

1. A steel scale that also serves as a slide
2. A protractor head that has direct reading double gradations with a full 0° to 180° in opposite directions
3. A square head that can be used to check and measure 45° and 90° angles, as a level, depth gauge, and height gauge
4. A center head that is used to locate the center of cylindrical objects

Scribing and Marking Tools.

Lines are scribed onto sheet metal by a *scriber*. Scribers are composed of a thin steel rod, with one end usually sharpened into an angular point of about 15° that is mounted into a body. They are used in exactly the same manner as a pencil would be used on a sheet of paper, except that a little more pressure would be applied to the scriber to ensure a clear marking in the metal. The thinner and harder the point is, the finer the scribed line it produces.

A prick punch (Figure 7-3) is a layout tool used to mark the

171

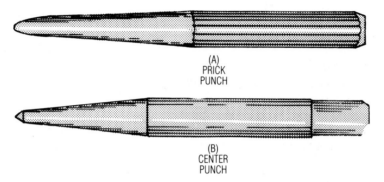

(A)
PRICK
PUNCH

(B)
CENTER
PUNCH

Fig. 7-3. Comparison between prick and center punches.

location of holes. These location markings are made after the lines have been scribed onto the work. Because layout lines are sometimes difficult to see, prick punch marks are often used as a guide. The angle of the prick punch point will range between 30° and 60°. A *center punch* looks similar to the prick punch, except that its point is ground to an angle of 90° and is used to enlarge prick punch markings.

Dividers are used to transfer measurements and to scribe circles and arcs. They have two straight legs that are pointed at the end. Unlike drafting dividers, these legs are sturdier and do not have removable points. To scribe a circle, place one point on the prick punch mark. Tip the divider slightly and scribe the circle into the metal. It is recommended that only one turn of the divider be made, for additional turns might leave multiple circle markings.

A *hermaphrodite caliper* is similar to the beam divider—it is used to scribe lines parallel to the blank's edge. In addition, the hermaphrodite caliper can also locate the centers of cylindrical workpieces. These calipers have one pointed leg that is similar to a divider, and one hooked leg (Figure 7-4) that resembles an outside caliper. This scribing tool is used by "hooking" or placing the hooked leg under the sheet metal and pulling it along the length of the metal as the scribing end marks the metal.

The last scribing tool to be considered is the *trammel*. Trammels are layout tools that measure distances between two points, as well as scribing large circles or arcs. The configuration of a trammel consists of a long rod or beam and two sliding heads. Scribing points

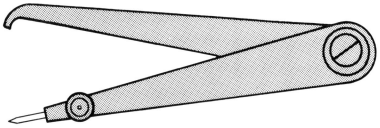

Fig. 7-4. Hermaphrodite caliper.

are mounted into the heads and are adjusted by a spring chuck.
These points may be replaced when worn by pencil leads or caliper
legs.

TECHNIQUES FOR LAYING OUT SHEET METAL BLANKS

There are several methods available to the sheet metal worker for
laying out sheet metal blanks. Each is designed for a particular
situation. It is therefore important that the sheet metal worker
become familiar with each technique.

Laying Out from a Sheet Metal Drawing

The laying out of a stretch-out from an actual sheet metal drawing
consists of transferring points, lines, contours, and dimensions from
a drawing to the sheet metal blank. It is frequently necessary to
actually develop the stretch-out on the metal blank from a multiple
view drawing. The actual procedures for developing these stretch-
outs are presented in Chapter 3. This section addresses those layout
procedures to be followed when the development has already been
constructed on a sheet metal drawing.

Laying out from a drawing is a time-consuming process and is
used in two cases: in making templates, and in customized or small
batch parts. Before laying out begins, the sheet metal worker should
carefully study the drawing and mentally plan a sequence for the
layout work. The recommended sequence (see Figure 7-5) that
should be followed is presented here:

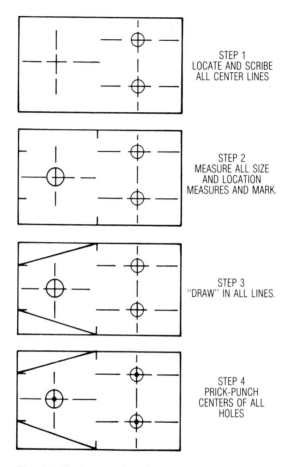

STEP 1
LOCATE AND SCRIBE
ALL CENTER LINES

STEP 2
MEASURE ALL SIZE
AND LOCATION
MEASURES AND MARK.

STEP 3
"DRAW" IN ALL LINES.

STEP 4
PRICK-PUNCH
CENTERS OF ALL
HOLES

Fig. 7-5. Basic procedure for sheet metal layout.

1. Locate and scribe all center lines. These lines can be first located by making small marks with a prick punch, and then connecting them with a scriber. It is a good practice to scribe in all horizontal center lines first, followed by vertical center center lines.

2. Actually measure out all size and location dimensions. It is poor practice to transfer measurements by using a divider, even when the drawing is prepared full sized (scale of 1:1).

3. All lines should be "drawn" with a scriber. The scriber should be held as a pencil so that the point is located directly against the straightedge and moved in one continuous, smooth motion. See Figure 7-6. It should be noted that when the layout is being prepared on aluminum sheet material, the markings are often made with a lead pencil, with the scriber used only to mark contoured lines along the material surface. Scribers are used only for contoured lines because they provide for a marked path the cutter can easily follow.

4. Punch marks are then made at the precise location where the holes' center lines intersect. The depth of these markings should not be so great as to deform the metal's flatness.

Laying Out from a Template

The most widely used method for laying out sheet metal products that are fabricated in large lots is by employing a template. This

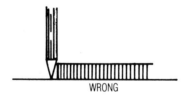

WRONG

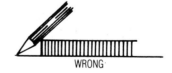

WRONG

Fig. 7-6. Correct scribing technique.

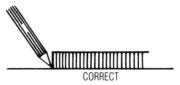

CORRECT

method is quite simple and straightforward, but it does require an accurately made template. The template itself is usually made out of metal, and sometimes is plastic. Of primary concern is that the material selected will be resistant to wear and distortion and possess good dimensional stability.

The actual making of the template starts with the pattern being laid out on the template material. This is similar to the procedure described under the section titled "Laying Out from a Drawing." Next, the template is carefully cut out or machined. Sometimes, the template is finished with a corrosion-resistant finish.

With a close tolerance template, the accuracy of the layout will depend on the correct grinding and use of the scriber (see Figure 7-9). The template should be kept stationary and held tightly against the metal. This can be accomplished by clamping or weighting down the template to the metal blank. The scriber must be held so that its point is tight against the template.

Layout errors are usually the result of an improperly secured template. Furthermore, the blank layout will be unusable if the scriber is dull or held in an incorrect position.

Laying Out with a Model and Mating Part

A model is frequently employed in repair jobs, where a sheet metal part already exists and must be replaced. Here, dimensions are taken directly from the broken or damaged part and transferred to the sheet metal blank. This method, however, is not generally recommended because of the inherent problems of wrongly placed parts and in accuracy.

The last method used for laying out a blank is by using a mating part. This is only done where large sized products are to be assembled. In this method, one of the parts is laid out with the mating part in the position they are to be joined in. Again, because of the problems of wrongly placed parts and inaccuracies, this method is not recommended unless no other procedure will work.

THE ECONOMICAL LAYING OUT OF SHEET METAL

In any job setting, profit is the ultimate goal. To obtain the highest rate of profit, one must be able to execute a job at the lowest possible rate so that the difference between actual cost and charge is maximized. One factor that directly contributes to the cost of a job is the amount of material used. Thus, the major objective of any sheet metal worker is to use as little material as possible to accomplish a given job.

In some cases, the cost of sheet metal materials is high, and they should be handled with a great deal of care and economy. Even a small amount of material savings can improve the margin of profit for a job. The cost of products can be significantly reduced if less metal is wasted. With this concept in mind, the sheet metal worker must select the most logical method of laying out parts.

Figure 7-7 presents economical and uneconomical methods for laying out several repeated patterns of a part. Note that the uneconomical method can easily be corrected on the same piece of metal, so that a savings of up to 30 percent of material can be realized (Figure 7-7a). Some blanks might be more convenient to cut, but their arrangement will cost in lost material (Figure 7-7b). Conversely, rearrangement may lead to both material savings and an easier cutting arrangement (Figure 7-7c).

In addition to multiple unit or repeat pattern layouts, material

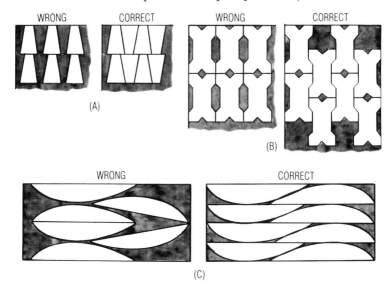

Fig. 7-7. Examples of metal saving by various methods of laying out.

savings can be realized by correctly laying out several different patterns on a single sheet of metal. Figure 7-8 shows an economical layout for several different patterns placed on a single metal sheet.

Provisions must be made for cutting allowances when several parts are laid out on the same sheet of metal. When templates are used, the cutting allowances are added to the template's dimensions. The exact amount of cutting clearance required will depend on the thickness of the metal and the type of shears used. For example, an allowance of about 0.039–0.079 in. (.991–2.007mm) should be left when cutting sheet metal 0.0197–0.079 in. (.5004–2.007mm) thick on lever-type or vibrator-type shears. Note that these close allowance figures are typically applied to production type settings where hundreds of thousands of units are produced, and if a small fraction of material can be saved, then a great amount of overall product cost can also be reduced.

An example of a procedure by which material can be economically used is shown in Figure 7-9. In the first case, an individual secures a sheet of metal sized 20×78 in. (50×198cm), with a total area of 1,560 sq.in. (9900cm^2) to lay out the part (Figure 7-9a). The area of the part is 561.1 sq. in. (3620cm^2). Thus, the part will take up only 35.97 percent of the total sheet, while slightly more than 64 percent will be waste. Obviously, this amount of waste is completely uncalled for and constitutes an extremely poor practice.

To make more economical use of material, let us now take another sheet that is 20×98 in. (50×249cm), with a total area of 1,960 sq. in. (12,645 cm^2). Two blanks can be laid out on this sheet (Figure 7-9b), with the total area 1,122.2 sq. in. (7,240cm^2). In this situation, the total amount of waste produced will be 42.7 percent— still impractical and wasteful.

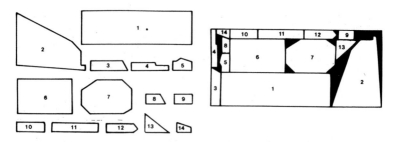

Fig. 7-8. Laying out different patterns on a single sheet of metal.

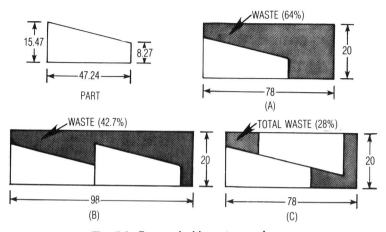

Fig. 7-9. Economical layout procedures.

The best solution to this problem is to lay out two blanks on the original 20 × 78 in. (50 × 198cm) sheet of metal in the arrangement shown in Figure 7-9c. If accomplished in a logical manner, this solution would result in a total waste of slightly more than 28 percent. Remember that the percentage of metal used will depend on the correct layout procedure. The sheet metal worker should compare various layout configurations and select the best one.

LAYING OUT PLATES AND HEAVIER STOCK

Sheet metal workers frequently find it necessary to lay out metal stock that is thicker than conventional sheet metal. These materials, with thicknesses up to 0.250 in. (6.35mm) are usually considered plate or bar material rather than sheet metal. They are used in the making of brackets, supports, and hangers for sheet metal units. The procedures here are similar to those used in laying out sheet stock, but tend to require more dimensional transferring than actual pattern development.

Layout Dyes

An aid that is often employed to make scribing lines stand out more clearly is coating the stock with a colored solution. The exact type of solution used will vary depending on the type of metal being worked. Generally, however, a dark blue layout dye is brushed onto the clean metal surface. This dye dries instantly and provides an opaque blue background that makes the scribed lines stand out.

The blue layout dye can be purchased or made. The mixture required for making the dye involves adding gentian violet dye to white shellac. This mixture is then diluted with denatured alcohol. The alcohol must be used to give the dye the proper consistency. Once mixed, the dye can be applied to the metal's surface with a small brush.

For rough layout work, where accuracy and close tolerances are not necessary, a mixture of white lead and turpentine can be used as a coating. Another common practice is the use of white or blue-colored chalk.

When close tolerances must be held and exact layouts are required on a smooth or finished surface, a special marking solution is recommended. This solution is made by adding a little nitric acid to a mixture of one part copper sulphate and four parts of water— usually 1 oz. to 4 oz. (.031kg to .124kg). This type of marking solution produces a copper-colored background on which scribing can take place.

Layout Procedures

Though the layout requirement for specific jobs will vary from one situation to another, several steps should be observed for most situations. The basic layout procedures recommended for most jobs are presented as follows:

1. Remove all dirt and oil from the surface of the metal. If there are any burrs or raised metal edges, remove them with a file. When possible, square the ends of the workpiece.

2. Apply a coat of layout dye to the surface of the workpiece that is to serve as the scribing surface.

3. Make sure that the metal is placed onto a flat, stable surface. In some shop situations, this may involve using a surface plate (which is a hardened steel surface specifically designed for close tolerance layout work).

4. It is a good practice to scribe a temporary line near the bottom of the workpiece that will serve as a checkpoint when scribing two or more parallel lines.

5. The more exacting the tolerance level, the sharper the scriber point should be.

6. When laying out the locations of holes, first scribe in the center lines along which they are to be machined or cut. Prick punch at the center of the intersecting center lines. If more than one hole is to be machined, it is good practice to use a divider as a means for spacing the holes. Make sure that the preceding intersection is prick punched before stepping off the next distance.

7. With a set of dividers, scribe in the circle. The prick punch should now be enlarged with a center punch.

8. Lines that are parallel to the edge of the stock should be scribed in with a hermaphrodite caliper.

9. Angular lines should be laid out with the aid of a universal or simple bevel protractor.

10. When using a steel rule, make sure that it is held firmly and parallel to the workpiece to ensure that all length dimensions are accurate.

11. To scribe perpendicular lines, hold a square firmly against the work. In this case, it is critical that the ends of the workpiece are squared, otherwise this technique should not be used.

SUMMARY

One of the most common operations performed by sheet metal workers is laying out sheet materials. Layout work consists of developing or transferring measurements for the scribing of a development onto sheet metal stock. The success and profitability of a job often depends on the layout competence of the sheet metal worker.

The most basic piece of equipment used in the layout process is the layout table. The table should be sturdy and provide for a smooth flat surface on which the work can be laid.

Layout tools vary greatly and conform to the type and accuracy of work performed. For example, shop layout work often requires producing a closer toleranced product than that performed in the field. In such cases, there will be differences in the types of layout tools used. Generally, however, the basic layout tools used by sheet metal workers are divided into three major groups: measuring, checking, and marking.

Examples of tools used in mensuration are beam dividers, scales or rulers, and protractors. Checking tools consist of squares and combination sets. Scribing and marking tools include scribers, prick punches, center punches, hermaphrodite calipers, and trammels.

There are several techniques used in laying out sheet metal stock. The two most common are laying out from a sheet metal drawing and laying out from a template. Less common because of the tendencies for inaccuracy is laying out with a model and mating part.

One of the most critical aspects in layout work is the economical use of material. Care must be taken to ensure that waste is minimized. This can be accomplished by placing more than one layout on a single piece of stock and/or rearranging the placement of layouts on the metal sheet.

Layout procedures on heavy metal stock are similar to those used on thinner sheet metals. The primary difference is that a layout dye is used to make the scribe lines stand out more clearly.

REVIEW QUESTIONS

1. What are the characteristics of a well-prepared sheet metal drawing?

2. Briefly describe the basic purposes of layout work in the sheet metal field.

3. What are the characteristics of a good layout table for shop and field work?

4. Briefly describe the desirable characteristics of the following tools when used in sheet metal layout: scales, beam dividers, protractors.

5. When using a prick punch, why should care be taken not to

make too deep a mark in the metal? When should a center punch be used?

6. What are hermaphrodite calipers used for?
7. Briefly describe the function of trammels.
8. List the basic procedures that should be followed when laying out from a sheet metal drawing.
9. List the basic procedures that should be followed when laying out with a template.
10. What are the differences between laying out on thin sheet metal stock and thick metal plates?

CHAPTER 8

Shear Cutting Sheet Metal

Once the development or pattern has been laid out, one of the first operations performed is cutting the sheet metal material itself. Several methods, as well as types of tools and equipment, can be used for cutting sheet metal. Sheet metals are cut with a variety of tools, including hand shears or snips, squaring shears, saws, drills, and hole punches. This chapter discusses those cutting methods that use shearing-type operations, tools, and equipment.

CUTTING OPERATIONS

Within the sheet metal industry, cutting operations are classified by either purpose or function of the cut or the cutting action itself. The basic classifications are presented in Table 8-1.

When a piece of sheet metal is cut from a larger sheet, strip, or coil, it is normally referred to as a blank. The blank, or workpiece, requires further working to turn it into a finished product. Additional processing may involve other cutting operations, as well as folding, forming, and fastening.

Most shearing operations are accomplished along a straight line, though some incorporate curvilinear lines. Straight-cut shearing is usually done on special machines known as squaring shears. Curved lines, by comparison, are frequently made by hand shears or snips. Shear cutting operations have the following purposes:

1. To cut large bulk sheet materials into blanks that can be handled more easily
2. To square the edges of sheets for the production of accurate blanks

Table 8-1
Classification of Cutting Operations

Classification	Name of Operation
Producing blanks	Shearing Cutoff Parting Blanking
Cutting holes	Punching Slotting Perforating
Progressive working	Notching Seminotching Lanching Cutoff
Size control	Trimming Slitting Shaving

3. To cut developments to shape

In production settings, where dies and large presses or brakes are common, there are specific types of cutting terminology and operations that are critical to the manufacturing of a product. These term, however, are rarely considered by sheet metal workers in the shop or construction setting. To avoid confusion, it would be helpful to the sheet metal worker to become familiar with such terms. The following is a listing and brief description of common cutting operations used in production situations:

1. *Cutoff* operations require that the cutting take place along a line, and may involve one or more cuts. The function of the cutoff operation is to remove a blank from a strip or sheet of metal.

2. *Parting* is similar to cutoff, except that when the blank is produced, a scrap piece is generated. A comparison between cutoff and parting is given in Figure 8-1.

3. *Blanking* occurs when the cutting operation generates a

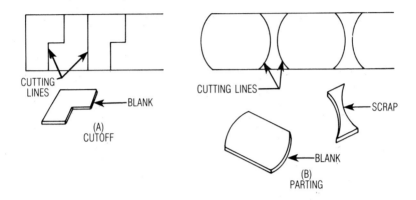

Fig. 8-1. Comparison of cut-off and parting cuts.

blank from a complete sheet or strip of metal. Here, the scrap appears as a skeleton strip of metal (Figure 8-2).

4. *Punching* is similar to blanking except that the metal removed from the sheet is the waste. Thus, this operation is used to cut holes in sheet materials.

5. *Notching* is a cutting operation that removes a piece of scrap from the edge of a sheet so that some type of bending or forming operation can be performed without material interference. A form of notching, known as *seminotching*, is used in progressive dies where pieces of metal must be removed, in progression, from a strip of metal in order for the next cutting or forming operation to proceed.

6. *Lanching* occurs when a cut is made only partway through the metal and no scrap is generated. Normally, lanching is used to permit metal bending at the cut location.

Fig. 8-2. Blanking.

7. *Trimming* operations are used to remove excess metal from the part.

8. *Shaving* is a unique cutting operation. It cuts off metal in a chipping fashion, and is used where close tolerance parts must be produced.

9. *Slitting* is an operation whereby wide strips or coiled sheets of metal are cut lengthwise to produce narrower width material.

CUTTING METHODS

Three basic methods are used to cut sheet metal, each representing the type of line(s) scribed during layout. The three cutting methods are straight, curvilinear, and combined straight-curvilinear cutting (Figure 8-3). Each is used to cut individual and repeat pattern parts of any shape or form.

Straight cutting is used to cut along non-curving lines, such as those used in box-type layouts. Cutting usually employs lever-type shears, shears with inclined knives, rotary gang slitting shears, or punching dies. The resulting shape of the sheet metal blank will be some form of polygon, such as a square, rectangle, or trapezoid.

Curvilinear cutting is employed to cut along circular, contouring, or curving lines, such as those found in discs. This cutting action is carried out by shears with curved knives, rotary shears, vibratory shears, and punching dies. In some production settings, milling machines are also used for cutting curvilinear patterns in sheet stock. The blank that is produced will take the form of a curved contour, such as a circle or ellipse.

Combined straight-curvilinear cutting is employed for layouts that have both straight and curving lines, such as those found in the development of funnels, or intricate shaped products. In this last method, the straight lines are normally cut first, followed by curvilinear lines.

HAND SHEARS

The most suitable shears used for cutting small sheets of metal are hand shears. They are best used after the layout has been cut away

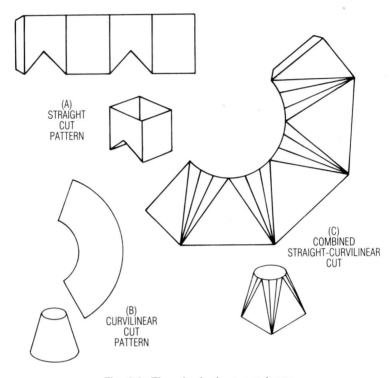

(A)
STRAIGHT
CUT
PATTERN

(B)
CURVILINEAR
CUT
PATTERN

(C)
COMBINED
STRAIGHT-CURVILINEAR
CUT

Fig. 8-3. Three basic sheet metal cuts.

from larger sheets of metal into a more suitable and manageable size. Hand shears are designed with either straight or curved blades, and are used in all types of cutting operations.

Types of Sheet Metal Hand Shears

Hand shears are also referred to as *snips*, and are used to cut steel sheets, strips, and bands up to .031 in. (.787mm) (between 21 and 22 U.S. Standard Gauge). Though they are sometimes used for greater thicknesses, hand shears are not recommended for use in cutting stock beyond this thickness because of the difficulty and physical exertion required and the potentials for cutting inaccuracy. For thick stock, mechanical or power shears are recommended.

The basic hand snip is similar in action to a pair of scissors, and is available in different sizes. A hand snip consists of two halves made of carbon alloy steel. The cutting edges (Figure 8-4) of the blades are ground to an included angle of about 85° and, when closed, the blades will overlap. The two halves will be joined by either a screw and nut or threaded pin arrangement. The joining must be properly done to assure that the halves are in tight contact and correctly aligned. When not properly joined, the snips will tend to jam and perform a poor cutting job. The basic types of sheet metal snips used in the industry are shown in Figure 8-5 and presented as follows:

- *Straight snips* are used for making straight cuts and come in sizes ranging between 2 and 4.5 in. (5 and 11.4cm). They are recommended for cutting sheet metals that are 22 gauge or thinner.

- *Double cutting snips* are specifically designed for cutting light gauge sheet metal pipe.

- *Hawk-billed snips* have narrow, curved blades, and are designed for making curvilinear cuts.

- *Aviation snips* are so named because they were first developed and used for sheet metal work in the aviation industry. They are used for cutting compound curves and other intricate designs. Aviation snips can be obtained in three designs (right, left, and universal), where each type is

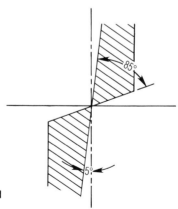

Fig. 8-4. Included angle of the cutting edges of hand shears.

Courtesy Niagara Machine and Tool Works
Fig. 8-5a. Straight snips and heavy duty straight snips.

Courtesy Niagara Machine and Tool Works
Fig. 8-5b. Double cutting snips.

Courtesy Niagara Machine and Tool Works
Fig. 8-5c. Aviation snips.

Courtesy Niagara Machine and Tool Works
Fig. 8-5d. Circular cutting snips.

specifically used for cutting curves in a right, left, or combination direction.

- *Circular cutting snips* are made of two narrow curved blades that tend to curve away from each other. They are widely used for making curved cuts on intricate patterns without bending the metal.

Making Cuts with Hand Shears

Before one begins to do any cutting, one should take care to assure that the snips are sharp and well maintained. If snips are dull, they can be easily sharpened on a grinding wheel to the proper included angle. After grinding, the snips should be reassembled by adjusting the blade tension with the nut and pivot bolt.

The proper methods for cutting with sheet metal snips are shown in Figure 8-6. The basic procedures are:

1. Make sure that you select the correct snips for the type of cut being made.
2. Open the blades as far as possible. When making the cut, make it almost as long as the length of the blade, allowing for a smooth, long cutting action.

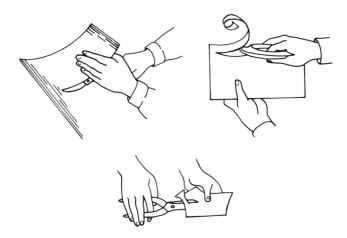

Fig. 8-6. Proper methods for cutting with handsnips.

3. When cutting to a line, cut slightly to the outside of the layout line. Where great accuracy is required, cutting through the center of the line is recommended. This latter technique, however, should only be attempted by individuals who have gained a high degree of skill in using hand snips.

4. In cutting outside curves, it is best to make a rough cut first, to within ⅛ in. (3.2mm) of the layout line. The finish cut can be made more easily.

5. When an inside curve must be cut, drill or punch holes in the waste stock to allow for easy access of the snips. Make a rough cut to within ¼ in. of the layout line, then finish the cut to size.

6. Sheets that are to be cut into wide strips should be held and slightly bent up by the non-cutting hand. This will not only make the cutting easier, but will also protect the cutting hand from injury.

7. When cutting notches, open the blades partway, and make the cut with the tip portion of the blades. When possible, try not to cut past the layout lines.

Portable Power Shears

In many situations, sheet metal can be cut much quicker and better by using portable power shears. These are hand-operated tools powered by either electricity or compressed air, and are available in various sizes and power ratings. Generally, portable power shears are used for cutting 12-gauge sheet metal or thinner. The cutting section of an electric portable shear is shown in Figure 8-7.

During the operation of a portable power shear, the operator should hold the tool with the right hand. The left hand is used to bend the cut blank away. To avoid injury by electrical shock, be

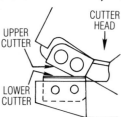

Fig. 8-7. Cutting section of a portable power shear.

sure that the shear is properly grounded. It is also recommended that the operator wear a pair of insulated gloves. Closer tolerances can be made with shears that have a higher operating frequency (cuts per minute).

Air-operated shears are engaged by an air-operated rotor type motor. In the head of the unit are mounted a small die and punch. When activated, a rod forces the punch through the die. Thus, the punch works in a reciprocating shearing motion.

MECHANICAL SHEARS

Mechanical shears are used when large sheets of metal must be cut into smaller pieces, or for heavy sheet metal stock. Manual-powered shears are designed for short-run or individual part cutting. Basically, these tools are made of two long hardened steel shear blades that can be employed to cut a variety of materials such as plastics, mica, leather, rubber, aluminum, lead, zinc, copper, stainless steel, brass, and cold rolled steel.

Squaring Shears

One of the most basic types of mechanical shears used in the sheet metal industry is squaring shears (Figure 8-8). The size of squaring shears is determined by the maximum shear width of the tool and the maximum gauge size or capacity that can be cut. Common hand shear sizes are 6 (15.2cm), 12 (30.5cm), 24 (61cm), and 36 in. (91.5cm) shears, while foot squaring shears come in sizes of 24-⅛ (61.3cm), 37-¾ (95.9cm) and 50 in. (12.7cm). Maximum gauge capacity for both types is 16 (mild steel).

Squaring shears used in shop and field situations can be either foot or hand operated. In both cases, their primary use is to trim and square stock to size. The basic elements of a squaring shear are the main base, upper shear blade housing and blade, and the power train.

The main base is usually cast iron and contains a smooth flat surface on which the sheet material is placed. Along the back end of the surface is a hardened and ground tool steel shear blade whose edge is level with the work surface. As a guide for the upper shear blade, two steel columns rise vertically from the base.

Courtesy Niagara Machine and Tool Works
Fig. 8-8. Foot operated squaring shears.

A number of different attachments can be used with the squaring shear's main base. These include a graduated steel rule that is mounted flush with the work surface and located on its right side, an adjustable protractor, and a quick-set micrometer spacing gauge located to the rear of the lower housing.

The steel rule serves two basic functions. The first is to act as a ready reference for cutting measurements to within ⅟₆₄ in. (.4mm). Second, since it is set at exactly 90° to the blades, is becomes a reference edge on all right-angle cuts. For closer tolerance cuts, generally to within .001 in. (.025mm), a micrometer nut can be used. Most micrometer gauges are set up so that the adjusting nuts will move by an inward pressure toward the screw thread. The protractor gauge is located to the left side of the work and is used to make standard angle cuts at 15° intervals, as well as other specific angles.

The movable section of the squaring shears is the upper shear blade housing. The blade itself is mounted in the housing, and at an angle to the base (see Figure 8-9). The amount of clearance between this blade and the base blade is at near zero. Such closeness is necessary to ensure a clean precise cut.

The power train is a cam combination assembly that produces the up-and-down motion of the shear blade. The actual drive mechanism can be hand, foot, or power driven, with one cam located at each end of the upper housing. By raising the hand or foot lever, the cams will raise the upper shear blade so that the work can be positioned for cutting. Lowering the lever will cause the upper shear blade to lower with a significant amount of power, so that shearing will occur easily and with little effort.

During the shearing operation, there are potentials for the workpiece to move and cause cutting inaccuracies. Generally, two types of motions occur. The first is for the workpiece to move away from the blade during the shearing action—this will usually happen when the blades are dull and need sharpening. Second, as the blade is cutting through the material, it will have a tendency to bow and lift up off the work surface. To prevent material movement, many shears are equipped with a series of metal fingers known as *holddowns*. These holddowns are located along the entire length of the upper blade housing and will typically be spring loaded. In effect, they act as clamping devices.

Cutting on Squaring Shears

The capabilities of squaring shears make them extremely useful to sheet metal workers. At the same time, they have the potential for causing significant injury to the operator if correct procedures are not followed. The basic operating procedures that should be followed on all squaring shears is as follows:

1. When cutting a large piece of stock, insert the sheet metal from the back of the machine. This is not necessary for smaller pieces.

2. If several pieces are to be cut to the same size, set the front gauge to the appropriate length. If several small pieces are to be cut to the same size, set the back gauge to the appropriate feed distance.

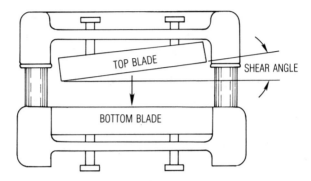

Fig. 8-9. Shear angle on squaring shears.

3. Securely press the left edge of the stock against the left gauge, while the end of the metal is against the front gauge.

4. With both hands, hold the sheet metal to the bed of the shears. If you're using hand shears, hold the work down firmly with one hand. *Make sure your hands are clear of the cutting blades.*

5. Apply pressure to the foot treadle with your foot (pull the hand lever evenly for hand shears).

Power Shears

The primary use of power shears is for shearing large-width sheet and plate materials. They may be powered by either electric or hydraulic systems that can be engaged by various triggering devices. Except for the power drive system, the actual function and appearance are generally the same as for manual equipment.

Power shears are found in the three general sizes of 24-⅛ (61.3cm), 37-¾ (95.9cm), and 50 in. (127cm) with a maximum shearing capacity of .250 in (6.35mm) for steel and .500 in. (12.7mm) for aluminum plate. When shearing thick material, however, shearing tolerances will seldom be less than ⅛ in (3.18mm).

The most typical shop power shears will have an electric motor with a high torque/high slip ratio. A clutching and flywheel configuration allows the operator to set the rate of shearing strokes up to 100 per minute or higher. This feature makes it possible for the operator to continuously feed stock into the shear for high-volume or production parts. Hydraulically operated shears are limited to large production settings where stock capacity often exceeds .250 in. (6.35mm).

Proper Care of Shears

The number one rule in caring for shears is *never* shear material thicker than recommended by the manufacturer. Attempts at forcing cuts on materials that exceed manufacturer's recommended maximum capacities will cause permanent damage in the form of housing warpage or cracking.

Blades should be routinely checked and examined for dulling or nicking, at which time they should be reground or rotated with new blades. As a safety precaution, when the blades are being replaced or reset on power shears, make sure that the power is turned off before any work begins. Also, checks should be made to see that blade clamping and backup screws are securely in place.

Refer to the manufacturer's instruction manual for lubrication procedures, especially for all moving and sliding parts. Whenever the shears are not going to be used for a while, apply a light coat of oil to the blades to prevent them from rusting.

BENCH NOTCHERS

One of the most efficient methods for making notches and tab cuts on a sheet metal product is to use sheet metal notchers. Such operations are important, especially in cutting out metal for boxes and chassis units.

Elements of the Bench Notcher

The bench notcher is a hand-operated tool that is similar in operation to the hand squaring shear. Two cutting blades, made of hardened tool steel, are mounted to the base work platen, and are at a 90° angle to each other. The top section of the notcher serves as a movable ram unit. To the ram are attached the upper shear blades, also set at a 90° angle to each other. The upper and lower shear blades are fixed into specially machined cavities that allow the blades to come in close contact with each other as the ram moves in a downward motion.

Notcher size is specified in terms of the material gauge limit and the maximum length that can be cut by the 90° blades. Perhaps the most common length found in the field is the 6 in., 16-gauge hand notcher. Here, the maximum shear length is 6 inches for sheet metal no thicker than 16 gauge. It should be noted that rectangular or smaller sized notches can also be cut on this unit by a gauging scale that is mounted to the work platen.

In addition to the length scale and gauge, bench notchers also come with two depth gauge stops. These gauges are mounted to the work surface and can be independently adjusted to make either square or rectangular cuts. Usually, the graduated scale fixed to the platen is used to indicate the position of the gauge stop, as measured from the corner point.

Notcher Operation

As can be surmised, the notcher can be a valuable tool to the sheet metal worker. In most cases, this piece of equipment is powered by a hand lever that is positioned to the top of the main body. The shearing blades are activated when the hand lever is pulled in a downward motion. The blades are then retracted as the lever is pushed up and toward the back of the machine.

There are also other notchers used for sheet metal work. One common type is known as a *power notcher*, and is operated from a floor pedal control. When used for high volume production, the power notcher can reach 180 strokes per minute.

Maintenance of notchers is critical. The shearing edges must be sharp and all moving parts kept properly lubricated. Specific maintenance directions are always provided by the manufacturer and should be carefully followed. When notchers are used for an extended period (e.g., high production runs), frequent checks should be made to see that all blades and stops are properly set and their fasteners are tight.

ROD PARTERS

Frequently, sheet metal workers need to cut rods of varying diameters to length, particularly in shop situations. Rods can be cut by hacksaw or handsaw. When rod length accuracy is important, however, sawing is not recommended. A tool designed to cut rods faster and more accurately is known as a rod parter. In some cases, as shown in Figure 8-10, rod parters are designed in combination with other tooling.

The most common type of rod parter used is the hand-powered version, which can easily shear various types of metal rods to specific lengths. Tool size is given in terms of the largest diameter rod that can be parted. The two most common rod parter sizes are ⅜ in. (9.5mm) and ⅝ in. (15.9mm). In the first size, a series of 11 holes are provided that range in size from ¹⁄₁₆ in. to ⅜ in. (1.59mm to 9.53mm), with hole graduations at ¹⁄₃₂ in. (.79mm) increments. The larger ⅝ in. (15.88mm) hole parter comes with 10 holes. Here hole sizes range from ¹⁄₁₆ in. to ⅝ in. (1.59mm to 15.9mm) at ¹⁄₁₆ in. (1.59mm) increments.

Shearing heads may also be ordered in terms of the type of rod

Courtesy Niagara Machine and Tool Works
Fig. 8-10. A combination rod and plate shear.

shape to be parted. Solid rod shapes that can be cut on the rod parter are round, square, rectangular, and hexagonal.

The shearing or parting action of the tool is accomplished by two *shear plates*. The first is known as the stationary plate, and is where the rod is inserted. The second plate is known as the shearing plate, and is attached to a handle that is cam driven. When the handle is pulled down, the shearing plate is rotated past the stationary plate. The clearance between the two plates is minimal and contributes to the accurate parting of the rod.

Parter Hole Clearances

Rod parter heads are typically designed to shear either cold- or hot-rolled steel rods. Consequently, hole clearances will vary between the two types of rod material. Generally, cold-rolled rods will be manufactured to closer dimensional tolerances than hot-rolled rods. The shear plate hole clearance for cold-rolled rods is 0.003 in. (.076mm) and only 0.015 in. (.381mm) for hot-rolled rods.

With minimum tolerance comes added clearance and more play. Thus, the parter blades will not be able to shear hot-rolled rods as accurately as cold-rolled rods. In addition, with the rod in a larger clearance hole, the rod will often have a burred and distorted shear end.

Shear Heads

The two circularly shaped shear heads are usually attached to their housing units by some form of screwing fastener. The shear heads are made of hardened tooled steel that are accurately ground with faces parallel to one another. Over time, the shear heads will become dull, burred, chipped, or mashed. When this happens, the heads should be rotated so that a new, sharp shear edge is exposed.

SUMMARY

One of the most basic types of cutting actions used with sheet metal materials is shearing. There are several ways in which cutting operations can be classified. One is by the use of the product, such as in producing blanks, cutting holes, progressive working, and size control. The second is by the nature of the operation itself. It should be noted that the cutting operations used in production settings are somewhat different from those used in the field and shop setting.

The three basic methods of cutting sheet metal are straight, curvilinear, and combined straight-curvilinear. One shearing tool that can make these three types of cuts is hand shears or snips. The hand shears used in sheet metal works are straight snips, double cutting snips, hawk-billed snips, aviation snips, and circular cutting snips. In many cases, sheet metal must be cut quickly and accurately, and therefore requires the use of portable power shears.

Mechanical shears are used to cut large sheets of metal to square and to obtain true edges for cutting and layout work. Squaring shears are one of the most common types of mechanical shears used. These shears can be hand, foot, or power activated.

Bench notchers are another type of shearing equipment used primarily to cut notches and tabs. The most common notchers found in the field are hand notchers, though power notchers are available for production purposes.

There is frequently a need for cutting rods of various diameters to length and sheet metal workers often use rod parters for this task. These tools are made up of a series of parter holes through which the rod is inserted and cut.

REVIEW QUESTIONS

1. What are the basic functions for shear cutting sheet metal?
2. Briefly describe what the following production cutting operations are: cutoff, parting, blanking, punching, notching, seminotching, lanching, trimming, shaving, and slitting.
3. Identify the three basic methods of cutting and give examples of where they are used.
4. Explain the primary application for the following types of snips: straight, double cutting, hawk-billed, aviation, and circular cutting snips.
5. Briefly describe the proper method for cutting with hand snips.

6. What are portable power shears?

7. What are the uses of squaring shears?

8. Describe the procedures that should be followed when making a cut with squaring shears.

9. What are notchers? Give the two primary types of cuts they are used for.

10. What are rod parters and how do they work?

CHAPTER 9

Holes

Once the sheet metal layout has been cut, many designs require the making of holes. In some cases, holes will be made prior to layout cutting. Generally, there are two techniques for making holes in sheet metal work: drilling and punching. A third technique, where hand snips are used to cut large holes, has already been described in the previous chapter. Presented here is a discussion of the various drilling and punching operations that can be used to make sheet metal holes.

DRILLING SHEET METAL

Drilling is a basic operation used to machine original holes in a piece of sheet material. Many times drilled holes are enlarged by other drilling, punching, or shearing operations.

Drilling Machines

Holes can be drilled by either manual or powered drilling devices. Most holes, however, are machined by powered drilling machines. These machines are capable of performing other operations, such as reaming, countersinking, threading, spotfacing, honing, and lapping. Because of the thinness of sheet metals, most drilling operations are limited to drilling.

Drilling machines come in many types and sizes. The bench drill press and floor-type drill press are most commonly found in sheet metal shops, while the portable drilling machine is usually standard for on-site work. Gang, radial, and sensitive drilling machines have proven to be valuable equipment for production work.

The sizes of vertical drilling machines are frequently designated by the largest diameter hole that can be drilled on center—normally ranging between 6 and 50 in. This technique, however, does not hold true for all types of drilling machines. Portable drilling machine sizes are given in terms of the largest diameter drill that can be mounted in its chuck.

The Twist Drill

The most common type of drill used for sheet metal work is the twist drill. Twist drills have commonly been categorized according to the type of method used to indicate their size. Some drills have a number size, ranging from 1 (0.228 in.) through 80 (0.0135 in.), that approximates the corresponding Stubs steel wire gauge. Another incorporates letter sizes from A (0.234 in.) through Z (0.413 in.), and a third category sizes drills by fractional measurements at ¹⁄₆₄ in. intervals. The final group of drill sizing is based on the metric millimeter that ranges from 0.5 to 10 mm at 1 mm intervals, and over 10 mm at 0.5 mm intervals.

Straight shank twist drills of fractional size are perhaps the most commonly used in sheet metal work. The actual length of these drills will vary according to diameter grouping (see Table 9-1). A taper shank drill is also available, but is primarily used on the floor-type drilling machine.

Generally, the design of twist drills is such that they are made up of three major sections: point, body, and shank. Figure 9-1 presents common nomenclature for both straight and taper shanked twist drills. The function of each section is as follows:

- The point is located at the the end of the drill and is the portion that actually does the metal cutting.

- The body is that section of the drill with two machined grooves that are located between the point and shank. The three functions of the flutes are to (1) form an appropriate cutting edge on the point, (2) provide a path for the chips to

Table 9-1
Nominal Sizes of Twist Drill Length Ranges

Type of Twist Drill	Drill Diameter Ranges (inch)	Increments (inch)
Straight shank	¹⁄₆₄ to 1-¹⁄₄	¹⁄₆₄
	1-¹⁄₄ to 1-¹⁄₂	¹⁄₃₂
	1-¹⁄₂ to 2	¹⁄₁₆
Taper shank	¹⁄₈ to 1-³⁄₄	¹⁄₆₄
	1-³⁄₄ to 2-¹⁄₄	¹⁄₃₂
	2-¹⁄₄ to 3-¹⁄₂	¹⁄₁₆

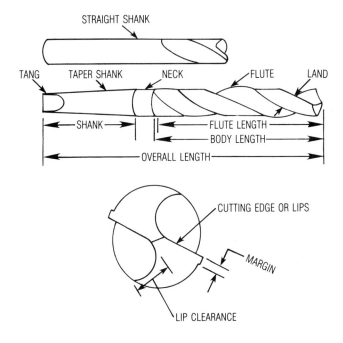

Fig. 9-1. Twist drill nomenclature.

be carried away, and (3) allow for the flow of cutting lubricant to the cutting edge. It should be noted that the body's diameter decreases from the point to the shank (back taper) to prevent binding during the drilling operation.

- The shank is that section of the drill that is clamped into the drilling machine's spindle or chuck. Its shape can be either straight or tapered according to its intended purpose.

Sharpening Twist Drills

The improper care of twist drills will often result in a product of poor quality. Inaccuracies and defects are only two of the most common problems resulting from poorly maintained drills. Table 9-2 gives a listing of common problems and their causes.

Drills will usually be sharpened by hand on an off-hand grinder or on a drill grinder. In some cases, a special drill sharpener is used. This sharpener operates like a pencil sharpener, where the drill is inserted into a round fixture and fed into a formed grinding wheel.

Sharpening of a twist drill involves three basic steps: grinding off of the worn section, thinning the web, and regrinding the web. The basic procedure recommended for sharpening twist drills by hand is as follows:

1. Be sure that the grinding wheel is dressed and true so as to provide for accurate metal removal.
2. Examine the drill itself. If the drill is dull and the margins are worn near the point, then it will be necessary to first grind off the entire point, and then regrind a new point.
3. As illustrated in Figure 9-2, hold on to the drill near its point with the right hand, while the left hand firmly grips the shank.
4. The lip of the drill is to be held at an angle of 59° to the face of the grinding wheel.
5. As the drill is ground, move the shank end downward—*do not twist the drill.* The downward motion will create a correct grinding arc on the back of the drill's cutting edge.

6. The shank should be kept below the level of the cutting lip; make sure that the clearance behind the cutting edge is maintained at about 12°.

7. Repeat the same procedures for grinding the other lip. Check to make sure that a negative angle has not been ground—otherwise the drill will rub behind the cutting edge.

8. After the second lip has been ground, check the drill point with a drill grinding gauge (Figure 9-3) to make sure that all cutting edges are the same length and appropriate angles.

Figure 9-4 gives three examples of incorrectly ground drills. In the first situation, the drill has be ground so that the lips are of unequal lengths, resulting in the machining of an oversized hole. The same result is observed in the second case where both angles

Table 9-2
Common Drilling Problems

Problems	Possible Causes
The drill cracks or breaks	Point is improperly ground. Dull drill. The drill's flutes are clogged with chips. The drill is being fed too heavily.
The cutting edges show signs of cracks or checks	The drill is overheated during sharpening, or quenched too quickly.
The drill's cutting edge chips	There is too great a lip clearance. The rate of drill feed is too great.
The drill's outer corners break	The drill's flutes are clogged. Lack of cutting compound at the drilling point.

Table 9-2
Common Drilling Problems (Cont'd)

Problems	Possible Causes
	Too high a cutting speed. Hard spots within the material being drilled.
Tang breakage	Improper socket and shank fit.
Drill breakage when drilling soft material	Clogging of the flutes with chips. Wrong type of drill for the job.
The drill splits along its center line	Too small a lip clearance. Too great a feed.
Hole finish is rough	The drill's point is either dull or improperly ground. Material improperly fastened. Either improper or no cutting compound. Too great a feed.
Finished hole size is too great.	The drill's spindle is loose. Unequal angle of the cutting edges. Unequal length of the cutting edges.
Character of the chip changes during the drilling operation	The drill becomes dull during drilling. The cutting edge is chipped.
Two different chips come out each flute	The point is improperly ground, so that only one lip is doing all the cutting.

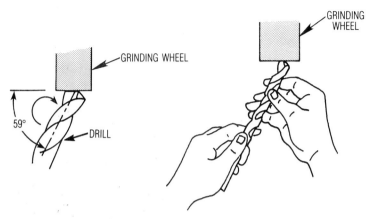

Fig. 9-2. Sharpening a drill by hand on a grinding wheel.

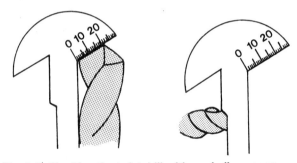

Fig. 9-3. Checking the twist drill with a grinding gauge.

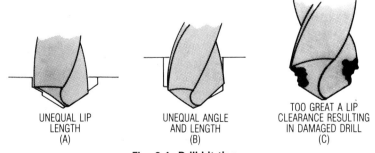

UNEQUAL LIP
LENGTH
(A)

UNEQUAL ANGLE
AND LENGTH
(B)

TOO GREAT A LIP
CLEARANCE RESULTING
IN DAMAGED DRILL
(C)

Fig. 9-4. Drill bit tips.

and lengths are unequal. The last example shows results of poorly ground drills, where a drill's edges have broken off because of too much lip clearance and the results of insufficient lip clearance.

Drilling Procedures

The first step in any machining operation is laying out the work. Once the center of the hole has been prick punched, a divider should be used to scribe a circle the same size as the hole to be drilled. When drilling thicker stock material, it is sometimes practical to prick punch four points about the scribed circle (see Figure 9-5). This is done to ensure that the drill will follow a true and accurate course. Another technique used is to scribe a smaller circle within the first one as a means of centering the drill accurately as the cut begins.

Cutting fluids are rarely used on thin stock and in short run situations. When thicker materials must be used or when production quantities are required, cutting fluids are recommended for extending the life of the drill and improving the cutting action. The ideal cutting fluid will act as both lubricant and coolant. Unfortunately, there is no one cutting fluid to be used for all situations.

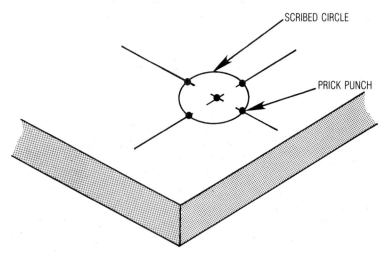

SCRIBED CIRCLE

PRICK PUNCH

Fig. 9-5. Laying out a hole for drilling.

Table 9-3
Recommended Cutting Fluid Use

Metals	Cutting Fluids
Aluminum and aluminum alloys	Soluble oil Kerosene Lard oil Neutral oil
Brass	Dry, soluble oil Neutral oil Kerosene Lard oil
Copper	Soluble oil Oleic acid compounds Winter-strained lard oil
Monel	Soluble oil Sulfurized mineral oil
Steel (ordinary)	Soluble oil Sulfurized oil Valve mineral oil
Stainless steel	Soluble oil Sulfurized mineral oil

Table 9-3 is a summation of recommended cutting fluids for drilling different types of metals.

The steps involved in drilling holes in metal are quite simple and straightforward and should be followed whether using a portable or upright drilling machine. The steps are as follows:

1. Select the proper dill size and type.

2. Mount straight shank drills directly into the drill chuck; mount taper shanked drills in the spindle or a drill sleeve and then the spindle.

3. Engage the power to make sure that the drilling machine is functioning correctly and that the drill is mounted properly.

4. When necessary, adjust the drilling machine's speed to the correct rate (rpm).

5. Secure the workpiece with a secure clamping mechanism. If drilling is to occur in an installed part, be sure that it is properly and securely fastened to eliminate any movement.

6. Line up the point of the drill to the punch mark on the metal and turn on the power.

7. Feed the drill into the metal, making sure that the drill is at 90° to the surface being drilled.

8. Check to see that the hole being drilled is true to the scribed circle. In metal plates or thick sheets, if the drill is not true, use the technique shown in Figure 9-6 to correct the alignment.

9. Apply even and constant pressure to the drill. Be sure not to apply too much pressure, otherwise there will be a chance of causing smaller drills to break and/or damaging the sheet material itself.

10. If the metal is thick, raise the drill occasionally to remove any excess chips.

11. When the hole is completed, remove the drill as it is turning, and then shut off the drilling machine.

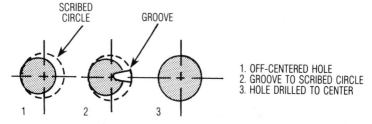

Fig. 9-6. Truing an off-center hole.

Other Drilling Machine Processes

In addition to drilling holes, other processes can be performed on drilling machines. These are:

- *Reaming.* This is an operation used to finish and size already drilled holes, and is employed where a fine surface finished and accurate hole is desired.

- *Boring.* The boring of a hole involves a rotating cutting tool that is similar to those used on lathes. Here, the holes are machined to a rough finish.

- *Countersinking.* When a machine hole must have a cone shape for the seating of flathead screws or other similar devices, then countersinking is used.

- *Counterboring.* This operation is used to enlarge an existing hole to a specific depth.

- *Spotfacing.* This is a finishing operation in which the workpiece is smoothed off and squared to a depth that will allow the seating of a washer, bolt head, or nut.

PUNCHING

The majority of sheet metal products begin as a development of shape and location dimensions that are laid out on a flat piece of material. After layout, the material is cut to shape. To this point, discussion has centered around the making of concentric holes. In addition to round holes, square, rectangular, hexagonal, and other geometric forms are commonly found in sheet metal design. These holes are used for fasteners, meters, valves, gauges, lights, and other items attached to the finished product.

Drilling is only one method used for making holes in sheet metal, and in particular small concentric holes. The method most often used in the sheet metal trade for producing irregularly shaped and larger concentric holes involves a punch and die (Figure 9-7). As shown, the punch and die must be used in combination. The male part of this tool is the punch; the die is the female part. The die is designed so that it will have a slightly larger dimension than the punch. The difference between the punch and die dimensions is known as the *die clearance*. Without the die clearance, it would be impossible to perform a punching operation.

Punching is a process whereby a specific hole shape is produced by a shearing action between the punch and die. Thus, the punch and die action should not be considered a cutting operation, but a punch type shearing process. Here, pressure is applied to the punch, which is forced against the sheet metal and die. This pressure then causes the metal to shear in the shape of the punch and die.

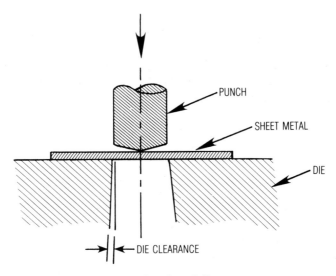

Fig. 9-7. Punch and die.

Hollow, Hand, and Chassis Punches

The hollow punch (Figure 9-8) is commonly used in the sheet metal shop and field situation where larger holes are required. This tool must be used prior to installation—and preferably before any metal forming or bending takes place—and on light gauge sheet metals.

The procedures recommended for using the hollow punch are given as follows:

1. Lay out the center of the hole and mark it with a prick punch.

2. Scribe a circle that is slightly larger than the diameter hole desired.

3. Select the appropriate size hollow punch.

4. Place the sheet metal on a flat, hardwood surface. In many shop situations, end-grain hardwood blocks are used.

5. Place the shearing edge of the punch in the center of the scribed circle.

6. Using a ball-peen hammer, strike the punch with a medium but firm blow. Raise the punch to make sure that it was properly centered.

7. Replace the punch over the first impression and strike it with a heavy blow so that the metal will be punched out.

8. If burr is generated, turn the metal so that the burr is face up and smooth it out with a mallet.

Courtesy Niagara Machine and Tool Works
Fig. 9-8. Hollow punch.

There are many situations where holes are best made with solid hand or chassis punches. One of the most common occurs when the part has been installed or assembled and changes must be made with the addition of new holes. Smaller holes can be easily made with a hand punch while larger ones are made with chassis punches.

Hand-held punches are a popular and useful tool that are designed to punch holes up to ½ in. (12.7mm) in diameter in 16-gauge mild steel. These solid punches are constructed so that they are able to accept various sized punches and dies. Perhaps the most common sizes are for hole diameters of $\frac{3}{32}$ (2.38mm), $\frac{1}{8}$ (3.18mm), $\frac{5}{32}$ (3.97mm), $\frac{3}{16}$ (4.76mm), $\frac{7}{32}$ (5.56mm), $\frac{1}{4}$ (6.35mm), and $\frac{9}{32}$ (7.14mm) in.

The lower assembly is equipped with an adjustable throat that can be regulated so that the punch can be inserted at various depths. There are ¼ in. (6.35mm) capacity punches that have a maximum throat depth of 1-¾ in. (44.45mm), while ½ inch (12.7mm) capacity punches have a throat depth to 2-¼ in. (57.15mm). A scaled gauge is available on several makes of hand punches, making it possible to punch many holes rapidly and accurately.

The dies and punches are installed by different methods. Dies are externally threaded and screwed into a tapped hole in the top half of the lower assembly. The punch, by comparison, is installed by slipping it into a throat casting T-slot. Whenever a new punch and die size are required, care should be taken to ensure that they are of the same size (i.e., proper mating)—improper mating will cause punch and die damage and a wrong sized hole.

The force produced during the punching operation is generated in the upper handle by a cam action arrangement. Here, two cams are mounted between the handles that provide for the downward movement of the punch. It must be emphasized that the punch should not be used on sheet metal gauges greater than those recommended by the manufacturer. By exceeding the limits of the tool, damage can occur to both the product and tool. The operation of the hand punch is quite simple, and involves the following steps:

1. Install the proper size punch and die unit.
2. For repeated hole punches of the same depth and size, adjust the punch's throat depth to the appropriate distance.
3. Line up the punch to the laid out hole so that it is positioned directly over the scribed circle.
4. Squeeze the punch so that the punch and die are in contact with the sheet metal. If the punch is off-center, adjust it.
5. Press down firmly and evenly until the punch takes hold.

The punching of larger holes is accomplished with a relatively simple hand tool known as the chassis punch. An inexpensive tool, the chasis punch is available in a variety of sizes and standard shapes. Common shapes are round, square, rectangular, triangular, and shapes that are frequently needed to install devices in the electronics field.

Chassis punches can be used on sheet material up to 16-gauge mild steel. These tools are composed of four basic parts: punch, die, draw bolt, and nut. The actual punching action is achieved as a result of drawing the punch and die together with the turning screw arrangement of the draw bolt and nut. In some cases, hydraulic pressure is used in portable units.

Both the punch and die are made of hardened tool steel. Through the center of the punch and die is a hole that permits the insertion of the draw bolt. The head of the draw bolt rests against the bottom of the die, while the nut rests against the bottom of the punch. The operation of the chassis punch incorporates the following procedures:

216

1. Lay out the shape of the hole (e.g., round, square, rectangular, etc.), and be especially careful with straight-sided shapes since their orientation in the object is frequently critical.

2. Locate the geometric center of the shape and prick punch it.

3. Drill a hole at the shape's geometric center. The diameter drilled should correspond to the draw bolt's diameter, or as specified by the manufacturer. The drilled hole should just allow the body of the draw bolt to slip through.

4. When possible, clamp the bolt's head in a secured vise, then place the die over the bolt so that the shear edge is face up.

5. Slip the sheet metal over the bolt so that it comes in contact with the die's shear edge.

6. Place the punch onto the bolt body.

7. Fasten the nut to the exposed threaded portion of the bolt body.

8. Using a wrench, tighten the nut so that pressure will enable the punch to shear through the material. Continue until the hole is completely punched out.

9. After the hole is punched, remove the nut, punch, draw bolt, and die.

In many cases, the hole punching process will be made more efficient by placing a light coating of grease or oil on the punch, die, and draw bolt threads. Where odd-shaped holes are punched, a *keyed chassis punch* is used. Here, a key is machined into the die so that its position will not change during the punching operation.

Punch Presses

Hand punch presses are special tools used to hold the punch and die assembly in alignment as a downward force is applied to the sheet metal. An example of a punch press is presented in Figure 9-9.

There are several techniques used to specify punch press performance. The first is the throat depth in inches. This size desig-

Courtesy Niagara Machine and Tool Works
Fig. 9-9. Punch press.

nation is the distance from the center of the punch and die to the back of the support frame. Thus, a 6 in. (15.24cm) punch will handle a sheet of metal with a diameter of 12 in. (30.48cm).

The second method used for specifying press performance is by work capacity. This is a rating given in tons, which pertains to the amount of force that can be exerted by the press. This rating is used for both hand and power operated presses.

The last method used for noting press performance is by material capacity, which is defined as the maximum diameter hole that can be punched for a given gauge metal. The maximum press performance for hand punch presses is a 4 in. diameter hole in 16-gauge mild steel. If a heavier material and/or larger diameter hole is desired, then a powered press will be used.

The main support frame of punch presses will be either cast or fabricated. The punching force of the press will be generated by a cam or gear activated lever that is connected to a ram located in a guide housing. The ram is sometimes referred to as a *turret* and is the portion of the press to which the punch is attached. Attached to the turret is a *stripper* that acts as a clamping device during the downward or punching phase of the press. As the turret is raised, the stripper will force or "strip" the metal away from the turret.

Below the ram is a platen to which the die is fastened. Within the platen is a die hole that is specified by letter size. These sizes are A, B, C, D, and E, which correspond to die diameters of 1-¼, 2-⅛, 2-¾, 3-¾, and 4-¾ in.

When accurate holes must be located and punched in a number of pieces, punch gauge stops are used. These gauges are located at the rear right side of the work surface and are at 90° to one another. Several gauge designs are used for this purpose. The first is relatively less accurate than other designs. It is made of stop plates that are locked onto a rod, so that as the metal is inserted it functions as a reference stop. The second design comes with a set of graduated dials calibrated to 0.100 in. per revolution. Where extreme accuracy is needed (to within 0.001 in.), small incremental dials can be obtained with a vernier screw.

A punch press used for short-run production shops is the turret punch press. These presses come with a number of turret stations, the most common having 12 and 18 turrets. This press is set up to accomplish a series of punching operations involving holes with diameters between ⅛ and 1-½ in. (3.18 and 38.1mm). The primary advantage of this tool is its speed in punching many holes of different diameters. Most turret punch presses will be equipped with a vernier travel dial for accurate metal positioning.

SUMMARY

Many sheet metal products require the inclusion of holes. Generally, there are two basic procedures used to make holes in sheet metal work. The first is by drilling operations and the second is by punching.

Drilling is a basic machining operation for making original holes in sheet material. Holes can be drilled by either manual or power drilling devices. The most common are power drilling machines, especially the floor-type press and portable drill.

Though there are a variety of drills used in machining holes, one is most frequently found in sheet metal work—the twist drill. Twist drills can be specified in various size designations, including letter, number, fractional, decimal, and metric drill sizes. In addition to size, twist drills are also found with two types of shanks: straight and taper.

Before working with a twist drill, care must be taken to ensure that it has been properly maintained and sharpened. Improper use and maintenance can cause severe damage or breakage to both drill and product.

Cutting fluids are used to reduce the friction generated by drilling and preserve the life of the drill. These fluids, however, are seldom used with thin sheet metals, but are commonly found in the drilling of plate material.

Drilling machines are not limited to the drilling of holes, for they can be used to perform other operations, such as reaming, boring, countersinking, counterboring, and spotfacing.

The majority of large holes found in sheet metal products are punched. Basically, punching involves the use of a punch and die for the cutting or shearing of a hole. Punches are sometimes categorized as solid and hollow, where the first are used for small diameter holes and the second for large holes.

The hollow punch is used on light gauge sheet metals, prior to any significant bending or forming, and must be used on a flat stable surface. The hand punch is a solid punch for making small holes. Its major advantage is that it can be used on products already installed. The most common type of punch used for larger holes is the chassis punch. Chassis punches are composed of a punch, die, draw bolt, and nut, and come in various standard shapes.

Punch presses are tooling used to punch holes of various diameters. The hand punch is a special tool that is hand powered and is capable of holding various sized punches and dies. A punch frequently used for short-run production situations is the turret punch press. This press is equipped with 12 to 18 turrets that can punch holes with diameters between ⅛ and 1-½ in.

REVIEW QUESTIONS

1. Identify the common type of drilling machines used in the sheet metal shop and for on-site jobs.

2. Identify the range of drill sizes for the following size designations: letter, number, decimal, fraction, and metric.

3. What is the difference between a straight and taper shank drill? What procedure is used to mount both types of shanked drills in a drilling machine?

4. Briefly list the procedures that should be used when sharpening a twist drill.

5. Identify the possible causes for the following drilling problems: cracked drill, the hole size is larger than the drill used, the hole finish is very rough, and the outer corners of the drill break.

6. What is punching, and how does it differ from drilling?

7. What is the basic difference between a hollow and hand punch?

8. What makes the chassis punch significantly different from other types?

9. Briefly list the procedures that should be followed when punching a hole with a chassis punch.

10. Describe how a punch press operates.

CHAPTER 10

Bending and Folding

The bending and folding of sheet metal can be grouped into two major types: straight and cylindrical bends and folds. These two types of bends and folds make up a majority of sheet metal forming procedures. This chapter presents a discussion of the principles of metal bending and the basic bending tools and procedures used in the sheet metal industry.

PRINCIPLES OF METAL BENDING

During bending, sheet material is subjected to a combined action of compression and tensile stresses. As shown in Figure 10-1, a sheet of metal is bent to a given form. According to the notations, the original line (before bending occurs) on the top of the metal (ab) is equal to the length of line $a'b'$ in the middle of the material, to line $a''b''$ at the bottom. However, after bending, arc ab is smaller than arc $a'b'$, which is also smaller than arc $a''b''$.

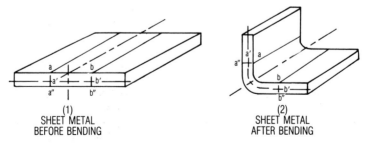

(1)
SHEET METAL
BEFORE BENDING

(2)
SHEET METAL
AFTER BENDING

Fig. 10-1. Illustration of the results of tensile and compression stresses produced by bending.

222

As this example clearly illustrates, metal is stretched on the outside of the bend and compressed on the inside. Only the *neutral plane* (median line) undergoes no change. Depending on the type of metal and bend, the material deformation resulting will be either *permanent* or *recoverable.*

Permanent deformation occurs when the elastic limit is exceeded, and the metal will not return to its original shape. Recoverable deformation happens when the elastic limit has not been reached, and the metal will return to its original shape, resulting in a spring-back effect. Thus, whenever a bending operation is used, the elastic limited should always be exceeded.

BEND ALLOWANCES

When bending sheet metal, the problem always arises as to the length of stock required for each bend. This is solved by determining the amount of metal needed for each bend and then adding it to the lengths of the straight sections. In addition, consideration must be given to the type of metal used—different metals have different physical bending characteristics.

90° Bends

To calculate the allowances or bend length (L) for bending sheet metals at a 90° angle, two factors are considered. The first is the thickness of the metal, which is usually expressed in inches and noted by the letter "t." The second is the inside radius of the bend in inches, which is noted by the letter "r."

Tables 10-1 through 10-3 give bend allowances for different types of sheet metal. Each table is based on the use of formulas for calculating 90° bend allowances. These formulas are given as follows:

- Soft Brass and Copper

$$L = 0.55t + 1.57r$$

- Half-hard Copper and Brass, Soft Steel, and Aluminum

$$L = 0.64t + 1.57r$$

223

Table 10-1
Stock Lengths Required for 90° Bends of Soft Copper and Brass

Radius of Bend, r (inches)	Thickness of Material, t (inches)						
	$\frac{1}{64}$	$\frac{1}{32}$	$\frac{3}{64}$	$\frac{1}{16}$	$\frac{5}{64}$	$\frac{3}{32}$	$\frac{1}{8}$
$\frac{1}{32}$	0.058	0.066	0.075	0.083	0.092	0.101	0.118
$\frac{3}{64}$	0.083	0.091	0.100	0.108	0.117	0.126	0.143
$\frac{1}{16}$	0.107	0.115	0.124	0.132	0.141	0.150	0.167
$\frac{3}{32}$	0.156	0.164	0.173	0.181	0.190	0.199	0.216
$\frac{1}{8}$	0.205	0.213	0.222	0.230	0.239	0.248	0.265
$\frac{5}{32}$	0.254	0.262	0.271	0.279	0.288	0.297	0.314
$\frac{3}{16}$	0.303	0.311	0.320	0.328	0.337	0.346	0.363
$\frac{7}{32}$	0.353	0.361	0.370	0.378	0.387	0.396	0.413
$\frac{1}{4}$	0.401	0.409	0.418	0.426	0.435	0.444	0.461
$\frac{9}{32}$	0.450	0.458	0.467	0.475	0.484	0.493	0.510
$\frac{5}{16}$	0.499	0.507	0.516	0.524	0.533	0.542	0.559
$\frac{11}{32}$	0.549	0.557	0.566	0.574	0.583	0.592	0.609
$\frac{3}{8}$	0.598	0.606	0.615	0.623	0.632	0.641	0.658
$\frac{13}{32}$	0.646	0.654	0.663	0.671	0.680	0.689	0.706
$\frac{7}{16}$	0.695	0.703	0.712	0.720	0.729	0.738	0.755
$\frac{15}{32}$	0.734	0.742	0.751	0.759	0.768	0.777	0.794
$\frac{1}{2}$	0.794	0.802	0.811	0.819	0.828	0.837	0.854
$\frac{9}{16}$	0.892	0.900	0.909	0.917	0.926	0.935	0.952
$\frac{5}{8}$	0.990	0.998	1.007	1.015	1.024	1.033	1.050
$\frac{11}{16}$	1.089	1.097	1.106	1.114	1.123	1.132	1.149
$\frac{3}{4}$	1.187	1.195	1.204	1.212	1.221	1.230	1.247
$\frac{13}{16}$	1.286	1.294	1.303	1.311	1.320	1.329	1.346
$\frac{7}{8}$	1.384	1.392	1.401	1.409	1.418	1.427	1.444
$\frac{15}{16}$	1.481	1.489	1.498	1.506	1.515	1.524	1.541
1	1.580	1.588	1.597	1.605	1.614	1.623	1.640
1-$\frac{1}{16}$	1.678	1.686	1.695	1.703	1.712	1.721	1.738
1-$\frac{1}{8}$	1.777	1.785	1.794	1.802	1.811	1.820	1.837
1-$\frac{3}{16}$	1.875	1.883	1.892	1.900	1.909	1.918	1.935
1-$\frac{1}{4}$	1.972	1.980	1.989	1.997	2.006	2.015	2.032

Table 10-2
Stock Length Required for 90° Bends of Half-Hard Brass and Copper, Soft Steel, and Aluminum

Radius of Bend, r (inches)	Thickness of Material, t (inches)						
	$1/64$	$1/32$	$3/64$	$1/16$	$5/64$	$3/32$	$1/8$
$1/32$	0.059	0.069	0.079	0.089	0.099	0.109	0.129
$3/64$	0.084	0.094	0.104	0.114	0.124	0.134	0.154
$1/16$	0.108	0.118	0.128	0.138	0.148	0.158	0.178
$3/32$	0.157	0.167	0.177	0.187	0.197	0.207	0.227
$1/8$	0.206	0.216	0.226	0.236	0.246	0.256	0.276
$5/32$	0.255	0.265	0.275	0.285	0.295	0.305	0.325
$3/16$	0.304	0.314	0.324	0.334	0.344	0.354	0.375
$7/32$	0.354	0.364	0.374	0.384	0.394	0.404	0.424
$1/4$	0.402	0.412	0.422	0.432	0.442	0.452	0.472
$9/32$	0.451	0.461	0.471	0.481	0.491	0.501	0.521
$5/16$	0.500	0.510	0.520	0.530	0.540	0.550	0.570
$11/32$	0.550	0.560	0.570	0.580	0.590	0.600	0.620
$3/8$	0.599	0.609	0.619	0.629	0.639	0.649	0.669
$3/32$	0.647	0.657	0.667	0.677	0.687	0.697	0.717
$7/16$	0.696	0.706	0.716	0.726	0.736	0.746	0.766
$15/32$	0.746	0.756	0.766	0.776	0.786	0.796	0.816
$1/2$	0.795	0.805	0.815	0.825	0.835	0.845	0.865
$9/16$	0.893	0.903	0.913	0.923	0.933	0.943	0.963
$5/8$	0.991	1.001	1.011	1.021	1.031	1.041	1.061
$11/16$	1.090	1.100	1.110	1.120	1.130	1.140	1.160
$3/4$	1.188	1.198	1.208	1.218	1.228	1.238	1.258
$13/16$	1.287	1.297	1.307	1.317	1.327	1.337	1.357
$7/8$	1.385	1.395	1.405	1.415	1.425	1.435	1.455
$15/16$	1.482	1.492	1.502	1.512	1.522	1.532	1.552
1	1.581	1.591	1.601	1.611	1.621	1.631	1.651
$1-1/16$	1.679	1.689	1.699	1.709	1.719	1.729	1.749
$1-1/8$	1.778	1.788	1.798	1.808	1.818	1.828	1.848
$1-3/16$	1.876	1.886	1.896	1.906	1.916	1.926	1.946
$1-1/4$	1.973	1.983	1.993	2.003	2.013	2.023	2.043

Table 10-3
Stock Length Required for 90° Bends of Hard Copper, Bronze, Cold-Rolled Steel, and Spring Steel

Radius of Bend, r inches	Thickness of Material, t (inches)						
	1/64	1/32	3/64	1/16	5/64	3/32	1/8
1/32	0.060	0.071	0.082	0.093	0.104	0.116	0.138
3/64	0.085	0.096	0.107	0.118	0.129	0.141	0.163
1/16	0.109	0.120	0.131	0.142	0.153	0.165	0.187
3/32	0.158	0.169	0.180	0.191	0.202	0.214	0.236
1/8	0.207	0.218	0.229	0.240	0.251	0.263	0.285
5/32	0.256	0.267	0.278	0.289	0.300	0.312	0.334
3/16	0.305	0.316	0.327	0.338	0.349	0.361	0.383
7/32	0.355	0.366	0.377	0.388	0.399	0.411	0.433
1/4	0.403	0.414	0.425	0.436	0.447	0.459	0.481
9/32	0.452	0.463	0.474	0.485	0.496	0.508	0.530
5/16	0.501	0.512	0.523	0.534	0.545	0.557	0.579
11/32	0.551	0.562	0.573	0.584	0.595	0.607	0.629
3/8	0.600	0.611	0.622	0.633	0.644	0.656	0.678
13/32	0.648	0.659	0.670	0.681	0.692	0.704	0.726
7/16	0.697	0.708	0.719	0.730	0.741	0.753	0.775
15/32	0.736	0.747	0.758	0.769	0.780	0.792	0.814
1/2	0.796	0.807	0.818	0.829	0.840	0.852	0.874
9/16	0.894	0.905	0.916	0.927	0.938	0.950	0.972
5/8	0.992	1.003	1.014	1.025	1.030	1.048	1.070
11/16	1.091	1.102	1.113	1.124	1.135	1.147	1.169
3/4	1.189	1.200	1.211	1.222	1.233	1.245	1.267
13/16	1.288	1.299	1.310	1.321	1.332	1.344	1.366
7/8	1.386	1.397	1.408	1.419	1.430	1.442	1.464
15/16	1.483	1.494	1.505	1.516	1.527	1.539	1.561
1	1.582	1.593	1.604	1.615	1.626	1.638	1.660
1-1/16	1.680	1.691	1.702	1.713	1.724	1.736	1.758
1-1/8	1.779	1.790	1.801	1.812	1.823	1.835	1.857
1-3/16	1.877	1.888	1.899	1.910	1.921	1.933	1.955
1-1/4	1.974	1.985	1.996	2.007	2.018	2.030	2.052

● Bronze, Copper, Cold-rolled Steel, and Spring Steel

$$L = 0.71t + 1.57r$$

Bends Other Than 90°

There are many bends other than 90° ones, and Figure 10-2 illustrates some common sheet metal bends. To calculate the length of material needed for these bends, use the 90° bend formula (per type of metal) and multiply it by the angle ($x°$) of the bend divided by 90°. In other words:

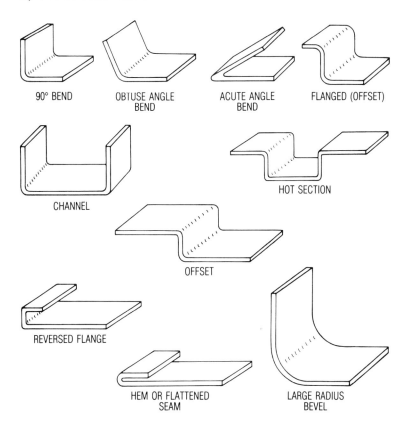

90° BEND

OBTUSE ANGLE BEND

ACUTE ANGLE BEND

FLANGED (OFFSET)

CHANNEL

HOT SECTION

OFFSET

REVERSED FLANGE

HEM OR FLATTENED SEAM

LARGE RADIUS BEVEL

Fig. 10-2. Common sheet metal bends.

- Soft Brass and Copper

$$L = (0.55t + 1.57r) \times (x°/90)$$

- Half-hard Copper and Brass, Soft Steel, and Aluminum

$$L = (0.64t + 1.57r) \times (x°/90)$$

- Bronze, Hard Copper, Cold-rolled Steel, and Spring Steel

$$L = (0.71t + 1.57r) \times (x°/90)$$

When specifying the bend angle, take care to give the actual angle through which the metal is bent. Thus, the bend angle may not be the angle indicated in the drawing. As an example, in Figure 10-3a the angle shown on the drawing is 60°, but is not the angle through which the metal is bent. Here, the actual bending angle is 120° (180° − 60°). Figure 10-3b is a 60° bending angle, and Figure 10-3c also has a bending angle of 60° (90° − 30°).

To calculate L for parts and products that require more than one bend at the *same* radius, determine L for one bend and then multiply it by the number of bends. The resulting product will give the total bend allowance for the part.

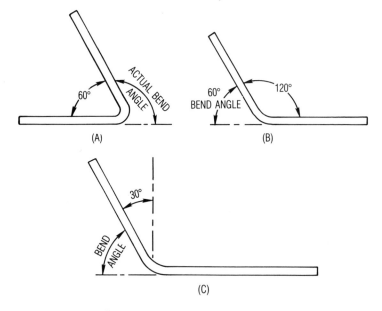

Fig. 10-3. Determining bend angles.

BENDING SHEET METAL BY HAND

There are situations where hand bending of sheet metal may be more convenient than by machine, especially when machines are not available or when bends must be made on installed sections. The development of hand bending competencies, therefore, will prove to be of valuable benefit to the sheet metal worker. Presented in this section is a discussion of the basic tools and procedures used in hand bending sheet metal.

Bending Equipment

Thin and small blanks are easily bent on *metal stakes*. There is a wide range of stakes used in the sheet metal industry. Some of the more common are shown in Figure 10-4. A description of these stakes follows:

- *Bench plate.* Also referred to as a *stakeholder*, the bench plate is used to securely hold individual metal stakes during the bending operation. The plate is made of a cast-iron material and is rectangular in shape. Within the plate are rectangular holes tapered so that individual stakes can be inserted in various positions (Figure 10-4a).

- *Beakhorn stake.* This commonly used stake is of value for most standard forming, riveting, and seaming operations. It is one of the larger stakes designed with a thick, tapered horn at one end and a long rectangularly shaped horn at the other (Figure 10-4b). Hence, both flat and contoured products can be used on this stake.

- *Bottom stake.* The bottom stake has a beveled edge that is fan-shaped. It is used for various operations such as flanging and burring circular parts (Figure 10-4c).

- *Coppersmith stake.* The stake that is considered a general-purpose stake is the coppersmith stake. It has a flat surface with one rounded and one square edge that are used to make straight or curved bends (Figure 10-4d).

- *Common square stake.* Another general-purpose stake, the common square has a flat surface with straight edges that is used for making straight bends and to support the part for riveting or seaming operations. Compared to other stakes, the common square tends to have a long stake (Figure 10-4e).

- *Beveled-edged stake.* This stake is designed so that its shank is off-set. It has a flat rectangular shaped head commonly used to make double seams (Figure 10-4f).

- *Double-seaming stake.* The double-seaming stake is used to support cylindrical parts while a double seam is made. It is designed with two round horns of different lengths at each end (Figure 10-4g).

- *Round-head stake.* The forming of contours is usually accomplished on the round-head stake, which is made of a solid domed-shaped head (Figure 10-4h).

Courtesy Niagara Machine and Tool Works
Fig. 10-4a. Bench plate or stake holder.

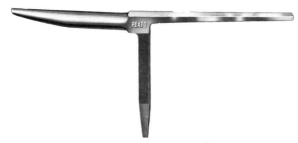

Courtesy Niagara Machine and Tool Works
Fig. 10-4b. Beakhorn brake.

Fig. 10-4c. Bottom stake.

Courtesy Niagara Machine
and Tool Works
Fig. 10-4d. Coppersmith stake.

Fig. 10-4e. Common square stake.

Courtesy Niagara Machine and Tool Works
Fig. 10-4f. Beveled-edge stake.

Courtesy Niagara Machine and Tool Works
Fig. 10-4h. Round-head stake.

Courtesy Niagara Machine and Tool Works
Fig. 10-4g. Double-seaming stake.

- *Hollow mandrel stake.* The hollow mandrel stake is used in forming large curved contours and laps as well as support parts for riveting and double seaming pans and boxes. This stake is designed with a lengthwise slot that houses a sliding bolt. The bolt is used as a means of fastening the stake to a working bench or surface at any desired length or angle (Figure 10-5a).

- *Solid mandrel stake.* A heavy stake used with hollow rectangular parts for forming and riveting operations is the solid mandrel stake. Shaped as a "T" on its side, this stake is usually clamped to the surface of a workbench (Figure 10-5b).

- *Double-seaming stake with interchangeable heads.* A stake that is used for all types of double seaming operations is shown in Figure 10-5c. This stake is made with a tapered rectangular hole, similar to bench plates, at one end. This end is used to insert various types of heads. The other end has a flat tapered surface used as a support for seaming, forming, and riveting operations.

- *Hand seamer.* The hand or *handy* seamer is made with two 3-½ in. (89mm) blades that can be adjusted with a screw gauge. As can be surmised by the hand seamer shown in Figure 10-6, this tool is hand held and is used for various seaming operations.

Courtesy Niagara Machine and Tool Works
Fig. 10-5a. Hollow mandrel stake.

Courtesy Niagara Machine and Tool Works
Fig. 10-5b. Solid mandrel stake.

Courtesy Niagara Machine and Tool Works
Fig. 10-5c. Double-seaming stake with interchangeable heads.

Courtesy Niagara Machine and Tool Works
Fig. 10-6. Hand seamer or handy seamer.

- *Riveting hammer.* When riveting must be done by hand, it becomes necessary to use a riveting hammer. This hammer has a squared and slightly curved face and beveled edges (Figure 10-7a).

- *Setting-down hammer.* The setting-down hammer has a slight resemblance to the riveting hammer, except that its face is square and flat. It is used to set down (make flat) hems and flanges. It is also employed for making certain types of hand seams (Figure 10-7b).

- *Forming hammer.* When contoured surfaces must be formed by hand, a forming hammer is used. A variety of forming hammers are available, and all have a rounded head (Figure 10-7c).

- *Mallets.* Because metal hammers have a tendency to dent and damage sheet metal, mallets are used for bending operations. Shown in Figure 10-7d is a wooden mallet. Other materials used for mallets are leather and rubber.

Making Hand Bends

The most common method for making hand bends utilizes a mallet and stake. Stakes should be selected according to the shape and radius of the bend and the type of metal deformation required. If a stake is not available, a solid, straight-edged block of wood can be used as a substitute. The procedures that should be followed in making a straight angular bend are as follows (see Figure 10-8):

Courtesy Niagara Machine and Tool Works
Fig. 10-7a. Riveting hammer.

Courtesy Niagara Machine and Tool Works
Fig. 10-7b. Setting down hammer.

Courtesy Niagara Machine and Tool Works
Fig. 10-7c. Forming hammer.

Courtesy Niagara Machine and Tool Works
Fig. 10-7d. Wooden mallet.

1. Select the appropriate stake and securely fasten it in a bench plate. If the stake cannot be fitted to a bench plate, clamp it ˙ to the work surface or in a vise.

2. Place the sheet metal onto the bending surface of the stake so that the bending line is even with the bending edge.

3. Bend the metal down with a mallet. *Do not* attempt to make the angle bend with a single blow of the mallet.

4. Bending will require a series of tapping strikes until the desired angle is achieved. If too great a bend is made at one time, the metal will buckle and distort, so that the edge is not smooth and straight.

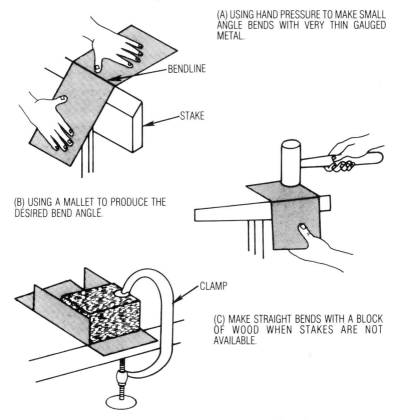

(A) USING HAND PRESSURE TO MAKE SMALL ANGLE BENDS WITH VERY THIN GAUGED METAL.

BENDLINE

STAKE

(B) USING A MALLET TO PRODUCE THE DESIRED BEND ANGLE.

CLAMP

(C) MAKE STRAIGHT BENDS WITH A BLOCK OF WOOD WHEN STAKES ARE NOT AVAILABLE.

Fig. 10-8. Technique for making hand bends.

Cylindrical parts can be made by forming the sheet metal about a cylindrically shaped surface. In addition to curved stakes, rods and pipes are also used. As a rule, the curvature of the form should be somewhat less than the finished part. The procedure used here is as follows (see Figure 10-9):

1. Place the metal over the curved stake, rod, or pipe.
2. Securely hold one edge of the sheet metal with one hand and strike the surface with a mallet.
3. Slowly form the sheet metal until the finished diameter is achieved.

With thin-gauged sheet metal, it may be possible to form the cylindrical part by slowly molding it with hand pressure. This is commonly used with tin plates, brass, and copper sheet metals.

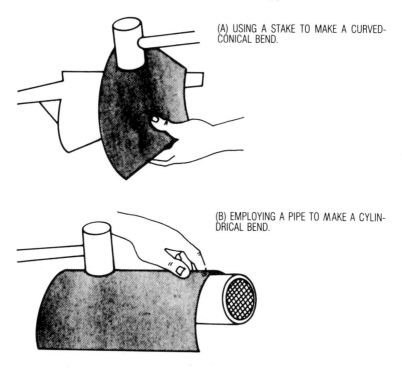

(A) USING A STAKE TO MAKE A CURVED-CONICAL BEND.

(B) EMPLOYING A PIPE TO MAKE A CYLINDRICAL BEND.

Fig. 10-9. Making cylindrical parts by hand bending.

Cone-shaped parts, such as those found in funnels and reducing sections, are formed in a similar sequence of operations. The only difference is the type of stake used. Cylindrical parts are formed around straight cylindrical forms; conical parts are formed about tapered cylindrical forms.

MACHINE BENDING

The vast majority of bending operations are performed on machines known as *brakes*. Except for production brakes, most machine bending operations are accomplished by hand-operated tools. Presented in this section are some of the more common types of brakes used for bending and folding operations.

Leaf Brakes

One of the most basic types of hand-operated brakes used to produce straight angular bends is the *leaf-box brake* or *box and pan brake* (Figure 10-10). This machine is used for bending sheet material of 16-gauge mild steel and thinner. The maximum length of stock that it can handle will depend on the length of the bending bars. Common sized leaf brakes found in the sheet metal trade are 6 (15.2cm), 12 (30.5cm), 24 (61cm), and 36 (91.4cm) in.

The leaf brake is capable of producing all the common bends shown in Figure 10-2. The most frequently made bend, however, is the right angle bend that is used in forming boxes. Angular bends that are greater or less than 90° can also be made on leaf brakes. Rounded folds can also be produced with the use of "fingers" that are designed with a given radius. A comparison of beveled and curved fingers is shown in Figure 10-11.

The basic component parts of the leaf brake are the main housing, forming bar, forming bar adjustment, front leaf assembly, and back gauges. The main housing of the leaf brake is of cast metal, and is designed for strength and durability. Within the main housing is a metal work surface that has been machined flat with a true edge. The metal clamping and bending action is accomplished by the forming bar that is lowered and raised by a cam-operated lever.

Individual forming bars are beveled to an angle that ranges

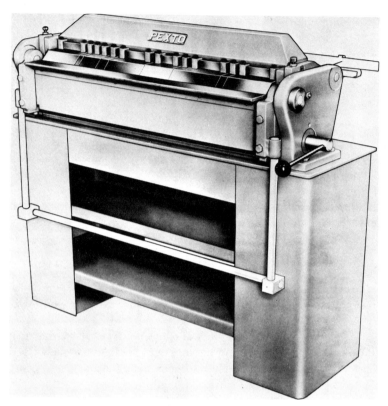

Courtesy Niagara Machine and Tool Works
Fig. 10-10. Leaf or box and pan brake.

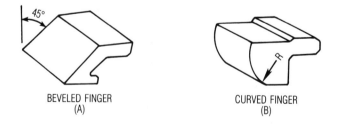

BEVELED FINGER
(A)

CURVED FINGER
(B)

Fig. 10-11. Comparison of beveled and curved leaf brake fingers.

between 125° and 135°. The angle of the bevel will therefore determine the maximum angle that the sheet metal can be bent to at one time. Great angles can be achieved by rotating the metal so that the forming bars will press down on the folded section of the metal.

At times, it may be necessary to move the forming bars closer or further away from the edge of the work surface. This is done by loosening two forming bar adjustment screws, and sliding the bar to the appropriate location. As a rule of thumb, the thicker the stock being bent, the further from the work surface edge the forming bar is placed.

The leaf or apron assembly of the brake is composed of a flat steel plate. This plate is connected to the end bearings of the main housing so that it can be rotated. The normal position of the leaf assembly is in line with the metal work surface plate. In this arrangement, the sheet metal can be easily inserted and withdrawn with no interference. When bending is desired, the leaf bar is rotated by the leaf handle. This action pushes up on the sheet material and causes it to bend at the edge of the form bar. This sequence is shown in Figure 10-12.

The angle of the bend can be accurately controlled by use of two adjustable stop gauges that are located at the ends of the leaf assembly. These stops are either of a dowel pin or leaf design. The stop gauges come in contact with the leaf bar as it swings up, stopping it at the desired bending angle. These adjustable gauges are frequently used where several common bend angles are needed (e.g., 30°, 45°, 60°, and 90°).

The back stop gauge is used when several bends must be made at the same length. These stops are located at the back of the main

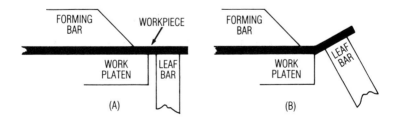

Fig. 10-12. Bending action of the leaf brake.

housing and control the length of the material inserted into the brake. Some brakes are equipped with a micrometer adjustment so that adjustments can be made to within .001 in. (.025mm).

The procedures recommended for bending with a leaf brake are presented as follows:

1. Insert the metal onto the work surface and lower the forming bar so that the finger's edge is just outside the bend line.

2. Set the bending gauges to the appropriate bend angle (when necessary).

3. Draw the front leaf up until the sheet metal is bent to the desired angle. Because of metal "spring-back," it is recommended that this bend slightly exceed the bend angle. The exact amount of excess bend will depend on the metal's gauge and physical properties.

4. Draw the front leaf back to its original position and raise the forming bar so that the metal can be removed.

Bar Folder

The bar folder (Figure 10-13) is used for making narrow bends and folds and is particularly helpful for producing straight hems. Bar folders come in various sizes, which are specified in terms of working length. The more common sizes found in the field are 21 (53.3cm), 30 (76.2cm), 36 (91.4cm), and 42 (106.7cm) in., while sheet metal capacity for most bar folders does not exceed 20-gauge mild steel. Common folds made on this machine are shown in Figure 10-14.

The principal parts of the bar folder are the frame, folding bar, wing, adjustable gauge, and fold stops. The frame is usually made of cast iron or steel for stability and strength. The folding bar in the frame is mounted and is made of a machined piece of hardened steel, which provides the edge around which the metal is folded. The wing is the portion of the folder that pushes up on the metal; it is activated by a hand level that is cam actuated by a spring-action configuration.

The adjustable gauge is used to set the length of the width of the folds, which can range from $\frac{3}{16}$ to 1 in. (4.76 to 2.54mm)— maximum diameter for round folds will be $\frac{1}{4}$ in. (6.6mm). The width of the fold is specified by turning an adjusting screw that is connected

Courtesy Niagara Machine and Tool Works
Fig. 10-13. Bar folder.

RIGHT ANGLE   ACUTE   HEM   DOUBLE HEM RIGHT ANGLE ROUNDED
  FOLD   ANGLE (2 OPERATIONS) (4 OPERATIONS)   FOLD   FOLD
             FOLD   (2 OPERATIONS)

Fig. 10-14. Common folds made with a bar folder.

to a scale. This scale provides a readout to the nearest ¹⁄₁₆ in. As the adjusting screw rotates, it moves a slide that is attached to the gauge bar. Once set, the slide is held in position by a locking screw.

A second gauge is available for adjustments according to metal thickness. Here, the screw knob is used to change the gap between the folding bar and wing. The normal operating range for this gauge is between ³⁄₃₂ and 1 in. (2.38 and 2.54mm).

Three stops are provided on the bar folder. The first two are positive stops for 45° and 90° bends. The third is an adjustable stop that can be set for any desired bending angle.

Folding with a bar folder is an extremely easy operation. The procedures that are normally followed are presented here:

1. Set the width gauge to the appropriate setting. This should correspond to the width of the bend desired. Once the setting is made, lock the gauge in position so that it will not move during folding.

2. Set the metal gauge to correspond with the approximate metal thickness.

3. Set the angle stop gauges to the appropriate bend angle (when necessary).

4. Insert the metal in the folder and hold it against the gauge tightly with the left hand.

5. Grasp the wing lever with the other hand and draw it up until the metal is folded to the appropriate angle.

6. Return the wing lever to its original position and remove the metal.

Cornice Brakes

The cornice brake is similar to the leaf brake, except that it has a solid bending edge rather than a series of forming bars or fingers. Because of this feature, cornice brakes are usually employed to make single straight bends, as compared to multiple bends (e.g., in the making of a box).

As the name implies, the "cornice" brake was first designed to bend sheet metal for use as architectural cornices and related products (e.g., projection moldings for the crowning of buildings and other structures). Today, these brakes are commonly used for making long straight bends required in the construction of ductworks and gutters and siding or roofing installation. Figure 10-15 shows a cross-section finger assembly of this tool.

There are several designs used in the manufacturing of cornice brakes. All, however, employ the same basic elements: work surface, forming bar, and wing (Figure 10-16). The work surface consists of a long straight machined surface on which the metal is placed. The forming bar is attached to a clamping lever that is used to hold down the work during the bending operation. The wing is used to push the metal up and bend it to the appropriate angle. It should be noted that the maximum bend angle that can be achieved at one time is determined by the beveled angle of the forming bar. At the

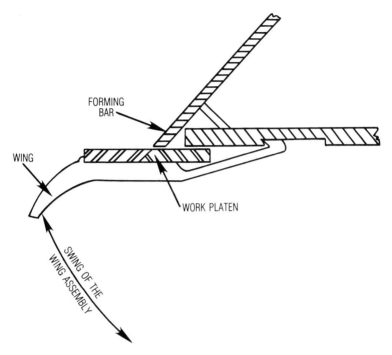

Fig. 10-15. Cross section of the finger assembly for the cornice brake.

ends of the wing is normally some type of counterweight that minimizes the amount of physical force needed to make a bend.

Use of the cornice is quite simple. The sheet metal is inserted onto the work surface and the forming bar is lowered and clamps the work in place. The forming bar is positioned just to the outside of the bend line. Once in place, the metal is bent by pushing on the wing's counterweights. This action swings the wing up and bends the metal. Since there is usually some type of metal "spring-back," the actual bend made should slightly exceed the desired bending angle.

Universal Brake and Folder

The universal brake and folder is an all-around piece of equipment that is a cross between the leaf brake and bar folder. In appearance

Fig. 10-16. Cornice brake.

and operation, however, it is probably more closely allied with the bar folder than the leaf brake (Figure 10-17).

The universal brake and folder is more versatile than traditionally designed bar folders, in that it can produce a fold of any width as well as along the edge of a sheet of metal. Because the main body frame is stationary during bending, it provides the stability needed for working with large sheets of metal. With the use of attachments, this machine is also capable of producing rounded folds.

Universal machine size is normally specified in terms of working length in inches. The two most common sizes found have working lengths of 30 and 42 in. Sheet metal gauge capacities will seldom exceed 20-gauge mild steel.

SUMMARY

The two most common types of folds and bends used in sheet metal work are straight and cylindrical. During the bending or folding

Courtesy Niagara Machine and Tool Works
Fig. 10-17. Universal brake and folder.

operation the sheet metal is subjected to a combined action of compression and tensile stresses. These stresses will result in either a recoverable or permanent deformation.

Bend allowances identify the amount of additional material length that is needed to achieve a bend without loss to the straight sections of the part. All angular bend allowances can be calculated by standard formulas, each designed to take into account the nature and characteristics of the metal.

Bending metal by hand is sometimes required of the sheet metal worker, especially when bending or folding equipment is not available. Hand bends performed in the shop and in some field situations are made on metal stakes. There are a wide range of stakes used in sheet metal work, the more common being the beakhorn stake, bottom stake, coppersmith stake, common square stake, beveled-edged stake, and double-seaming stake. Other sheet metal stakes used include hollow mandrel stakes, solid mandrel stakes, and double-seaming stakes with interchangeable heads. Hand tools used for bending operations are hand seamers, riveting and setting-down hammers, mallets, and forming hammers.

The vast majority of bending operations are performed on machines known as brakes. One of the most versatile types is the leaf or box and pan brake. This brake has interchangeable fingers that are used to make either curved or straight bends. As its name implies, it is easily used to make box-type products.

The bar folder makes narrow bends and folds and is extremely useful for producing straight hems. Unlike the leaf brake, bar folders can only make bends of limited lengths. The length of material that it can handle, however, normally ranges between 21 and 42 in.

Cornice brakes are similar to leaf brakes except that they have a solid bending edge, rather than a series of forming bars or fingers. This equipment is commonly used to produce sheet metal products that require long bends, as in ductwork and gutters. The universal brake and folder is a combination between a leaf brake and bar folder that offers flexibility in bending operations.

REVIEW QUESTIONS

1. Explain what is meant by the expression that bending incorporates a combined action of compression and tensile stresses.

2. What is the difference between permanent and recoverable material deformation?

3. Calculate the bend allowances required for the following material bends:

    Soft copper, 0.0156 in. thick, with a bend radius of 0.250 in., and a bend angle of 90°.

    Aluminum, 0.156 in. thick, with a bend radius of $\frac{1}{32}$ in., and a bend angle of 90°.

    Copper, 0.0625 in. thick, with a bend radius of 0.5625 in., and a bend angle of 90°.

    Cold-rolled steel, $\frac{1}{32}$ in. thick, bend radii of $\frac{1}{16}$ in. and $\frac{1}{8}$ in., and both bend angles of 90°.

Soft steel, 0.0469 in. thick, with a bend radius of ³⁄₆₄ in., and a bend angle of 120°.

4. What are metal stakes? Briefly describe how they are used in bending operations.

5. Briefly describe the procedures that you would use to make a simple 90° straight bend by hand.

6. What are brakes and how are they used?

7. Briefly describe what a leaf brake is and how it operates.

8. What are the unique features of a cornice break?

9. What are bar folders and their uses?

10. Describe what a universal brake and folder is.

CHAPTER 11

Forming Operations

The forming operations that can be performed on sheet metal material are almost as numerous as the products or parts that can be made. There are, however, several basic forming operations that are basic to all sheet metal work. Because of the design and nature of many forming operations, care must be taken in planning the specific *sequence* of steps used by the sheet metal worker. If improper sequencing is selected, it will not only be difficult, but sometimes impossible to make the desired form.

It is, therefore, the intent of this chapter not only to review basic forming operations used in the sheet metal trade, but also to describe the recommended sequence of steps involved in their fabrication. There is usually no "one way only" of accomplishing a specific forming operation—this will be pointed out in a few of the forming operations presented here.

EDGES AND HEMS

The forming of edges and hems usually serves as a means for improving the strength of a product and/or its appearance. Both forming operations are usually performed around the periphery of the part. In the making of a part, edges and hems are commonly made before any bending occurs. Thus, if a boxed container is the desired product, all hems or edges will be formed first, followed by the straight bending of the sides and tabs.

Single and Double Hems

The two most common types of hems made are the single and double hem. Both are frequently made on a bar folder. If desired, these hems can also be made by hand forming. The sequence of bends, however, will be the same in both cases. Figure 11-1 is an illustration of the making of a single hem on a bar folder. The sequential steps recommended are given as follows:

1. Set the gauge of the bar folder to the width of hem required (common hem widths are ¼ (6.35mm), ⅜ (25.4mm), and ½ (12.7mm) in.). Also, adjust the folder to accept the thickness of metal being used.

2. Adjust the bend stop gauges to permit the metal to be bent to the maximum angle.

3. Insert the metal into the bar folder until the entire edge of the part is in contact with the back stop. This is critical, otherwise the hem will be uneven.

4. Pull the folder's handle forward as far as possible, making a maximum angle bend.

5. Push the handle back to its original position and remove the part.

6. Hold the sheet metal *back* on the beveled part of the folder and pull the handle forward as far as possible. This operation closes the hem.

7. Push the handle to its original position and remove the finished hem.

In making a double hem (Figure 11-2), the operations are the same as for the single hem with the exception of repeated steps. Once the single hem is formed, the entire process is repeated so that a second hem can be produced. Hence, it is possible to have a triple hem by repeating the same procedure. It should be noted

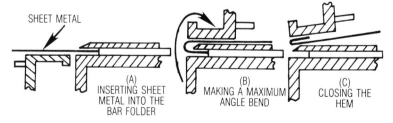

Fig. 11-1. Making a single hem on a bar folder.

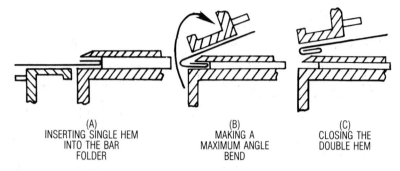

(A)
INSERTING SINGLE HEM
INTO THE BAR
FOLDER

(B)
MAKING A
MAXIMUM ANGLE
BEND

(C)
CLOSING THE
DOUBLE HEM

Fig. 11-2. Making a double hem on a bar folder.

that the single hem is the most common type followed by the double hem. Rarely are triple hems used.

Wired Edges

A wired edge is intended to add strength to the edges of a part. The diameter of the wire selected should conform to the general size of the part, as well as being able to withstand the expected load and stresses. Similar to other forming processes, wired edges can be constructed by hand (Figure 11-3), though this approach is seldom used in the trade today.

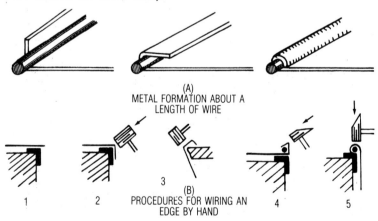

(A)
METAL FORMATION ABOUT A
LENGTH OF WIRE

1   2   3   4   5

(B)
PROCEDURES FOR WIRING AN
EDGE BY HAND

Fig. 11-3. Forming a wired edge by hand.

Most wired edges are constructed with the aid of a rotary machine. This machine (Figure 11-4) is designed for a variety of operations, such as burring, crimping, trimming, flanging, edging, and beading. The versatility of the rotary machine results from the wide variety of rollers available. Examples of some of the more common types of rollers found are shown in Figure 11-5.

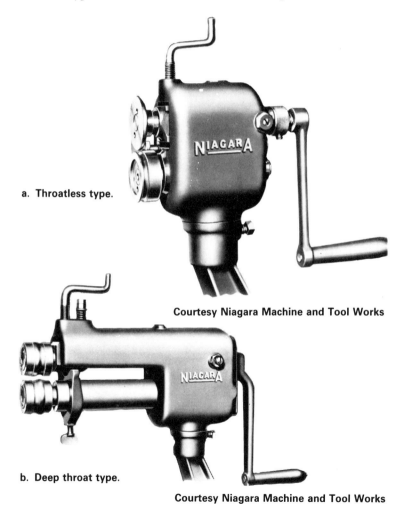

a. Throatless type.

Courtesy Niagara Machine and Tool Works

b. Deep throat type.

Courtesy Niagara Machine and Tool Works

Fig. 11-4. Two common rotary machines.

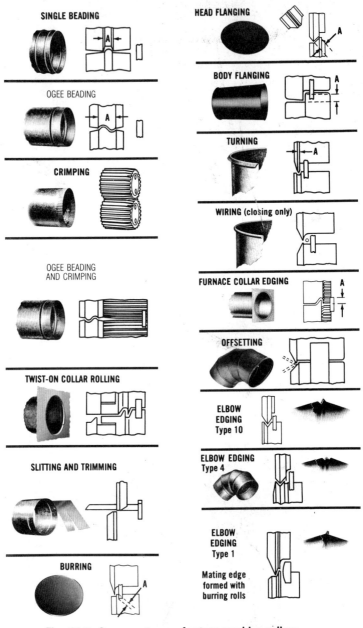

Fig. 11-5. Common types of rotary machine rollers.

Courtesy Niagara Machine and Tool Works

Common types of hand rotary machines are capable of handling sheet stock up to 24-gauge mild steel. Power machines are also found, usually arranged in multi-drive power table (Figure 11-6). In some cases, the rollers may be designed for a single purpose or for two operations, such as shown in Figure 11-7.

When constructing a wired edge on a rotary machine, two types of rolls must be used: turning and wiring rolls. Two sequences used for constructing a wired edge are illustrated in Figure 11-8. The most common and simplest method used is presented as follows:

1. Insert and secure the turning rolls on the rotary machine and set the gauge distance equal to 2.5 times the diameter of the wire. Note that this distance is measured from the gauge to the center of the groove.

2. Place the sheet metal between the two rolls so that the metal's edge comes in direct contact with the gauge.

3. Lower the upper roll with the crank screw to make a slight depression in the metal. Turn the handle until the metal has passed through the rollers the entire length of the edge.

4. Continue to lower the upper roll until a complete groove is formed. During each pass through the turning rolls, raise the work slightly until it is in the vertical position.

5. Cut the wire to length and slip it in the formed groove.

6. Remove the turning rolls and replace them with wiring rolls. Adjust the gauge so that it will be equal to the diameter of the wire plus 2 times the thickness of the metal.

7. Insert the part so that the wired edge is face up.

8. Lower the upper roll so that it grips the work. Turn the handle until the metal is formed over the wire. To ensure a tight form, raise the work up slightly so that the edge of the sheet metal is forced under the wire.

9. Raise the upper rolls and remove the work.

Beading and Crimping

Both beading and crimping are operations that can also be performed on a rotary machine. Beading can be accomplished on flat or cylin-

Fig. 11-6. Multi-drive power table with rotary machines.

Courtesy Niagara Machine and Tool Works

drical pieces to strengthen or enhance their appearance. In some cases, beads are placed on the ends of tubing and sheet metal pipes for connections with rubber or neoprene hosing. The physical dimensions of a bead will depend on the thickness of the material.

Generally, there are two types of beading rolls: single and ogee. In single beading rolls, the three most common diameters (of the bead) are ⅜ (9.5mm), ½ (12.7mm), and ¾ (19.1 mm) in. Common double diameters for ogee beading rolls are 9/16 (14.3mm), ¾ (19.1mm), ⅞ (22.2mm), 1 (25.4mm), and 1-¾ (44.5mm) in. Products that use multiple beads, such as a triple bead, will often require

Fig. 11-7. Combination bending and crimper roller mounted on a rotary machine.

more than one pass through the rotary machine. Shown in Figure 11-9 are examples of single and ogee beading.

The basic procedure used in beading are presented as follows:

1. Insert and secure the proper type and sized beading roller in the rotary machine.

2. Set the gauge at the appropriate distance. The setting should be equal to the distance from the edge of the part to the centerline of the bead.

3. Lower the upper roller until there is a slight impression in the metal, and turn the handle until the metal passes through the rollers.

4. Continue to lower the roller and make passes until the bead is completely formed.

Crimping is used to form a corrugated surface and for reducing the end of sheet metal piping. An example of a crimping roller is shown in Figure 11-10. The crimping operation entails the following steps:

1. Select the appropriate sized crimping roller and securely attach it to the rotary machine.

2. Adjust the rotary machine gauge to the desired length or position of the crimp.

3. Insert the metal so that it is held securely against the gauge.

4. Lower the upper roller until the crimp begins to form and rotate the rollers until the metal passes through.

5. Continue to lower the roller and make passes until the crimp is completely formed.

SEAMING

An operation used for the permanent joining of metals is seaming. Seams are made by folding two or more edges together to form a

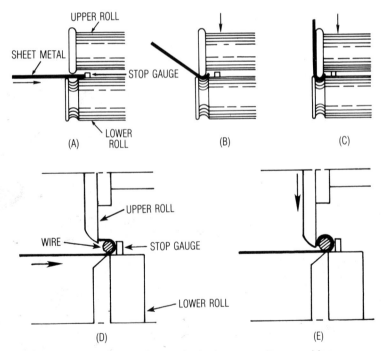

Fig. 11-8. Constructing a wired edge on a rotary machine.

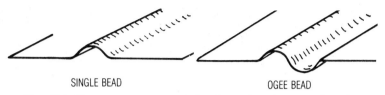

SINGLE BEAD   OGEE BEAD

Fig. 11-9. The two most common beads used in sheet metal work.

CRIMPING

Courtesy Niagara Machine and Tool Works   **Fig. 11-10. Crimping roll.**

permanent connection. Seaming is extensively used in the manufacturing and fabrication of all types of sheet metal products, and is frequently used in combination with other joining techniques such as welding, soldering, and riveting. Examples of products designed with seams are air ducts, shaped parts of plenum and ventilation systems, and containers used to hold liquids and loose materials.

As already presented in this book, there are a number of different types of seams used in the sheet metal industry. Some of the more common (Figure 11-11) and their uses are as follows:

- *Flat lock seams* are used to form longitudinal or lengthwise joints of various types of air ducts. These seams are used where a high degree of airtightness is not required.

- *Double flat lock seams* are used for parts that must be held together by a strong, tight seam.

- *Standing seams* are used in combination with grooved seams for increasing the strength and rigidity of the product.

- *Corner seams* are frequently used to make rectangularly shaped products that are joined at the corners.

- *Bottom seams* are used in the fabrication of articles connected on the bottom side of the object, such as tanks and pails.

257

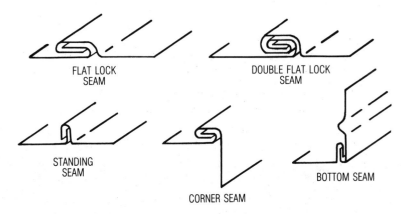

FLAT LOCK
SEAM

DOUBLE FLAT LOCK
SEAM

STANDING
SEAM

CORNER SEAM

BOTTOM SEAM

Fig. 11-11. Common seam types.

Flat Lock Seam

Perhaps the simplest type of seam used is the flat lock or *grooved seam*, which is sometimes made by hand operations. Here, a hand groover (Figure 11-12) is used to form the finished seam. The basic steps used in making a grooved seam require that the ends of the joining edges be folded. These folded edges are referred to as *locks*.

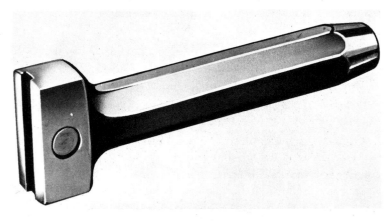

Courtesy Niagara Machine and Tool Works
Fig. 11-12. Hand groover.

258

The two edges are hooked together and are then formed to a finished dimension and locked together with a hand groover.

Grooving tools have a machined channel at one end and come in a variety of sizes. Grooving tool sizes are specified in terms of a number. This number is equivalent to a specific dimensional width. Common groover numbers and their corresponding width dimensions are presented in Table 11-1.

The specific steps used to fabricate a flat lock seam by hand are as follows:

1. Make the connecting locks to size on the bar folder.

2. Hook the locks together and securely hold them in place. With a mallet, lightly tap the locks together so that they are brought into contact with each other.

3. With the appropriate sized groover, place the channeled groove over the locks and tap with a mallet or riveting hammer. Continue this the entire length of the seam.

   NOTE: In selecting the proper sized groover, an allowance should be made for the amount of metal used to form the lock. A rule of thumb allows for 3 times the lock width (Groover Size = $3w$) for 24-gauge mild steel and thinner, and 3 times the lock width plus 5 times the thickness of the metal (Groover Size = $[3w + 5t]$) for mild steel 22-gauge or heavier.

4. Repeat the tapping action on the groover until the seam is formed to specifications.

Table 11-1
Grooving Tool Sizes

Size Number	Equivalent Size in Inches
0	$\frac{3}{8}$
1	$\frac{11}{32}$
2	$\frac{5}{16}$
3	$\frac{9}{32}$
4	$\frac{7}{32}$
5	$\frac{5}{32}$
6	$\frac{1}{8}$

Grooving can also be accomplished on powered or hand-operated grooving machines (Figure 11-13). These machines are frequently used to produce single and Pittsburgh lock seams. Grooving machines are often capable of handling sheet metal thicknesses to 18-gauge mild steel. With grooving machines, care must be taken to use the appropriate sized groover to form the seam. This will be determined by the finished seam width, whose dimensions are a function of the metal's thickness or gauge. Table 11-2 contains recommended seam width sizes for given gauge thicknesses.

A modification of the flat lock seam is the double flat lock seam. Procedures here are similar, with the addition of a few more forming sequences. The procedure is illustrated in Figure 11-14 and outlined as follows:

1. Make the first edge bend with a bar folder for each end to be joined.

2. Adjust the bar folder gauges to accept the metal sheet with the first bend. Insert the working end of the metal piece into the bar folder and make the second bend. Repeat operation for other metal piece.

3. Carefully slide the two working ends together so that the folds mate appropriately, and secure in place by tapping with a mallet along the length of the seam.

4. Set down the seam on a grooving machine, hand groover, or steel bar and hammer.

Table 11-2
Seam Widths for Grooving Machines

Gauge	Finished Seam Width (inches)
20	7/16
22	3/8
24	5/16
26	1/4
28	7/32
30	3/16
32	5/32

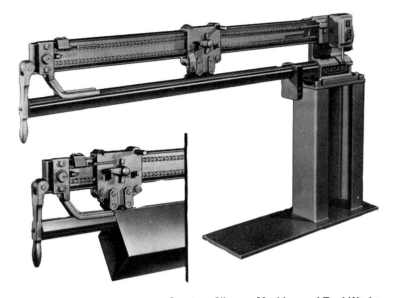

Courtesy Niagara Machine and Tool Works
Fig. 11-13. Grooving machine.

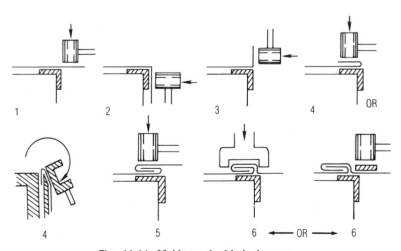

Fig. 11-14. Making a double lock seam.

Standing Seams

Standing seams are used in the fabrication of a large number of sheet metal products. The two most common types of seams are the single and double lock standing seams. The height of standing seams will vary according to the type of part being made, though most standing seams will range in height from ½ to 1 in. (12.7 to 25.4mm). Illustrated in Figure 11-15 are the procedures that should be used to construct a single standing seam. The sequence is as follows:

1. On one of the ends, make the appropriate sized lock bend on the bar folder.

2. Adjust the bar folder so that it will accept the lock end of the metal. Insert this end into the folder and bend it 90° so that the lock is above the outside surface of the part.

3. With the bar folder, make a 90° bend on the end of the other metal piece so that it is above the outside surface of the part.

4. Fit the two ends together, and set with a mallet or with a flat roller on a rotary machine.

The construction of a double lock standing seam (Figure 11-16) is similar to the single lock, with the addition of one fold per end. The procedure used here is as follows:

1. At the end of both metal pieces, make a standing lock on a bar folder so that it is 90° to the outside surface of the part.

2. Select one of the pieces and fold down the standing lock until it becomes a double lock.

3. Bend the double lock until it stands 90° to the outside surface of the part.

4. Slide the single and standing locks together and set with a mallet or rotary machine.

Corner Seams

One of the most common types of corner seams used on square or rectangular products is the double seam. Similar to other seams,

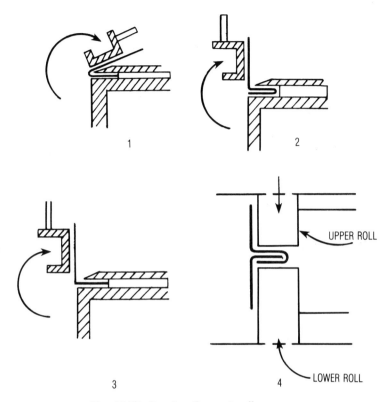

Fig. 11-15. Constructing a standing seam.

the double seam is frequently constructed on a rotary machine with several types of rollers. The fabrication sequence is illustrated in Figure 11-17 and outlined as follows:

1. Make a 90° bend with a bar folder on the edges to be seamed together. If a bar folder is not available, this step of the operation can also be accomplished on a rotary machine that is equipped with a burring roll.

2. Securely install two setting down rolls in the rotary machine and insert the two folder edges until they come in contact with the rollers.

3. Lower the rollers until the bottom flange starts to bend over the side flange, and make one pass through the rollers.

4. Continue to lower the rollers until the flange is pinched tightly.

5. Install a set of seamer rollers in the rotary machine.

6. The first operation on the seamer requires that the pinched flange be bent toward the wall of the part. This process uses both upper and lower rollers and should be carried on until the maximum bend angle is achieved.

7. With the upper roller, set the double seam.

HOLLOWING

The process known as hollowing is used to form sheet metal into convex shapes. Thus, the work is "hollowed" on a stake, die, or block. Hammer blows or forming presses are used to deform the sheet metal blank to size. As the metal is struck, it will thin out and take on the form of the die or stake. Shown in Figure 11-18 is a simple illustration of how the metal deforms to shape in hollowing.

Hollowing by Hand

Convex shapes are formed by hand by striking the metal with a mallet, planishing hammer, and/or ball-peen hammer over a stake.

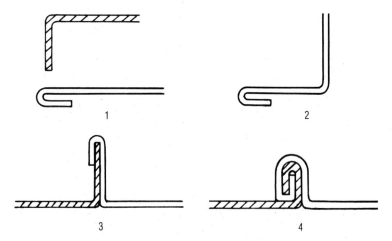

Fig. 11-16. Bending sequences for a double standing seam.

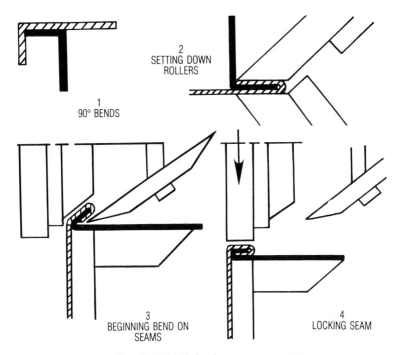

1
90° BENDS

2
SETTING DOWN
ROLLERS

3
BEGINNING BEND ON
SEAMS

4
LOCKING SEAM

Fig. 11-17. Fabricating a corner seam.

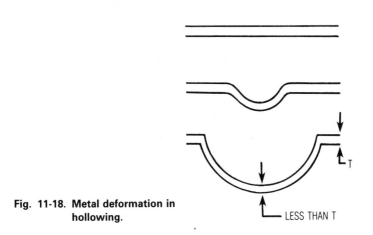

Fig. 11-18. Metal deformation in
hollowing.

T

LESS THAN T

265

The stake will take on the image of the inside surface of the part. Thus, the size and shape of the stake selected must conform to those of the end product. Stake surfaces should always be well polished and free from dents, corrosion, and deep scratches, otherwise they will leave an impression on the part itself.

The basic sequence of operations in hand hollowing is presented as follows (see Figure 11-19):

1. Select the appropriate size and shaped stake.
2. Cut out the metal blank to size.
3. Bend down the edges of the work by a series of gentle strikes beginning at the center of the work and continuing out in a spiral pattern.
4. As the work begins to take shape, the edges will be deformed with crimps, similar to a corrugated pattern. At this time, the crimps should be smoothed out.
5. Continue to make gentle blows with a mallet until the part reaches the desired size and shape.
6. If a very smooth finish is desired, continue the striking process with a mallet.
7. Final evening is accomplished on a round stake with a planishing hammer.
8. Check the work and remove any burrs.

Hollowing Press Hammers

Sheet metal can also be hollowed on power presses. The principal working components of press hammers are shown in Figure 11-20

1.
BENDING DOWN
OF EDGES

2.
SMOOTHING OUT
OF CRIMPS

3.
HOLLOWING THE
INSIDE WITH
HAMMER

Fig. 11-19. Hollowing by hand.

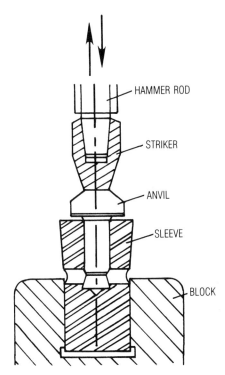

HAMMER ROD

STRIKER

ANVIL

SLEEVE

BLOCK

Fig. 11-20. Cross section of a working hollowing hammer.

and consist of a hammer rod, striker, anvil, sleeve, and block. The striker and anvil are the male and female parts of the die and are made of hardened tool steel.

Actual hollowing of the blank can be accomplished by a series of strikes or with one single strike of the hammer. With small shop-type hammers, several strikes are usually required. Production-type presses normally use a single stroke action for hollowing.

FREE FORMING

One of the first methods used to form and shape metal was by free forming techniques. These techniques were useful in producing tools, weapons, and artwork. Today, however, most free forming is limited to art metalcraft. Though sheet metal workers are seldom called on to produce metal artwork, it is important that they at least

267

understand the principles involved in free forming. There are times when these techniques can prove helpful in installation and repair work.

The primary objective of this section is to briefly discuss basic free forming operations. Artistically inclined individuals should seek additional information and training if they are truly interested and talented in the area of metalsmith artcraft.

Basic Forming Operations

The most basic forming process employed in art metalwork is hammering. Hammering can be used to thin out a piece of sheet metal stock as well as shape it to a given form. In earlier days, many hammering operations required the metalsmith to heat the metal before work began.

Generally, there are three basic hammering processes used in free forming:

1. *Forming* or *silversmith* hammering is the most basic type of forming operation. This technique is used to shape bowls and trays. The hammers used here are made of hardened forged steel with highly polished and rounded faces. The resulting work produces a smooth impression on soft metals such as copper, silver, brass, and aluminum.

2. *Raising* is an operation used to make objects such as bowls or vases. Here, the metal is worked on the outside surface so that it is driven or raised to shape.

3. *Planishing* is used to smooth off any surface irregularities in the product. This operation is executed after the product has been shaped or embossed. Planishing produces a smooth and bright finish.

There are several basic hand tools used in free forming operations. The first are forming hammers that are categorized as forming, raising, and planishing hammers (Figure 11-21), and are used for the three operations just described.

Mallets are primarily used for rough forming over anvils. In some products, such as pewterware, mallets can be used throughout the forming process. Unlike steel hammers, mallets will leave no

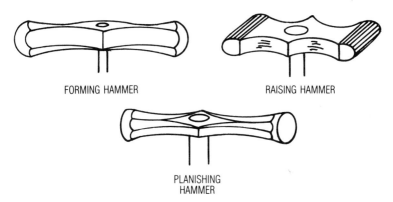

Fig. 11-21. Three categories of free forming hammers.

marks in the metal if handled correctly. Examples of common types of mallets used in free forming are hardwood, double wedge, round end, and leather-faced forming mallets (Figure 11-22).

Decorative Surfaces

A decorative surface frequently produced in hand forming is known as a *wrought iron effect*. This surface is often seen on flat metal surfaces found in door hinges, straps, lock assemblies, and light

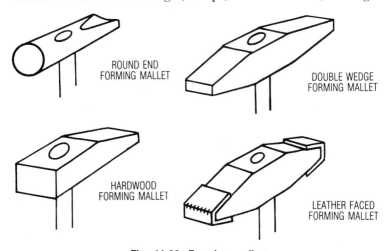

Fig. 11-22. Forming mallets.

housings. It is produced by hammering onto a flat sheet of metal with the rounded end of a forming hammer.

To complete the wrought iron effect, the entire surface of the part must be hammered. The impressed circles or dimples produced will vary in diameter and depth since each strike of the hammer will also vary in force. To produce an attractive and true wrought iron effect, it is critical that the amount of force used to strike the work piece varies. In addition, none of the original metal's surface should be left. This decorative surface is commonly used on steel, aluminum, copper, and brass.

Another decorative surface finish that can be achieved is to buff only the raised surface of the metal. This technique is often used with copper and brass products. By not allowing the buffing wheel to penetrate the dimples, only the high points will appear shiny, offering an attractive contrast. If a buffing wheel is not available, a fine grade of steel wool can be used.

Finally, the product can be further treated with a sprayed or brushed on finish. Lacquer is a popular choice for it not only produces a clear finish but also protects the metal from tarnishing or dulling.

Forms

A number of forms can be used to shape metal. In each case, these forms provide a solid surface that supports the metal as it is hammered. Consequently, the shape of the form will dictate the finished shape of the metal and will function as a mold or die.

Four common types of products used to support and form metal are stakes, wooden flat surfaces, female-formed cavities, and a sandbag. Artmetal stakes come in a vast array of designs and configurations. Some are designed for bending, forming, raising, and planishing, while others are manufactured for forming a specific shape such as a bowl or cup. Flat wooden surfaces are used because they will not damage or mar the metal being shaped. These surfaces may be either a bench top or wooden block.

Pre-formed female cavities are usually custom made by the metalsmith for the sole purpose of producing a specific shape or design. These cavity forms are made of hardwood, such as maple or oak, and serve as an inexpensive method of free forming. Sandbags or leather shot bags are used in both raising and forming operations. Made of either canvas or leather, they are filled with fine sand or metal shot. The main function of this support is to produce special free form depressions in the metal.

Forming Metals

Not all metals are conducive to free forming. Only those with high malleability and a soft temper state are successful. Perhaps the most common free forming metals used today are aluminum, soft brass, copper, gold, lead, and silver.

Some metals, such as copper and brass, exhibit a unique characteristic known as *work hardening*. Work hardening is the change in temper state as the metal is worked. In other words, as these metals are worked, they become harder. Once the metal loses its soft temper, further forming is not only difficult, but can also produce stresses and strains that result in metal cracking and deformation.

A practice used to handle work hardening problems is annealing. Annealing is a heating and cooling process that returns the metal to a soft temper state by rearranging its internal structure. Annealing procedures recommended for common free forming metals are as follows:

- *Copper* is easily annealed by heating it to a red glow temperature and immediately quenching (cooling) it in cold water.

- *Brass* is annealed by heating it to a red glow temperature and letting it cool to room temperature at a very slow rate. The cooling process is frequently accomplished with the aid of an oven.

- *Silver* is annealed by heating it to a high temperature and quickly quenching it in cold water.

- *Aluminum* is also annealed by raising its temperature followed by rapid quenching in cold water.

One of the best free forming metals recommended for the beginner is copper. This metal not only works well but also produces a very attractive product.

Free Forming Procedures

Though there are a number of different free forming operations available to the metal worker, several basic steps are common to most operations. Presented here is a discussion of each step:

1. *Preparation of the backing block.* This is one of the most important steps involved in free forming, since it will dictate the shape or form of the finished product. Here, the worker will examine a drawing of the product and prepare a "negative" or "reverse" form in the backing block. In some cases, a backing block will not have to be made if such a form is already available.

2. *Metal preparation.* Once the backing block has been made or selected, the metal must then be prepared. This may involve an annealing process, but in most cases will be limited to cutting out a blank. For example, if a bowl is being made, then a circular blank will be cut from stock.

3. *Initial forming.* The blank is then centered onto the backing block. To begin with, all hammering strikes should be light and cover the entire area of the metal. If too heavy a blow is made, the metal may be damaged or disfigured. Care should be taken to ensure that the forming process is gradual and made along the entire surface area of the metal.

4. *Finish forming.* Once the metal has been initially shaped, it must then be formed to finished size and shape. This is again accomplished by a series of small, light taps with the hammer. These strikes are normally made closer together and at a higher rate. Small irregularities are worked out with a small hammer and light blows. It must be noted that free forming is a long and painstaking process, and any attempt to speed up the process will often lead to a defective product.

Embossing

Free forming cannot be adequately covered without some mention of embossing techniques. Embossing is a process where an image or design is made in metal without any material removal. Impressions are made by raising and/or depressing the metal's surface.

Metals used in embossing are very soft and thin. Examples of metals with good embossing characteristics are copper and lead. Here, a tool that is harder than the metal is used to produce the desired effect. The tool can be struck with a hammer or impressed with hand pressure, causing the workpiece metal to be displaced.

The first step in embossing is a drawn pattern or design, which is often prepared on paper. The drawing is then either transferred to the metal by carbon paper or is taped directly to the workpiece. Tools are then selected that will produce the desired effect. Embossing begins when these tools "trace over" the drawing, leaving an impression in the metal.

SUMMARY

A number of basic forming operations are common to most sheet metal products. Of great importance in each is the sequencing of folds and bends. Without proper sequencing, many operations would be difficult, if not impossible, to execute.

The fabrication of edges and hems are two forming processes used to improve the strength and/or appearance of a product. Single and double hems are perhaps the most common types of hems used on sheet metal products. Wired edges, by comparison, are used primarily for increasing the strength of a part's edge. Beading is an operation also used to improve the strength and appearance of many cylindrical and some flat products. Crimping, on the other hand, is used for either forming a corrugated surface or for reducing of sheet metal piping ends.

Seaming is a forming process to connect pieces of sheet metal by folding operations. Common seams used in construction and manufacturing settings are flat lock, double flat lock, standing, corner, and bottom seams. These seams can be made entirely by hand tool operations or sheet metal machinery such as rotary and grooving machines.

Hollowing is an operation employed to form convex-shaped objects. These products can be formed by hand on stakes or on powered equipment such as hollowing press hammers. Unlike free forming, hollowing is usually executed to specific tolerances.

Free forming is an art metalworking operation where the metal is formed without great dimensional tolerance. Basic free forming operations include forming or silversmith hammering, raising, and planishing. Another technique unique to art metalwork is decorative surfacing such as wrought iron effect. Examples of forms used in the shaping of art metalwork are stakes, wooden flat surfaces, female-formed cavities and sandbags. Common free forming metals used by craftspeople are copper, brass, aluminum, lead, and silver. Another important free forming technique is embossing, a process where an image is made in the metal without any material removal.

REVIEW QUESTIONS

1. Briefly explain the importance of proper sequencing in forming sheet metal products.

2. Explain the tools and procedures you would use in forming a double hem.

3. What are wired edges used for? Give examples of products that use a wire edge.

4. Briefly describe the function of a rotary machine and its applications.

5. What is the primary function of beading?

6. How is crimping used to fit two cylindrical pipes together with the same dimensions?

7. List the procedures you would use to form a single lock seam with a hand groover. Identify the differences when using a grooving machine.

8. Explain how a rotary machine can be used in making a corner seam.

9. Identify the two methods for sheet metal hollowing.

10. What is free forming and how does it differ from other sheet metal operations?

11. What is embossing?

CHAPTER 12

Notching and Clipping

One of the primary objectives of sheet metal workers is to produce an attractive and functional product. To accomplish this, one must be able to fabricate seams and hems that are both functional and pleasing to the eye. A problem commonly faced in such fabrications is the overlapping of seams and edges. To avoid this problem, the sheet metal worker must be able to cut away the overlapping portion of material and still maintain the form and function of the product.

Two basic operations designed to eliminate the problem of material overlap are known, as notching and clipping. To be a successful sheet metal worker requires knowledge in the laying out and cutting of notches and clips. Presented in this chapter is a discussion of how notching and clipping are successfully employed in the fabrication of sheet metal products.

NOTCHING VS. CLIPPING

Both notching and clipping are methods used to cut away sections of metal that might otherwise overlap and bulge. The basic difference between a notch and clip are illustrated in Figure 12-1. As can be seen, a notch and a clip are considered two separate operations, but are used to accomplish the same goal.

Notches

There are several common forms of notches used in sheet metal work. The first is the square notch for making square or rectangular containers such as boxes and pans. As shown in Figure 12-2, square

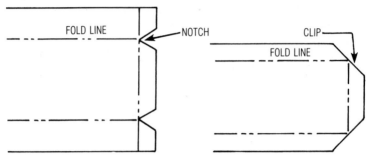

Fig. 12-1. Comparison between notching and clipping.

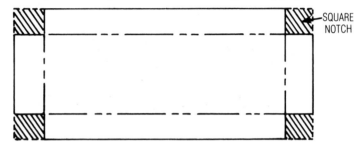

Fig. 12-2. Square notched layout.

notches enable these products to be easily folded and fitted. The dimensional size of the notch is predetermined by the location of the product's bend lines.

Another notch often used in sheet metal products is the 45° notch. Formed in the shape of a "V," the 45° notch is primarily used for one of two situations: for the fabrication of a double seam end and 90° bend with an inside flange. Shown in Figure 12-3 is an illustration of the 45° notch.

Not all notching involves angular cuts. There are times when a straight notch, sometimes referred to as a slit edge, is of benefit. An example of straight notching is shown in Figure 12-4.

Clipping

The most common use of clipping is in forming a hem. Here, the material is cut or clipped at the corners where the hem will meet at right angles. The angle of cut will usually be at 45°, though other

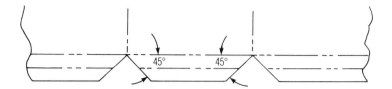

Fig. 12-3. 45° notch for a double seam.

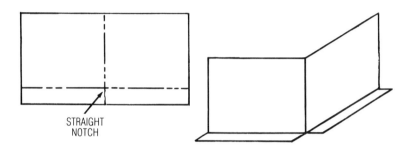

Fig. 12-4. Straight notching.

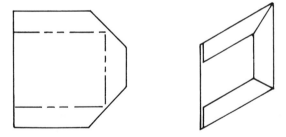

Fig. 12-5. Clipping for a single hem.

angles may be used according to the part's shape and angle of bend. Shown Figure 12-5 is an example of clipping for a single hem.

NOTCHERS

There are special tools available designed to produce notches. Shown in Figure 12-6 is one such machine—an air-powered notcher.

Courtesy Niagara Machine and Tool Works
Fig. 12-6. Air-powered notcher.

In addition to this type, there are also hand operated and electrically powered notchers.

The operation of notchers is similar to that of shears. The lower work platen functions as a blade holder for two blades that are set at 90° to each other. Above the blades is the filler block and upper blade that are connected to a movable ram. As the ram is lowered, the upper and lower blades provide a shearing action as they pass in close contact.

Notcher size is specified by the length of the 90° cut and its material capacity. Two common sized notchers are 6 in. (15.2cm), 16-mild-steel gauge and 5 in. (12.7cm), 14-mild-steel gauge notchers. These descriptions simply translated mean that the length of the 90° cut is either 6 or 5 in. (15.2 or 12.7cm), on sheet materials that have a thickness equivalent to either 16- or 14-gauge mild steel. Power notchers are also specified in terms of cuts or strokes per minute (spm). A common spm capacity for a power notcher is approximately 40.

Other cuts, such as small sized notches or rectangularly shaped notches, can also be made by stop gauges. These gauges are positioned on the bottom work platen at 90° to each other. Gauge scales can be obtained in either inches or millimeters.

278

Stops that are set to the gauging scales will indicate the distance from the corner of the work to the cut line. Thus, if the stop is set at the 2 in. (5.1cm) mark, this would mean that the cut would be made 2 in. (5.1cm) from the corner. Rectangular cuts can be set on the stop gauges by positioning each gauge independently to correspond to the length of each side of the rectangle.

Notches Greater than 90°

Notches that are greater than 90° can also be cut on a notcher by a simple procedure. Consider the obtuse angle notch of 140° shown in Figure 12-7, where the sides of the notch are equal.

To cut the 140° notch, two cuts must be made. The first cut will be made at 90°, so that the second cut must be at 50° (140 − 90 = 50). To make this second cut, one of three procedures can be followed. The first is achieved by laying out the 140° line prior to any cutting, and then cutting along the line during the second cut. A second method uses stops on the work platen. These stops are set according to the length of one side of the angle. The third and perhaps easiest method is used where the platen is equipped with protractor gauging assembly. Here, the desired cut angle is set so that the workpiece can be inserted at the given angle.

Each of the three methods used for cutting obtuse angles offers differing advantages. The first method is quick and can be used where great accuracy and tolerances are not required. The second is best suited for multiple operation work, and the last is most advantageous in achieving great accuracy with minimal set-up time.

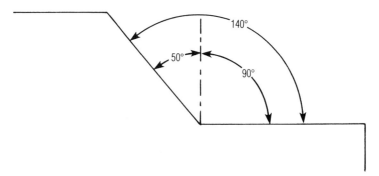

Fig. 12-7. Notching for angles greater than 90°.

Tabs

Cutting tabs is another operation that can be successfully achieved on a notcher. Tabs are metal sections that extend beyond the bend line of parts for the purpose of providing additional strength and/ or for a convenient method of fastening to maintain the final product shape. Shown in Figure 12-8 is an illustration of how tabs are used in the fabrication of a box.

Tab cuts are easily made on notchers by modifying the blades. This procedure requires adjustment in both the upper and lower blades of the notcher. As an example of how this is accomplished, consider the cutting of the tabs shown in Figure 12-9.

The first cutting operation consists of making a conventional

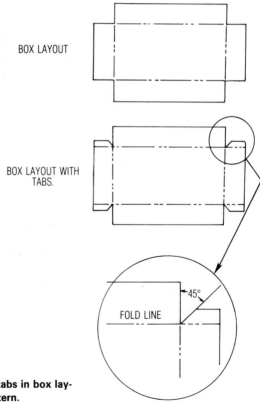

BOX LAYOUT

BOX LAYOUT WITH TABS.

45°

FOLD LINE

**Fig. 12-8. Use of tabs in box lay-
out pattern.**

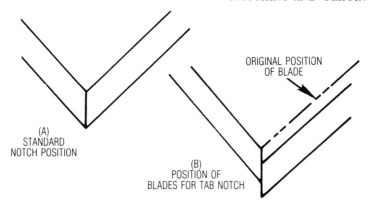

ORIGINAL POSITION
OF BLADE

(A)
STANDARD
NOTCH POSITION

(B)
POSITION OF
BLADES FOR TAB NOTCH

Fig. 12-9. Notcher blade positions for standard and tab notching.

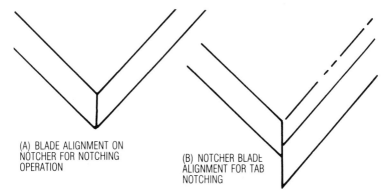

(A) BLADE ALIGNMENT ON
NOTCHER FOR NOTCHING
OPERATION

(B) NOTCHER BLADE
ALIGNMENT FOR TAB
NOTCHING

Fig. 12-10. Blade alignments on notcher.

90° cut, after which the tab section must be fabricated. To do this, many notchers are designed so that the two top and bottom blades will work independently. Where the blades can function separately, loosen one so that it can be moved forward (Figure 12-10) a distance equivalent to the 45° cut length. On 6 or 5 in. (15.2 or 12.7cm) notchers, the maximum size tab that can be cut is 1 in. Critical in this procedure is that the top and bottom blades match each other.

SUMMARY

Notching and clipping are separate operations used to eliminate unnecessary overlapping and metal bulging where seams and hems meet. There are several types of notches used in the sheet metal trade, with the most common being the square notch, 45° notch, and straight notch. Clipping, on the other hand, is mostly made at an angle of 45°, though the cut angle can vary according to pattern shape.

Most notching operations can be performed on a machine known as a notcher, which can be either hand operated or powered. In addition to making 90° notches, these machines can also make obtuse angle cuts. A useful application of notching is making tabs, which are used to strengthen and/or fasten metal together.

REVIEW QUESTIONS

1. Explain the difference between notching and clipping.
2. Sketch a pattern for a simple sheet metal box and identify where the notches and clips are located.
3. Briefly describe what a notcher is and how it functions.
4. Explain how one can make a 135° cut on a notcher.
5. What are tabs and how can they be cut on a notcher?

CHAPTER 13

Fabrication of Round and Cylindrical Parts

Sheet metal workers often encounter work that involves the making and fabrication of round and cylindrically shaped parts. These items cannot be formed in conventional methods used for making straight bends on flat surfaced work, but require the the use of specialized tools and procedures. Presented in this chapter is a description of tools, equipment, and procedures frequently used by sheet metal workers to fabricate round and cylindrical parts.

CUTTING AND FORMING ROUND PARTS

Cutting and forming circular patterns in the sheet metal industry are frequently done by hand shears and methods. When work is required for large diameter circles, conventional procedures often prove to be time consuming and not highly accurate. Though special types of snips and forming tools are sometimes used for unique cutting and bending operations, many sheet metal workers find that the manual methods conducive to smaller part fabrication are totally inadequate for larger objects.

Ring and Circle Shear and Flanger

To cut and form a large diameter arc or circle, it is often most economical (in terms of time and material) to use a specially designed piece of equipment known as a ring and circle shear and flanger. Because of the design and operation of this machine, its most frequent use is in shop and production settings.

Ring and circle shears and flangers (Figure 13-1) are designed

283

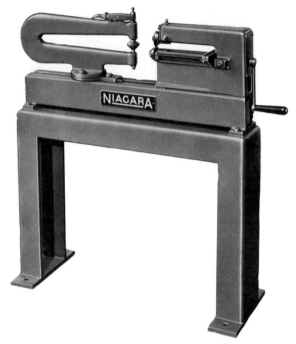

Courtesy Niagara Machine and Tool Works
Fig. 13-1. Hand operated ring and circle shear and flanger.

with two major component parts: cutter and circle arm units. As its name implies, the cutter unit houses the cutters, which are made of a hardened tool steel, are either hand or power activated, and mounted into a cast metal base. The circle arm unit is designed both to hold the workpiece in place and rotate it about a central axis.

The cutter heads are of two basic designs. The first are circle cutters, where cutting begins at the edge of the metal blank. As the metal rotates about a central axis, the part is sheared in one revolution. The second type of cutter is a ring shear used to cut out sheet metal rings. After the square or octagonal blank is initially cut with a circle cutter (producing a circle blank), the ring shear cutter is inserted. Here, cutting begins inside the blank so that the off-cut material remains flat and workable.

A third type of head used for forming is known as a flanger.

Flanges are raised rims employed for strength, guiding, or attachment to other parts. Illustrated in Figure 13-2 is a comparison between a circle, ring, and flange. The maximum height of flanges depends on the diameter of the part and the thickness and ductility of the metal. Thus, higher flanges can be produced on thick stock and larger diameter parts. For maximum height flanges, partial bending may be required before finishing. Table 13-1 shows the maximum height of flanges, for a ⅜ in. (9.5mm) bend radius, that are dictated by material thickness.

Hand-powered machines are capable of handling sheet metal thicknesses equivalent to 16-gauge mild steel or less, while powered machines can handle material to 8-gauge mild steel. The cutter

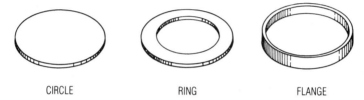

CIRCLE   RING   FLANGE

Fig. 13-2. Basic parts produced on a ring and circle shear and flanger.

Table 13-1
Maximum Flange Heights (⅜″ Bend Radius)

Mild Steel Gauge Number	Maximum Overall Outside Height of Flange (inches)
8	1.500
10	1.500
12	1.375
14	1.250
16	1.125
18	1.000
20	0.875
22	0.750
24	0.500
26	0.500

frame throat depth will vary, with the most common maximum depth measure being 9-¼ in. (23.5cm).

The circle arm unit is mounted onto a T-beveled base. This permits one to position the material clamp to be moved at specific distances from the cutter head. The circle arm's throat will vary from 16 to 34 in. (40.6 to 86.4cm) for hand operated machines, and 16 to 52 in. (40.6 to 132.1cm) for powered equipment. Thus, a circle arm that has a throat depth of 16 in. has a maximum material handling capacity of 32 in. (81.3cm) (diameter). A workpiece clamp is raised or lowered by a threaded shaft. The actual clamping surface is fitted to a bearing surface on the shaft so that it can rotate during machine operations.

When mounting the work onto the circle arm unit, it is critical to locate its center, otherwise the finished product will be dimensionally incorrect. Centers can be located on square or octagonal blanks by diagonal intersections. On some machines an adjustable centering gauge is available for centering unmarked blanks.

Ring and Circle Shear and Flanger Operation

Before any cutting or forming operation can be executed on the ring and circle shear and flanger, the workpiece blank must be prepared. This blank will usually be square, octagonal, or circular in shape. Octagonal and circular blanks are often used when the diameter of the finished circle is close to the circle arm's throat capacity, and when minimal material waste is desired. Once the blank is prepared, the following steps should be observed:

1. Insert the the proper cutting or flanging rolls into the cutter unit.

2. Locate the center of the blank.

3. Clamp the blank to the circle arm at the center of the blank. Make sure that the piece is securely clamped, for any movement will result in cutting or forming errors.

4. Lower the cutting or flanging rolls to the workpiece. If flanging is to be accomplished, it should be noted that several passes through the rolls may be required. Here, the rolls would be lowered at each pass.

5. Activate the rolls. Cutting will normally require only one pass—avoid multiple passes to minimize material movement and operation inaccuracies.

6. Once the cutting or forming is completed, raise the roller and loosen the circle arm clamp, and remove the finished workpiece.

It should be noted that some rotary machines come with optional attachments that enable them to ring and circle, shear and flange. Though the design of these attachments may vary, their operation is similar to those just described.

SLIP ROLL BENDERS

The vast majority of cylindrically and conically shaped objects are made on roll benders. Of these benders, *slip rollers* are perhaps the most widely used (Figure 13-3). Slip rollers are forming machines specifically designed to take flat sheets of metal and form them into cylindrical sections, large radius sections, or flat and curved seg-

Courtesy Niagara Machine and Tool Works
Fig. 13-3. Slip roll bender.

ments. As in the case of other equipment, slip rollers can be either hand or power driven.

Slip Rolling Concepts

All roll benders are equipped with three cylindrical rollers that are housed in a cast metal frame. Each roll has a specific function within the forming process, an illustration of which is shown in Figure 13-4. A description of each roll is presented as follows:

1. *Power roll.* Also known as the *fixed roll*, the power roll rotates during the forming process, with its position remaining stationary. It should be noted that at the bottom ends of the housings are two adjusting screws to raise and lower the power roll. They are used to make adjustments for metal thickness only. This roll rotates within the two end housings of the bender on a set of bearing sleeves. Its primary function is to supply turning power so that the sheet metal can be fed through the rolls. Power rolls can be powered by hand crank or electric motor.

2. *Clamping roll.* Directly above the power roll is the clamping roll. This roll can be moved in an up and down direction at either end. As its name implies, the roll's primary function is to "clamp" the workpiece as it is fed through the rolls. The

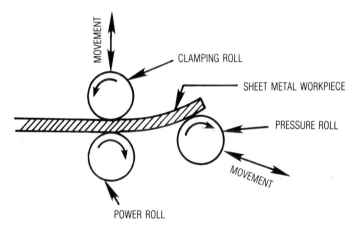

Fig. 13-4. The three rolls used in slip roll benders.

positioning of the clamping role will be dictated by the gauge size metal being formed. For optimal forming, the clamping roll is usually lowered until it just touches the workpiece. The clamping roll also functions as the first roll to help position the workpiece in the machine. The diameter of this roll will dictate the minimum diameter cylinder that can be formed on the bender.

3. *Pressure roll.* The third roll is known as the pressure roll. This roll is also adjustable and is located directly behind and slightly above the power roll. The major function of the pressure roll is to apply an upward force to the metal so that it bends and turns up toward the clamping roll as it is fed through the bender. Adjustments are made only to control the diameter of the cylinder being formed. Hence, the pressure roll serves as a gauge mechanism to produce products with a specific bend radius. As the pressure roll is moved toward the power and clamping rolls, more pressure is applied to the workpiece. When pressure increases, so does the tendency of the metal to bend. Thus, as the pressure roll's distance decreases from the power and clamping rolls, so does the radius of the metal bend. During operation, the pressure roll is adjusted gradually until the workpiece is formed to the desired bend radius (the minimum diameter of which will equal to the diameter of the clamping roll).

A common problem faced by the novice sheet metal worker is how to remove the finished cylinder workpiece from the roll bender without bending it. This may seem like a perplexing dilemma, but is quite easy to solve. The clamping roll is equipped with a split bearing at one end. When the clamping roll release is moved out of position, this roll can be raised. Once raised, the work can then be "slipped" off the roll—hence, the name *slip roll forming machine*.

As mentioned, there are two housing units, known as the left- and right-hand housings. These units not only provide a place for the roll ends to rest, but also contain the gears that rotate the rolls. The drive mechanism, hand or motor, will be attached to the right-hand housing.

Roll benders are usually specified in terms of the minimum diameter that can be formed, or the roll diameter. These diameters in turn dictate the maximum material thickness that can be formed. Presented in Table 13-2 are common gauge capacities for different roll diameters.

Table 13-2
Roll Bender Specifications

Roll Diameter (inches)	Gauge Capacity (Mild Steel)	Thickness Capacity (Inches)
1	28–30	—
1-½	24–26	—
2	16–24	—
3	14–18	—
4	10–18	—
5	8–16	0.1875 (maximum)
6	10–12	0.3125–0.1875

Slip Roll Forming

All forming operations begin with a flat sheet of metal cut to specifications. Before any forming operation can be accomplished on the slip roll, or any other roll bender, consideration must first be given to the treatment of abutting edges. That is, what method is used to join them, such as a lock joint seam. In the majority of cases, these ends should be bent prior to roll forming. Thus, all straight forming bends are first made on leaf or press brakes prior to cylindrical, curved, or conic forming.

The basic steps recommended for slip roll forming are presented as follows. Note that these steps are preceded by pattern cut-out and abutting edge treatment.

1. Adjust the position of the power roll for the appropriate gauge metal stock being used.
2. Insert the sheet metal piece and lower the clamping roll so that it just comes in contact with the work. Lock in position.

3. Ease back the pressure roll so that it will allow easy entrance of the workpiece.

4. Make one complete pass of the sheet metal through the rolls. Remove the metal and completely flip it over to the other side so that a second pass will be made of the opposite side. This operation is referred to as *breaking the sheet* and is used to reduce the surface strength of the material, allowing for an increase in forming flexibility. If breaking the sheet is not performed on the workpiece, then its surface will tend to have a series of bend lines in it rather than a smooth even surface.

5. Move the pressure roll closer to the power roll and make another pass of the workpiece so that the bend radius of the metal will decrease. This process should continue until the final bend radius is achieved.

6. When cylinders are made, release the clamping roll so that it can be raised at one end. When that end is raised above the end housing frame, slip the formed cylinder off the roll.

7. Return the clamping roll to its original position and lock in place.

There is one fact that must always be remembered when slip forming: roll forming is a forward moving process. The workpiece should never be reversed rolled while in contact with the pressure and clamping rolls. If the workpiece is reversed rolled while engaged with the pressure and clamping rolls, the bend radius will increase, which can result in completely ruining all work accomplished to that point. Therefore, all roll contact must be disengaged for all backout operations.

Conical shapes, such as those used in funnels and circular reducing sections, can also be formed on the slip role. What must be remembered is that in conical sections one end will have a smaller diameter than the other, thus the layout must be fed into the slip roll former so that more bend occurs at the small diameter end.

Shown in Figure 13-5 is an illustration of how conical forming is achieved. The concept here is that arcs A and B must both pass through the forming rolls in proportion to each other. This is illustrated by the center lines shown on the layout in our figure. For

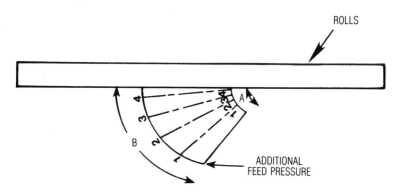

Fig. 13-5. Conical forming on a slip roll bender.

each travel distance between element lines along A (i.e., A-1, A-2, etc.), a greater, but proportional, distance between element lines along B (i.e., B-1, B-2, etc.) must be achieved.

To achieve the appropriate bending of conical products, the following steps should be used:

1. Insert the metal workpiece along one side of the layout.

2. Before the workpiece is passed through the rolls, adjust the clamping roll so that there is more pressure applied to the small diameter end of the workpiece. Depending on the difference in end diameters, little or no pressure is applied at the large diameter end. It should be noted that this type of clamping pressure arrangement makes the small diameter end function as a pivot point around which the layout is formed.

3. Turn the rolls and feed the workpiece so that more feeding pressure is applied at the large diameter end. Here, distance A-1 should be covered at the same time as distance B-1, as is A-2 and B-2, A-3 and B-3, and so on.

4. After the first pass, move the pressure roll in closer to the power roll. This movement must be made at small parallel increments until the final diameters are achieved.

In shops that are required to do a large number of cone rolling operations, it becomes inefficient to continually perform material feeding by hand pressure. In these cases, it is more economical to obtain a cone rolling attachment (Figure 13-6). This attachment consists of a hardened steel set that feeds the workpiece into the rolls so that more feed pressure is applied to the large diameter end of the cone.

Forming Rods, Tubes, and Bars

Circular segments can be made on rods, tubes, and bars by using roll benders. Though these materials have different cross sections (round, square, rectangular, etc.), the only limitation that they have on roll bender work is material thickness.

Conventional rolls are flat and should not be used to form material other than flat sheet stock. If tubing or bars were to be formed on these smooth rolls, it is most probable that permanent damage, such as cracking and denting, would occur. Thus, special rolls must be used to form rods, tubes, and bars on roll benders.

Figure 13-7 is an illustration of grooved rolls that can bend roll materials that are not flat sheet stock. Several groove designs are used. The first is when a groove is machined into the power and pressure rolls. Here, the groove will have a radius and is designed for roll forming round cross-sectional materials such as rods. Without the radius groove in both rolls, rods would have a tendency to flatten out and distort during rolling.

The second design includes flat bottom grooves with straight sides. These grooves are used for bending square and rectangular

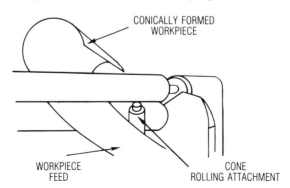

CONICALLY FORMED
WORKPIECE

WORKPIECE
FEED

CONE
ROLLING ATTACHMENT

Fig. 13-6. Cone rolling attachment.

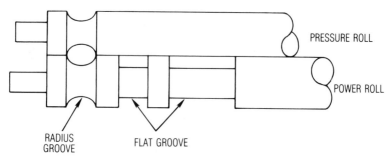

RADIUS
GROOVE   FLAT GROOVE

Fig. 13-7. Roll bender grooves.

bars and strips. Because the sides of these shapes are flat, the groove is only cut into the power roll. Thus, no distortion will occur when one side of the workpiece comes in contact with the non-grooved pressure roll.

Not only are grooved rolls used for forming special-shape materials, but they are also useful in forming parts that have been pre-formed or worked, such as wire edging or flanging. The procedure in working with grooved rolls is the same as for flat sheet stock, except that the pre-formed edge is placed in the appropriate groove. All other adjustments, such as those made with the clamping and pressure roll, are the same as for conventional roll forming.

It should be noted that the grooved section of the roll will have a determination in the thickness of material that can be formed. Generally, the deeper the groove, the greater the reduction in its rated capacity.

CIRCULAR BENDING OF PIPE AND OTHER MATERIALS

Though sheet metal workers are primarily concerned with bending and forming sheet material, there are times when they must also work with other materials. These materials include rods, tubes, bars, and pipes.

Bent pipes are extensively used as fuel and lubricant lines in cars, aircraft, and ships. Tubing and piping are used in heating and air-conditioning systems to transport oil and gases to furnaces, compressors, and coils. Other materials encountered by sheet metal workers are rods, L-shaped channels, bars, and strapping. These shapes will be made out of a variety of different metals such as aluminum, duralumin, steel, copper, and brass.

Bending Methods

Materials can be bent into circular forms by one of two methods. The first is known as *crush forming*. An example of this technique is the free form bending of a metal bar, rod, or tube by hand. Here, the material is not bent around any die or form. The primary disadvantages of this technique are lack of great accuracy and a material defect known as *puckering* (Figure 13-8).

The second bending technique is called *wiper forming*. This technique is popular in the bending of thin-wall sections that are commonly found in tubing, channels, and pipes. Conversely to crush forming, wiper forming employs a die or form about which the material is bent. Figure 13-9 is an illustration of wiper forming with a hand-made system.

The bending of pipe is somewhat different from other types of materials in that there are two material "walls" that must be con-

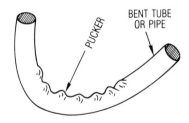

Fig. 13-8. Puckering defect.

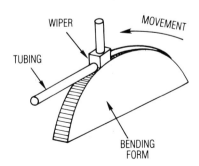

Fig. 13-9. Principle of wiper bending.

sidered. Illustrated in Figure 13-10 are examples of compressed and stretched walls. Note that the internal wall is always compressed, while the external wall is stretched. The exact amount of material deformation will depend on the material used, pipe diameter, bend radius, bend angle, and the method of bending.

Circular Bending

The circular bending of non-sheet materials can be accomplished by either hot or cold methods. Of primary concern in this book, however, is cold bending.

The basic tool used to make circular bends on various materials is the hand or powered bender. This tool is capable of making crush and wiper formed bends on a variety of strip and tubing material. Benders are usually specified in terms of the maximum radius that they can form. The most common sizes found in the sheet metal shop are 2 (5.1cm), 6 (15.2cm), 9 (22.9cm), and 12 (30.5cm) in. benders. Examples of basic circular forming applications of this tool are shown in Figure 13-11.

There are a number of different bender designs on the market. The basic theory employed by most, however, is consistent in most products. First, a work base or table is used to hold a series of pins and forming dies around which the material is formed. Attached to the work table is a rotating arm that provides for the forming power

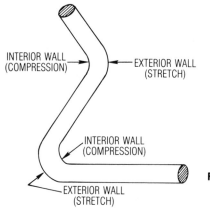

INTERIOR WALL (COMPRESSION)

EXTERIOR WALL (STRETCH)

INTERIOR WALL (COMPRESSION)

EXTERIOR WALL (STRETCH)

Fig. 13-10. Two material "walls" involved in tube and pipe bending.

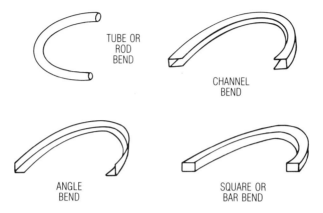

Fig. 13-11. Applications of circular forming.

to shape the workpiece about the pins or dies. An illustration of this concept is shown in Figure 13-12.

The most common types of bends made on hand and power benders are centered eyes, zero bends, and circular forms. Presented here are the procedures used for each type of bend:

1. *Centered eyes.* The three basic steps used to form a centered eye are illustrated in Figure 13-13. Here, the specified radius pin is attached to the work table, along with a lock pin. The nose of the rotating arm is then adjusted to

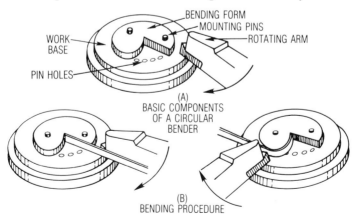

Fig. 13-12. The circular bender.

provide adequate forming pressure on the material. The material is inserted between the lock and radius pins. The arm is then rotated until the circular eye is formed. At that time, the straight section of the stock is off-set to an appropriate angle.

2. *Zero radius forming.* The making of zero radius bends is common on products composed of small rectangular brackets or rods. As shown in Figure 13-14, this procedure is quite simple. First, a preformed angle block is mounted to the work table, along with a lock pin to hold the workpiece in place. The nose of the rotating arm is then rotated in such a way as to move along the material and form.

3. *Circular forms.* The use of circular forms is somewhat different from the previous two bending methods. Here, a form block with the desired forming radius is mounted onto the work table. Instead of using a stationary rotating arm nose, a *nose roller* is employed. In some situations, a *wiper block* is also used (Figure 13-15). The forming procedure progresses as in other bending operations. The metal is inserted between the form block and nose roller. At that time, the rotating arm swings the nose roller and wiper block around the material and form until the part is formed to size.

Fig. 13-13. Center eye.

Fig. 13-14. Zero bend.

Fig. 13-15. Circular bend.

Tube forming can be accomplished on the bender, but it requires the use of forms and rollers equipped with a radius groove. Similar to the rolls of a roll bender, this groove protects the tube from being flattened and distorted. In cases where wiper blocks are used, grooving may or may not be machined into the wiper block— this, however, will be determined by the diameter of the tubing. When channel, angle, and squaring material are used, form blocks with square grooves are needed.

Pipe bending often requires pipe bending machines. Pipes are made of heavier gauged metal and therefore require more bending forces. There are, however, four basic bending methods used to form piping. These are illustrated in Figure 13-16 and described as follows:

1. *Draw bending.* Also known as rotary bending, this technique is done on a machine with a bending die that rotates and a fixed die clamp or wiper block. The pipe is clamped to the dies and is bent when the die begins to rotate.

2. *Compression bending.* Another name for this procedure is stationary die bending. Here, the pipe is clamped into the die while it is bent by a moving wiper block. There is no movement of the bending die.

3. *Roll bending.* One of the most popular methods used for producing a circular bend is by roll bending. This technique uses two pairs of rolls, and each pair consists of opposing positioned rolls. As the grooved rolls rotate, the pipe can be bent. Unlike other bending techniques, this procedure can bend pipe into a complete circle.

4. *Stretch bending.* A bending procedure that applies two forces to the pipe during forming is known as stretch bending. A die form pushes down on the pipe as it is being pulled.

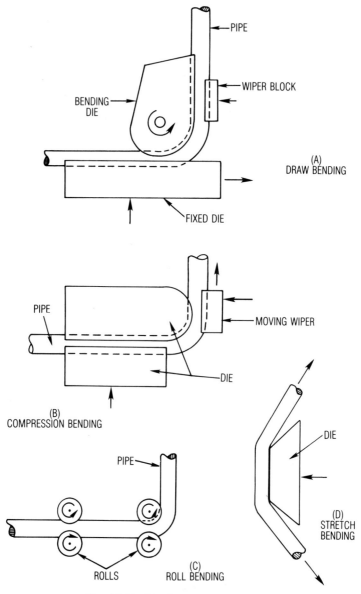

Fig. 13-16. Pipe bending methods.

CALCULATIONS

Several important calculations must be made when making circular and cylindrical bends. Presented in this section are some basic formulas that are commonly used in the sheet metal trade.

Disc or Circle

The primary formulas used in circle (Figure 13-17) calculations are for determining the area (A) and circumference (C) of a circle. These, and related formulas, are given as follows:

$$A = \pi r^2 = 3.1416r^2 = 0.7854d^2$$
$$C = 2\pi r = 6.2832r = 3.1416d$$
$$r = C/6.2832 = \sqrt{A/3.1416} = 0.564\sqrt{A}$$
$$d = C/3.1416 = \sqrt{A/0.7854} = 1.128\sqrt{A}$$

Arc length for center angle of $1° = 0.008727d$
Arc length for center angle of $n° = 0.008727nd$

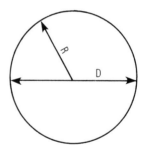

Fig. 13-17. Circle or disc.

Circular Sector

The basic formulas used when working with circular sectors (Figure 13-18) involves area (A), length of arc (l) and angle in degrees (a). These, and reated formulas, are presented as follows:

$$A = .5r \ l = 0.008727 \ ar^2$$
$$l = (ra \ 3.1416)/180 = 0.01745ra = 2A/r$$
$$a = 57.296 \ l/r$$
$$r = 2A/l = 57.296 \ l/a$$

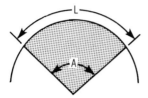

Fig. 13-18. Circle sector.

Circular Segment

The formulas commonly used when working with circular segments (Figure 13-19) are presented as follows:

$$c = 2/h(2r - h)$$
$$A = .5[rl - c(r - h)]$$
$$r = (c^2 + 4h^2)/8h$$
$$l = 0.01745ra$$
$$h = r - .5\sqrt{4r^2 - c^2}$$
$$a = 57.296 \; l/r$$
$$h = r[1 - \cos(a/2)]$$

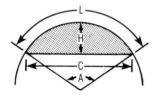

Fig. 13-19. Circle segment.

Rings

Area calculations are most often used when working with circular rings (Figure 13-20). These formulas make use of the major and minor diameter (D and d, respectively), and are presented as follows:

$$A = \pi(R^2 - r^2) = 3.1416(R^2 - r^2)$$
$$= 3.1416(R + r)(R - r) = 0.7854(D^2 + d^2)$$
$$= 0.7854(D + d)(D - d)$$

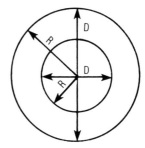

Fig. 13-20. Circular ring.

Ring Sectors

Similar to circular ring calculations, ring sector (Figure 13-21) formulas that are most often used in the sheet metal industry deal with surface area, and are presented as follows:

$$A = a\pi/360(R^2 - r^2)$$
$$= 0.00873a\ (R^2 - r^2)$$
$$= a\ \pi/1440(D^2 - d^2)$$
$$= 0.00218a\ (D^2 - d^2)$$

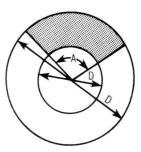

Fig. 13-21. Ring sector.

SUMMARY

The forming of round and cylindrical parts is frequently required of the sheet metal worker. Though cutting round parts is often done with hand snips, this has proven to be an inefficient method in shop and production settings, especially for cutting large radius circles and arcs. Tools used specifically for this function are ring and circle shears and flangers. These tools are capable of cutting out circular discs and rings. In addition, they can also perform the forming process of flanging.

Most cylindrically and conically shaped products are formed on roll benders. A roll bender that is most often used is the slip roll bender. These benders are equipped with three rolls: power, clamping, and pressure. The minimum diameter bend that can be performed on these tools will correspond to the diameter of the clamping roll, which will normally range from 1 to 6 in.

In addition to bending flat sheet stock, roll benders can also be used to bend rods, bars, and sheets with pre-formed or pre-worked edges. This is accomplished on benders that are equipped with grooved rolls. Conical shapes are achieved by use of a bender attachment or by hand processing.

Rods, tubes, bars, and pipes are other materials that are sometimes formed by sheet metal workers. There are two basic methods used for bending these materials: crush and wiper bending. The latter is best used for more precise bending.

Examples of common types of bends made on non-sheet material are centered eye bending, zero radius forming, and circular forming. Pipe bending often requires the use of special pipe bending machines, because they are made of heavier stock material. The basic forming or bending methods used on pipes are draw bending, compression bending, roll bending, and stretch bending.

In connection with circular cutting and forming operations, the sheet metal worker must be knowledgeable about basic mathematical calculations. Most of these calculations are related to finding surface area requirements of parts.

REVIEW QUESTIONS

1. Give examples of products that require cylindrical and conical forming.

2. Under what conditions are ring and circle shears more advantageous in cutting out circular parts than hand snip methods?

3. Briefly list the procedures that would be used in cutting out a large diameter circle on a ring and circle shear.

4. How is flanging accomplished on the ring and circle shear and flanger?

5. Identify and explain the factors affecting the maximum height of a flange that can be formed on a ring and circle shear and flanger.

6. What are roll benders, and how did the slip roll bender get its name?

7. Identify the three rolls used on roll benders and describe their function.

8. List the procedures you would follow to form a cylinder with a simple lock seam.

9. How does the forming process used to form a conical differ from that used to form a cylinder?

10. What are roller grooves and how are they used?

11. Explain the difference between crush and wiper forming.

12. What is puckering?

13. Explain what circular forms are and how they can be used to form rods and bars.

14. What special consideration must be given when working with tubing, rods, and pipes?

15. Identify the basic forming processes used to bend pipes.

CHAPTER 14

Metal Spinning

In some sectors of the sheet metal industry, many operations have become extensively mechanized. Work that is performed in this sector is distinguished by large-scale and small-scale operations. In the first case, products are produced by highly efficient and accurate machinery, and often involve little human contact with the working of the metal. Small-scaled operations often involve simple machines that are easy to operate, where only individual operations are mechanized.

Metal spinning is a process that falls into both categories of large- and small-scale operations. Within the context of this chapter, metal spinning discussion will be of greater detail in the area of small-scale operations.

METAL SPINNING CONCEPTS

Metal spinning involves shaping sheet metal discs into contoured forms by pressing against them as they are rotating. Because of the nature of the process and the forming techniques used, metal spinning is limited to work on symmetrical articles that have a circular cross section. This process is performed on a *speed lathe* which is similar in appearance to a conventional wood lathe, with the exception that in place of a tailstock there is some device or method used for holding the work against the form (Figure 14-1).

"Spun" products are usually formed against a *chuck* that is shaped to specifications. These formed chucks are frequently turned from hard wood and attached to a face plate that is mounted to the

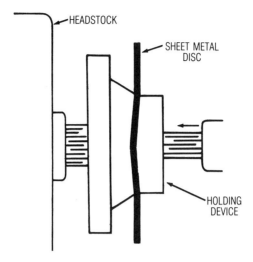

Fig. 14-1. Metal spinning set-up on speed lathe.

head stock of the lathe. For production-type jobs, the chuck would normally be made out of steel. Steel-formed chucks are employed where extensive usage might produce wear that would result in interior imperfections.

To form the metal around the chuck, a blunt hand tool is used. This tool presses the metal against the form as it rotates at speeds ranging from 480 to 2750 rpm.

Spinning is considered an "art" rather than a precise technical process by many individuals. The reason for this is that it was first developed as an metal craft by the Egyptians and later used to produce fine silver and copperware. Today, however, spinning produces a wide variety of products, including various fine household wares, aircraft parts, missile components, funnels, processing kettles, and light fixtures.

METALS AND LUBRICANTS

A significant amount of skill and technical knowledge is required to successfully spin metal parts. Central to this is an understanding of the metals best suited for spinning and the effective use of lubricants.

Spinning Metals

Not all metals can be successfully spun. The characteristics that are desirable for spinning metals are: high ductility, formability, and resistance to work hardening. An important material behavior here is work hardening. This refers to the property of metal to become hard and brittle as it is worked. An example of this behavior occurs when you take a piece of metal and keep bending it back and forth. After several bends the metal will become hard and brittle, and eventually break or fracture. The rate at which this happens will vary in different metals.

Most metals used in spinning will show some form of work hardening. Those that show the least degree of work hardening are often used for metal spinning. Aluminum is perhaps one of the best metals available for metal spinning because softer grades will work harden very little. The best aluminums recommended for spinning are series 1100 and 3003. For this reason, aluminum is one of the spinning metals recommended for the beginner. Table 14-1 is a list of common spinning metals.

The thickness of spinning metal blanks or discs will vary according to the design of the product spun. Most spinning metals range between 28 and 12 gauge, with 20 to 18 gauge being the easiest to work with.

Some spinning metals require a great deal of skill to work with. They work harden quite easily and must be *annealed*. Basically, annealing is a process whose primary function is to soften metal so that it may be more easily worked. This is accomplished by raising the temperature of the metal so that all stresses are relieved and the internal structure of the metal is the same throughout. The metal is then cooled at a given rate so that the new stress-relieved structure is maintained until cooled. Table 14-2 lists recommended annealing temperatures for common spinning metals.

After reviewing the annealing temperatures of common spinning metals, you will note that britannia requires no annealing. Britannia is also known as modern pewter and is an extremely soft metal that does not work harden during spinning operations. Because of its high ductility and no lead content, it is popular in the making of many utensils.

Table 14-1
Common Spinning Metals

Metal Category	Alloy
Aluminum	Non-heat treatable
	1100
	3003
	3004
	5052
	5083
	5454
	Heat treatable
	2014
	2024
	2219
	6061
	7034
Copper	101
	102
	220
	230
	260
	262
	270
	280
	350
	356
	462
	510
	521
	655
	715
	754
Steels	1006
	1007
	1008
	1010
	1012
	1014
	1016
	1018
	1020
	4130
	4340

Table 14-1
Common Spinning Metals (Cont'd)

Metal Category	Alloy
Base metals	Gold
	Lead
	Nickel
	Platinum
	Silver
	Zinc
Other alloys	Brass (leaded)
	Britannia
	Monel
	Gar-alloy

Table 14-2
Annealing Temperatures for Spinning Metals

Metals	Gauge Thickness Number	Temperature	
		°F	(°C)
Aluminum	18 to 22	650	(343)
Copper	20 to 26	1000	(537)
Brass	20 to 26	1000	(537)
Britannia	No annealing is required		
Monel	20 to 26	1700	(926)
Steel	24 to 26	1200	(648)
Zinc	20 to 26	212 to 190	(100) to (374)
Gar-alloy	18 to 24	270	(132)

Lubricants

During metal spinning, a great amount of heat is generated as a result of friction between the rotating workpiece and spinning tool. Excessive heat generation is not a desirable outcome, for it may not only damage and distort the spun product, but also cause unnecessary wear on the spinning tool itself. The acceptable method employed for reducing friction is the application of lubricants.

Depending on the characteristics of the metal being spun, many types of lubricants can be used. The property that is closely examined when selecting a lubricant is known as *viscosity*. Briefly, viscosity is the property of a liquid to resist flow. Lubricants with high viscosity ratings are best suited for situations where considerable heat is generated.

Lubricants are available in either liquid or stick form, with the latter being the most common. Both naphtha soap and mutton tallow are widely used lubricants. In some cases, sheet metal spinners will make their own lubricant mixture. An example of a common mixture is a combination of one part oil to four parts tallow (i.e., 4 oz oil to 1 lb tallow). These ingredients are then heated and mixed until they are combined.

Examples of lubricants often used with different spinning metals are presented in Table 14-3.

SPINNING LATHES, TOOLS, AND CHUCKS

The proper selection and use of spinning lathes, tools, and chucks is critical in the making of quality products. Presented in this section will be a discussion of three major topics: the spinning lathe, spinning tools, and chucks used in metal spinning.

Spinning Lathes

The most important piece of equipment used in spinning is the lathe. Special lathes known as speed lathe (Figure 14-2) are specifically designed for spinning operations. This does not mean that other lathes cannot be used for spinning. In fact, it is not uncommon to find wood and metal lathes used for certain spinning operations.

311

Table 14-3
Spinning Lubricants

Lubricant	Spinning Metal
Stick wax	Aluminum
	Copper
	Brass
	Britannia
	Gar-alloy
Cup grease	Aluminum
	Copper
	Brass
	Gar-alloy
Tallow	Aluminum
	Copper
	Brass
	Zinc
	Gar-alloy
Laundry soap	Aluminum
	Copper
	Brass
	Monel
	Steel
	Zinc
	Gar-alloy

Spinning lathes are usually specified in terms of *swing size.* This pertains to the largest diameter of work that can be mounted to the head stock without hitting the lathe's ways or bed rails. Thus, a 15-inch (38.1cm) lathe is one with enough clearance between the center of the headstock spindle and bed rails to accept work 15 inches (38.1cm) in diameter.

Speed lathes are the simplest of all lathes, and consist of a bed, headstock, tailstock, and an adjustable slide used to support the tool. A variable speed motor is usually built into the head stock unit or can be driven by a belt to step-cone pulley arrangement. Because spinning requires the use of hand tools, the lathe must be able to achieve high speeds that will sometimes exceed 2800 rpm. Since the lathe spindle is exposed to significant amounts of high pressure during spinning, it must be designed in such a way as to withstand

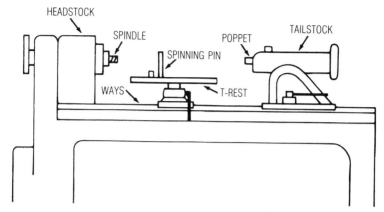

Fig. 14-2. Typical speed lathe design.

these pressures. Thus, thrust bearings that are capable of withstanding excessive pressures must be used.

The lathe speed selected for a particular spinning operation will be inversely proportional to the diameter of the work. In other words, the larger the diameter of the work, the slower the speed. A good practice for the beginner is to start off at a slow speed until skill and confidence are gained, then slowly work up to faster speeds.

If a standard wood or metal lathe is used, the tailstock will usually be equipped with a handwheel. However, for many spinning speed lathes, a cam lever and sliding spindle are used (Figure 14-3). Both handwheel and cam lever designs are adequate for moving the tailstock's spindle toward or away from the workpiece.

Another component of the spinning lathe that must be used during processing is the *spinning T-rest*. As its name implies, the T-rest is used to rest the spinning tool on during forming. Figure 14-4 shows a simple T-rest design often found on speed lathes.

In the spindle of the tailstock is often fitted the spinning center (Figure 14-5). This center is used to hold the work in place during forming. Note that the center's flat or blunted point is fitted into a bearing sleeve that rotates along with the workpiece. If the center point were unable to rotate, excessive friction would build up and cause damage to the workpiece and chuck.

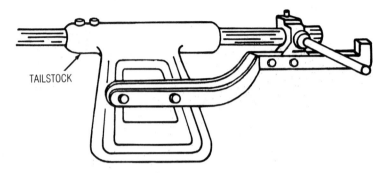

Fig. 14-3. Cam lever sliding spindle.

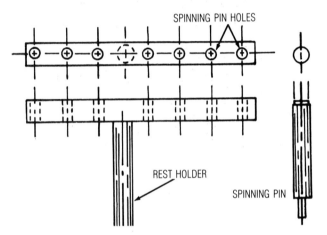

Fig. 14-4. Typical spinning T-rest design.

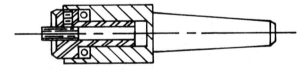

Fig. 14-5. Cross section of a typical spinning center.

Spinning Tools

The number and types of spinning tools required for metal spinning are based on the competence and experience of the worker. Many tool designs are available. Shown in Figure 14-6 are only a few of

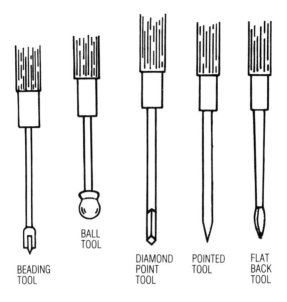

BALL
TOOL

DIAMOND
POINT
TOOL

POINTED
TOOL

FLAT
BACK
TOOL

BEADING
TOOL

Fig. 14-6. Common types of spinning tools.

the more common types used. These tools are categorized into three general groups: blunt or round-nosed tools, trimming or cutting tools, and beading tools.

For most spinning operations, five basic spinning tools will meet most forming requirements. These tools are made out of tool steel, and are described as follows:

1. *Flat back tools* are considered one of the more important metal spinning tools, since most operations are accomplished with them. These tools are designed with one side flat and the opposite rounded.

2. *Pointed tools* are used in the formation of corners and small radii. The tip of this tool is similar in shape to that of a cone.

3. *Trimming tools* are employed to reduce the size of sheet metal discs as well as truing it to size and shape. Critical here is keeping the point of the tool sharp. Unlike the pointed tool, trimming tools, such as the diamond-point tool, are usually ground from a square bar.

4. *Ball tools* have a spherically shaped end. They are used in the initial forming and shaping operations for heavier gauged metals.

5. *Beading tools* are equipped with a *beading wheel* that will vary in diameter from 1 to 2 in. (2.5 to 5.1cm). As the name implies, they are primarily used to form beads on the edges of the spun workpiece.

Not all tools are made from tool steel. Those that are used to spin steel are often made from brass and bronze alloys. Other "tools" may consist of nothing more than a rod made of a hardwood such as maple or hickory. These special non-tool steel materials are recommended where workpiece marring might become a problem.

Spinning Chucks

Two general types of chucks are used for spinning operations: solid and sectional. Solid chucks are made out of a single "solid" piece of wood or metal, while sectional chucks are constructed from two or more sections of wood or metal.

Chucks that are custom made are usually made of wood. Commercially produced chucks are available in either laminated hardwood or cast iron. In many small shop production settings, wooden chucks will have an exterior metal skin to prolong their work life.

Chucks are held on a metal faceplate that screws onto the threaded spindle of the headstock. An example of how this is accomplished is shown in Figure 14-7. Since the chuck is either screwed

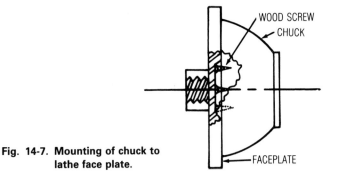

Fig. 14-7. Mounting of chuck to lathe face plate.

or glued onto the faceplate, the faceplate should be considered a permanent part of the chuck. If the faceplate is frequently removed or changed, there exists a danger of screw hole wear, which will off-set the position of the chuck during turning and result in a defective and untrue product.

When spinning centers are not used to hold the metal blank against the chuck, then *follow blocks* can be incorporated. Follow blocks are usually made out of hardwood such as maple or oak and fit snugly against the metal blank. Similar to the spinning center, the hollow block must be able to revolve freely along with the chuck. These blocks are usually a minimum of 1 in. (2.5cm) in thickness, and are never larger than the diameter of the base of the workpiece. If the follow block is too small, the metal will tend to spin back over the block. On the other hand, if the follow block is made too large, then it will prevent accurate work at the base of the workpiece.

The follow block is constructed so that it will fit into the tailstock center and is centered directly in line with the chuck. The tailstock is then moved closer to the chuck so that the follow block matches directly with the workpiece's base.

Chucks that are custom made are turned on a wood lathe. When turning begins, it is recommended that a template be used. This template should be a precise profile of the finished product; it functions as a quality control measure. Care should be taken to make sure that sufficient clearance is allowed between the lathe's headstock and the blank. Chucks that are used to spin bowls and trays are made so that they are slightly concave at the base, which allows for a more secure and stable end product.

Articles that require a deep spin will have to be spun in stages. This process is referred to as the *break-down process*. Here, a series of chucks are used that gradually work the sheet metal to finished size and shape. By forming the metal over a series of break-down chucks, there will be less tendency for the metal to become too thin in certain sections or develop flaws and distortions. This process is illustrated in Figure 14-8.

Products that have varying diameters along their body or are spun open end down to a smaller diameter must make use of a sectional chuck. If a solid chuck were used, the spun part could not be removed from the chuck without damage. Sectional chucks therefore make it possible to remove the product unharmed. This is

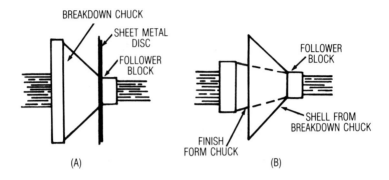

Fig. 14-8. Use of a breakdown chuck.

possible because the sectional chuck is made of segments that are fastened to a backing block. When removed from the backing block, the sections of the chuck collapse and are taken out. A sectional chuck is shown in Figure 14-9.

Since sectional chucks are used in many forming operations, it is important to the sheet metal worker to have an understanding of

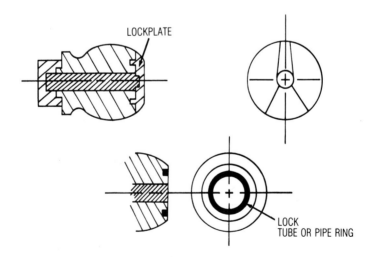

Fig. 14-9. Sectional chuck.

how they should be constructed. Presented here are the basic procedures used to construct a sectional chuck:

1. Select a piece of hardwood large enough to make the entire chuck. If the selected block is too small, it may be necessary to glue several pieces together.
2. Fit a mandrel through the center of the block by drilling an appropriate sized hole.
3. Mount the mandrel on a wood lathe between centers and turn to shape by using wood turning tools.
4. Screw a piece of wood to the faceplate. This wood will not be part of the forming chuck itself, so be sure that it is of suitable thickness.
5. Turn a small recess in the end of the chuck large enough to hold a ring. The ring will be cut from a piece of pipe or tubing, depending on the radius of the chuck.
6. Remove the chuck from the lathe after all shaping operations are completed.
7. Determine the number and location of desired sections and lay out with a pencil.
8. With a fine tooth band saw or backsaw, cut the chuck sections. Be sure the chuck is cut lengthwise along the vertical.
9. Since the cut chuck will be undersized, because of the saw kerfs, fit an appropriate shim material into the kerfs.
10. Lock the sectional chuck with the cut pipe or tube ring.

Another type of chuck is used for "spinning on air." Here, two chucks are used somewhat similar to breaking down chucks. As shown in Figure 14-10, the first chuck provides initial shaping. Once formed, the spun part is removed and placed onto a second chuck for special shaping. Since the entire part is not in contact with the second chuck during spinning, it is said to be spun "on air."

METAL SPINNING PROCEDURES

Metal spinning should be viewed as a process that is similar to the molding of clay on the potter's wheel. Like the "throwing" of a clay

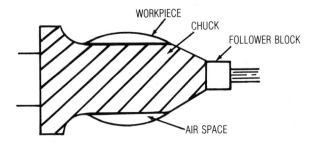

Fig. 14-10. On-air spinning.

pot, metal spinning requires time and patience, and is not a skill
that can be picked up immediately.

During the spinning process, the metal will have changes in
thickness, so that excessive pressure in any one location will cause
the metal to thin or even break. In addition, as the metal is formed
about the chuck where its circumference decreases, it will have a
tendency to form a series of wrinkles. This undesirable characteristic, however, can be corrected by further working with a backstick
and flat back tool.

It is recommended that novice sheet metal spinners begin with
a simple, shallow bowl until they get comfortable with the flow of
the metal and can successfully make it work for them. Presented
here is a step-by-step description of how metal spinning should be
accomplished:

1. Make sure that all preliminary work is accomplished with
   great care and accuracy. This involves the preparation of
   working drawings, the turning or securing of a chuck, and
   the selection of the appropriate metal to be spun.

2. Calculate the diameter of the sheet metal disc to be cut out.
   The basic formula used here is: Disc diameter $= D + 2H$,
   where D is equal to the diameter of the base and H is the
   height of the part measured from the base to the top edge
   (see Figure 14-11).

3. On a sheet of metal, lay out the appropriate sized disc with a
   set of dividers and cut it out to size. It should be noted that
   standard sized discs can be purchased ahead of time.

4. Center the disc between the chuck and follow block. This is accomplished by holding the disc against the chuck while the tailstock is moved in close to the headstock; then bring the follow block in contact with the metal blank.

5. Set the T-rest so that it is about 2 in. from the disc and lock it in place.

6. Check to make sure that the disc is truly centered on the chuck. This is accomplished by rotating the chuck and lightly holding a straight, flat piece of wood against the edge of the disc. The wood should resting securely on the T-rest.

   If the disc is centered, the wood will be in constant contact with it through an entire revolution. However, if the disc touches the wood at certain points only, the disc is off-centered. Push the disc in toward the center at that point until the disc becomes centered. The follow block is then tightened against the disc and locked in position. Make sure that when the chuck is rotated the follow block rotates with it.

7. Select the appropriate working speed for the spindle. This will vary from metal to metal, and is based on the diameter of the chuck. Beginning spinners should start off at a slightly slower speed than recommended. Examples of cutting speeds for various diameter chucks are presented in Table 14-4.

8. Select the appropriate spinning tool. The selection should be based on the type of spinning operation to be accomplished, plus the kind of metal being worked on.

9. Next, select a spinning pin and place it in the T-rest. The T-rest should then be adjusted so that when the spinning tool is inserted against the pin, it will be at a slight angle to the face of the disc.

10. Apply a suitable lubricant on the disc as it is rotating. The lubricant should be applied to the surface that will be in direct contact with the spinning tool.

11. As the disc is turning, hook it to the chuck to minimize the danger of its flying off the lathe.

12. The spinning tool should be held with the right hand so that

the handle is braced under the right arm. The left hand is used as a guide and is positioned around the tool and the spinning pin.

13. Bring the nose of the tool in contact with the disc at a point just below center. As you apply pressure, move the tool downward and to the left. The metal should always be spun *toward the headstock.*

14. Continue to work the metal with various spinning tools until the part is spun to finished size and shape.

15. Lay down the final edge by trimming and filing.

16. Remove the the chuck from the lathe after all spinning operations are completed. If the spun part is held too tightly to the chuck and cannot be removed without damage, drill a small hole (approximately ⅛ in. (25.4mm) diameter) through the chuck so that air will come in contact with the metal. Another technique would be to place the chuck back on the

DISC DIA = D + 2H

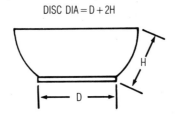

Fig. 14-11. Circular disc diameter.

Table 14-4
Spinning Speeds for Aluminum Discs

Chuck Diameter (inches)	Recommended Speeds (rpm)
3 to 6	2,000 to 3,400
7 to 10	1,500 to 2,300
11 to 14	1,000 to 1,200
15 to 20	500 to 800

lathe and re-spin the metal with a planishing tool so that the part will be spun at a slightly larger size for easy removal.

POWER SPINNING

Conventional spinning processes have limited applications, especially when it comes to production runs and products requiring a high degree of tolerance. A spinning process that has gained wider acceptance in these areas is power spinning. Power spinning not only can produce a product that possesses all the advantages of spinning, but it is also capable of meeting the production and tolerance requirements set by industry. In addition, power spinning can deliver products of significantly larger sizes and thicknesses than those formed by hand spinning. As an example, many power spinning lathes are capable of handling metal blanks in excess of 170 in. (432cm) in diameter and over 2 in. (5.1cm) thick.

An example of the basic steps used in power spinning is presented in Figure 14-12. Instead of using a chuck, a steel *mandrel* forms the metal. Holding the blank in position is a "live" metal holder that rotates along with the blank. Instead of stationary spinning tool, a set of roll formers is used.

When the lathe is turned on, the blank begins to spin. At the same time, the roll formers are activated to rotate in an opposite direction to the lathe spindle. As the formers rotate, they also apply uniform pressure in the direction of the headstock. This pressure forces the metal back against the mandrel. The lathe continues to run until the metal is completely formed about the mandrel.

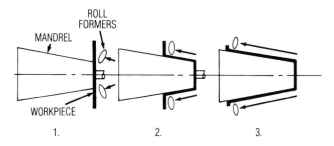

Fig. 14-12. Power spinning.

323

Because the mandrel and roll former rotate at the same time, the pressure applied to the metal is made in a continuous spiral pattern. This type of pressure causes the metal to flow smoothly and to form rapidly. Several benefits derive from this type of pressure: material savings, an increase in the strength of the product, reduction in production costs, and an excellent surface finish.

In some power spinning operations, heat is applied to the workpiece to make it easier to form. In these situations, the operation becomes a hot metal process. This technique, however, is seldom required because of the easy flow of most metals. In turn, since power spinning is accomplished so rapidly, annealing is seldom necessary during the forming process.

Unlike conventional spinning, power spinning can be performed on a larger variety of metals. In addition to metals used in hand spinning, examples of nontraditional spinning metals used in power spinning are: steel forgings and plate, 300 and 400 series stainless steels, molybdenum, tungsten, Inconel, Monel, K-Monel, titanium TI-14-A, timken 16-25-6, hastalloy B, C, and X, and zirconium.

It should be noted that the term "power spinning" is sometimes considered a generic term for a number of different spinning procedures. Examples of these are hydrospinning, spinforging, floturning, shear spinning, and compression spinning. In reality, these other terms are given by machine manufacturers that produce power spinning lathes.

SUMMARY

The metal spinning field is one of the more mechanized sectors of the sheet metal industry. Though spinning is a relatively simple process, it is widely used in both small- and large-scale operations. Basically, metal spinning is the operation of shaping sheet metal discs into contoured forms by pressing against them as they rotate on a lathe.

Spun products are formed around a chuck that is mounted to a faceplate. The faceplate, in turn, is screwed onto the spindle of the lathe. The lathe specifically designed for metal spinning is the speed lathe, though wood and metal lathes are sometimes used for metal spinning operations.

Not all metals can be successfully spun. Only those that exhibit high ductility and workability and will not become work hardened easily are used for metal spinning. Examples of metals that meet these criteria are aluminum, copper, lead, silver, brass, and britannia. Because most metal do exhibit some degree of work hardening, it often becomes necessary to anneal them during the forming process.

During spinning, a great deal of heat is generated as a result of friction between the workpiece and spinning tool. Though most lubricants are available in either solid or liquid form, solid lubricants are often preferred by metal spinners. Examples of common lubricants used during spinning are stick wax, cup grease, tallow, and laundry soap.

Spinning lathes are capable of reaching high speeds. They are normally specified in terms of the maximum amount of swing allowed. The essential parts of this lather are the headstock, tailstock, and T-rest.

A number of different spinning tools are available. Though many are made out of tool steel, others are available in wood and brass. Common tools used are blunt or round-nosed tools, trimming or cutting tools, and beading tools.

Chucks are generally categorized into two groups. The first, and most common, are solid chucks that are used to form objects such as bowls and dishes. The second chuck category includes sectional chucks, which are made of several pieces of wood that can be disassembled after spinning. Sectional chucks are often used where there are undercuts and intricate formations along the length of the part.

Within large production settings, power spinning has become a popular processing method. This technique makes use of a mandrel and set of form rolls during the spinning operation. In concept, power spinning is a combination spinning and metal extrusion process.

REVIEW QUESTIONS

1. Briefly describe what metal spinning is.
2. Explain how metal "flows" during the spinning process.

3. What is the difference between a chuck and mandrel?

4. Explain the difference in construction and use between solid and sectional chucks.

5. What is a speed lathe?

6. Identify the characteristics necessary for a successful spinning metal. Give examples of these metals.

7. Why are lubricants necessary during metal spinning?

8. Briefly describe how to set up a lathe for metal spinning.

9. Why is spinning always accomplished toward the headstock?

10. Briefly explain what power spinning is and its advantages over conventional metal spinning.

PART IV

FASTENING SHEET METAL

CHAPTER 15

Mechanical Fastening of Sheet Metal

There are times when sheet metal parts must be fastened by various forms of mechanical hardware. In most cases, mechanical fasteners are used because the sheet material or product is too heavy or large to bend or the design and use of the part dictate that it be disassembled for shipment and/or servicing. The most common types of mechanical fasteners used in sheet metal work are rivets and screws.

RIVETED JOINTS

Riveting is an operation in which a permanent joint is fabricated with the use of rivets. Though riveting can be either hot or cold, those riveting processes used in sheet metal work are cold. Since different sheet metal parts that are fastened together often serve different purposes, different requirements must be met by riveted joints. In some cases, the joint may be required only to be strong, while others may need tightness or a combination of strengh and tightness.

Two general methods are used to categorize rivet joints. The first is by application, where there are three major types of rivet joints:

1. Pressure vessel rivet joints
2. Structural rivet joints
3. Machine member rivet joints

The second method is based on the general characteristics or features demanded of the joint. The three basic categories here are:

1. High strength rivet joints
2. Tight rivet joints
3. High strength and tight rivet joints

Comparing the two categories of joints, high strength joints would be somewhat similar in requirements to structural and machine member rivet joints, and high strength and tight rivet joints are employed in pressure vessel construction. Tight rivet joints, however, are limited to holding gases or liquids under a small load, such as in the fabrication of gasoline, oil, and water tanks.

Rivet Joint Factors

A number of factors must be considered when selecting a particular joint for fabrication. In addition to the category of rivet joint required, other factors such the spacing of rivets, the type and size of rivets, the type and size of hole, and the material to be riveted must all be considered.

When determining the spacing of joints, there are several terms that may be encountered. These are:

- *Pitch* is a term used to indicate the measured space between rivet centers.

- *Back pitch*, also referred to as *transverse pitch*, indicates the measured distance between the center line of rows of rivets.

- *Diagonal pitch* is a measurement given to identify the distance between the closest rivet centers in different rows.

- *Margin* is the distance from the edge of the workpiece to the center of the closest row of rivets.

When preparing work for riveting, it is critical that care be taken to ensure accurate spacing of rivets. In sheet metal work this is particularly important, since inaccurate spacing will lead to material buckling and material deformity.

The size and type of rivet selected will be determined by the gauge of the sheet metal and product use. As a rule of thumb, the approximate diameter (d) required for riveting a given thickness (t) of material will be calculated between the following ratios:

$$d = 1.2/t \text{ and } 1.4/t$$

In preparing sheet metal for riveting, care must be taken in determining the appropriate size and type of rivet hole. Generally, rivet holes are either drilled, punched, or punched and reamed (the last technique is primarily used for plate and other heavy gauge materials). The size of the rivet hole should provide minimum clearance so that the hole will be completely filled by the rivet. (A comparison to hole size occurs when hot riveting is used. Here, the rivet holes are usually made approximately 1/16 in. (0.0625 in. (1.588 mm) larger than the rivet diameter.)

Another important consideration is the type of sheet material being used. This will vary from one industry to another and will greatly influence the type and design of rivet selected. As an example, rivets that are used for structural work and joining machine members will be made of wrought iron or soft steel. Rivets used in the aircraft and marine industry, however, have different requirements and usually must meet minimum weight specifications and be resistant to corrosion. Corrosion-resistant rivets are made out of materials such as copper, aluminum, Monel, or Inconel.

Rivets

Rivets are similar in design to screws, except that they are not threaded. They have a particular head design, body diameter, and length. The type of rivet design available will depend on the body diameter required. In larger rivets with diameters ranging from 1/2 to 1-3/4 in., there are six general rivet designs (Figure 15-1): button head, high button head, cone head, pan head, flat countersunk head, and oval countersunk head. Size specifications for these rivets

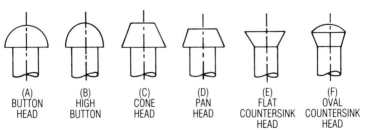

| (A) | (B) | (C) | (D) | (E) | (F) |
| BUTTON HEAD | HIGH BUTTON | CONE HEAD | PAN HEAD | FLAT COUNTERSINK HEAD | OVAL COUNTERSINK HEAD |

Fig. 15-1. Six basic rivet head designs.

can be obtained in the American National Standard Large Rivets standards ANSI B18.1.2-1972, R1977.

Smaller rivets are of most interest to sheet metal workers. These designs will have a body diameter that ranges from ⅟16 to ⁷⁄16 in. (0.0625 to 0.438 in.) (1.588 to 11.113mm). The smaller rivets fall into four general styles: flat head or tinner's rivets, flat countersunk head, button head, and pan head (Figure 15-2).

The most desirable property a small rivet material can have is malleability. That is, it must be easily formed to shape. For this reason, there are a number of different malleable metals used in the manufacturing of rivets. Examples of metals used to manufacture small rivets include aluminum, copper, Monel, brass, steel, and stainless steel.

Small rivets are usually specified in terms of their head design and shank diameter. Table 15-1 lists the specifications for small rivets. Note that the specification notations are keyed to those identified in Figure 15-2.

There is another method used for specifying rivets that is found for rivets on the smaller end of the scale. Here, rivets that have a body diameter between 0.081 to 0.347 in. (2.06 to 8.81mm) are indicated in terms of weight per 1000 rivets. A common rivet falling into this category is the *Tinner's rivet*, which is a form of flat head rivet. Presented in Table 15-2 are the specifications for this rivet (again, letter dimensions correspond to Figure 15-2).

Types of Rivet Joints

Sheet metal sections that are riveted together may serve different purposes. For this reason, different specifications are set for se-

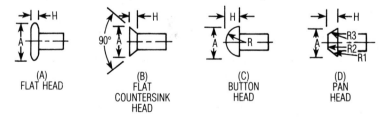

(A) FLAT HEAD   (B) FLAT COUNTERSINK HEAD   (C) BUTTON HEAD   (D) PAN HEAD

Fig. 15-2. Small rivet head designs.

Table 15-1
Small Rivet Specifications (Approximate) (All Measures Given in Inches)

Shank Diameter D	Flat Head A	Flat Head H	Flat Counter-sunk A	Flat Counter-sunk H	Button Head A	Button Head H	Button Head R	Pan Head A	Pan Head H	Pan Head R1	Pan Head R2	Pan Head R3
1/16	.130	.022	.114	.027	.112	.047	.055	.108	.035	.019	.052	0.217
3/32	.190	.032	.170	.040	.172	.071	.084	.163	.054	.030	.080	0.326
1/8	.250	.042	.226	.053	.225	.094	.111	.215	.072	.039	.106	0.429
5/32	.312	.052	.283	.066	.279	.117	.138	.268	.089	.049	.133	0.535
3/16	.374	.062	.339	.079	.335	.140	.166	.321	.107	.059	.159	0.641
7/32	.440	.073	.399	.094	.392	.165	.195	.378	.126	.069	.186	0.754
1/4	.500	.083	.453	.106	.445	.188	.221	.429	.143	.079	.213	0.858
9/32	.562	.094	.510	.119	.501	.211	.249	.482	.161	.088	.239	0.963
5/16	.624	.104	.568	.133	.555	.234	.279	.535	.178	.098	.266	1.070
11/32	.686	.114	.624	.146	.611	.257	.304	.589	.196	.108	.292	1.176
3/8	.750	.125	.680	.159	.665	.281	.332	.644	.215	.118	.319	1.286
13/32	.812	.135	.737	.172	.721	.305	.358	.697	.232	.127	.345	1.392
7/16	.874	.146	.794	.186	.776	.328	.387	.750	.250	.137	.372	1.500

Table 15-2
Tinner's Rivet Specifications (Approximate) (All Measures Given in Inches)

Size Number	Length L	Shank Dia. D	Head Dia. A	Head Height H
6 oz.	1/8	.078	.203	.022
8 oz.	5/32	.088	.215	.030
10 oz.	11/64	.094	.240	.030
12 oz	3/16	.104	.255	.031
14 oz.	3/16	.108	.265	.032
1 lb.	13/64	.110	.275	.034
1-1/4 lb.	7/32	.119	.285	.039
1-1/2 lb.	15/64	.129	.305	.040
1-3/4 lb.	1/4	.133	.320	.042
2 lb.	17/64	.143	.330	.043
2-1/2 lb.	9/32	.147	.300	.062
3 lb.	5/16	.159	.316	.066
3-1/2 lb	21/64	.164	.335	.067
4 lb.	11/32	.175	.355	.069
5 lb.	3/8	.186	.375	.077
6 lb.	25/64	.202	.406	.083
7 lb.	13/32	.220	.418	.087
8 lb.	7/16	.223	.460	.093
9 lb.	29/64	.237	.475	.095
10 lb.	15/32	.237	.490	.096
12 lb.	1/2	.257	.515	.099
14 lb.	33/64	.282	.560	.104
16 lb.	17/32	.298	.580	.119
18 lb.	19/32	.341	.687	.146

lecting a specific type of rivet joint. When designing a rivet joint, several conditions, or "givens," are assumed. These are:

1. That any load or force applied to the joint will be carried equally by all rivets.
2. There will be no combination of stresses that will act on a rivet that will cause failure or fracture.
3. The shearing stress or force found in a rivet will be equal or uniform throughout its cross section.
4. Any bearing stress that is exerted on a riveted joint will be distributed equally over the anticipated area of the rivet.

The analysis of rivet joints is based on different measures and quantities per type of rivet joint. Generally, most rivet joints are categorized into one of six rivet joint types. The six basic types of rivet joints are illustrated in Figure 15-3, and are listed as follows:

1. Single riveted lap joints
2. Double riveted lap joints
3. Single riveted lap joints with inside cover plate
4. Double riveted lap joints with inside cover plate
5. Double riveted butt joints
6. Triple riveted butt joints

RIVETING OPERATIONS

Once the appropriate rivet joint has been selected, it is then necessary to determine what type of rivet is to be used and how it is to be formed. The traditional conception of a finished rivet is one with a rounded head. In fact, three different rivet potentials exist: rounded, flat, and countersunk. The specific type of finish, however, will normally be specified in the product's working drawings. Here, standardized symbols are used to denote a specific type of rivet finish. Figure 15-4 gives the conventional symbols used for identifying rivet finishes.

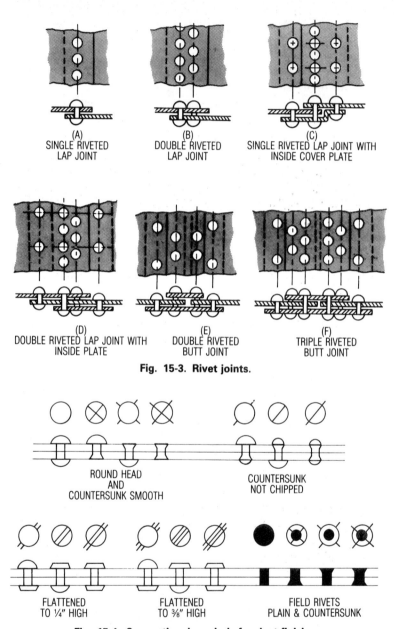

(A)
SINGLE RIVETED
LAP JOINT

(B)
DOUBLE RIVETED
LAP JOINT

(C)
SINGLE RIVETED LAP JOINT WITH
INSIDE COVER PLATE

(D)
DOUBLE RIVETED LAP JOINT WITH
INSIDE PLATE

(E)
DOUBLE RIVETED
BUTT JOINT

(F)
TRIPLE RIVETED
BUTT JOINT

Fig. 15-3. Rivet joints.

ROUND HEAD
AND
COUNTERSUNK SMOOTH

COUNTERSUNK
NOT CHIPPED

FLATTENED
TO ¼" HIGH

FLATTENED
TO ⅜" HIGH

FIELD RIVETS
PLAIN & COUNTERSUNK

Fig. 15-4. Conventional symbols for rivet finishes.

336

Hand Riveting

One of the more traditional methods used for riveting small, custom-made sheet metal products is by hand. To hand rivet, all one needs are two simple hand tools: riveting hammer and rivet set. The riveting hammer is used to "set" the rivet in place and apply pressure for head formation. The rivet set (Figure 15-5) provides the forms required for setting and head formation.

Courtesy Niagara Machine and Tool Works
Fig. 15-5. Rivet set.

The procedures recommended for hand riveting and head formation (Figure 15-6) are presented as follows:

1. Lay out the rivet holes according to the type of rivet joint to be used. Make sure that the rivet holes are properly spaced. As a rule of thumb, there are two rivet spacing standards commonly observed. The first is that the distance from the edge of the sheet metal to the center of the rivet hole should be approximately 2 times the diameter of the rivet. Second, the minimum distance between rivet centers should be approximately 3 times the rivet diameter. The maximum distance between rivet centers should never exceed 24 times the thickness of the sheet metal.

2. Center punch the rivet hole centers. Depending on the hole size and product requirements, the hole can then be drilled or punched.

3. Select the proper size and shape rivet and insert it in the rivet holes. Rest the head side of the rivet on a solid metal surface, bar, or stake. Make sure that the shank of the rivet is properly aligned through all matching holes.

4. Draw the pieces of sheet metal together by setting the rivet in place. This is accomplished by putting the appropriate

sized rivet set hole over the rivet and striking it firmly with the riveting hammer.

5. Once the rivet is set, remove the rivet set and *upset* the rivet by hitting it with the riveting hammer. This locks the rivet in place and provides for the initial formation of the rivet head.

6. Place the rivet set's pre-formed cavity over the upset end of the rivet and complete the forming process by striking the set with the riveting hammer.

There are times when riveting defects will occur, but most of them can be corrected. Presented in Table 15-3 and Figure 15-7 are common riveting defects and their causes.

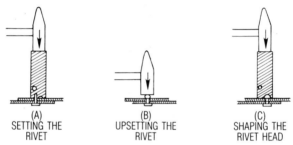

| (A) SETTING THE RIVET | (B) UPSETTING THE RIVET | (C) SHAPING THE RIVET HEAD |

Fig. 15-6. Hand riveting with a rivet set.

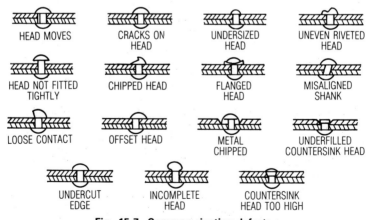

Fig. 15-7. Common riveting defects.

Table 15-3
Riveting Defects and Causes

Rivet Defect	Possible Causes of Defect
The rivet head shifts during hammering	The metal sheets are not properly set or clamped. Poor riveting.
The rivet is not fitted tightly to the metal sheets	Rivet's shank is too thick at the head. The head is not completely formed and tight against the sheet metal.
There is loose contact between the head and part	Rivet head was formed misaligned
Edges of rivet head are undercut	Defective rivet. Wrong-sized rivet set. Tooling misalignment.
Rivet head cracks	Defective rivet, low quality.
Rivet head chips off at periphery	Rivet set moved during head formation. Poor riveting.
Rivet head is offset	Pre-formed cavity of the rivet set was improperly aligned. Upsetting was not properly accomplished.
Rivet head is not completely formed	The rivet shank is too short. The metal sheets are

Table 15-3
Riveting Defects and Causes (Cont'd)

Rivet Defect	Possible Causes of Defect
	improperly set.
	Metal sheets are not properly clamped.
Undersized rivet head	Undersized rivet set.
Flange around the rivet head	Rivet shank is too long.
	Undersized rivet set.
Metal is chipped or marred about the rivet head	Rivet shank is too short.
	Oversized rivet set.
Rivet head has an uneven head	Poor quality rivet.
Misaligned shank	Holes drilled incorrectly.
	Rivet shank diameter is too small for the rivet hole.
Countersunk rivet head is underfilled	Rivet shank is too short.
	Incorrect countersink rivet.
Countersunk rivet head is too high	Rivet shank is too long.

Expanding Rivets

The design requirements of the aircraft, electronics, computer, marine, and other technical industries have put new demands on the way riveting is done. The expanding rivet was developed to meet the demands made by these industries. This rivet is frequently used on products that have no, or limited, access to the back side. Thus, conventional riveting procedures would prove either extremely difficult or impossible.

Riveting sheet metal parts, without access to the back side, is referred to as *blind riveting*. Blind riveting, also referred to as *pop riveting*, employs a rivet that is made up of two parts: a hollow rivet, and a *clinching mandrel* or steel pin which is inside of it (Figure 15-8). Similar to other types of rivets, expanding rivets are available in various shapes, which include a 100° countersunk head. Shank diameters are commonly found in sizes such as 3/32 (2.38mm), 1/8 (3.18mm), 5/32 (3.97mm), 3/16 (4.76mm), 7/32 (5.56mm), and 1/4 (6.35mm) in. Expanding rivets are also available in different materials such as Monel, copper, aluminum steel, stainless steel, and brass.

Blind riveting is quite easy to accomplish. The rivet's steel mandrel is inserted into the gripper jaws of a blind or pop riveter. The rivet body is then inserted into the pre-drilled hole of the metal sheets. The riveter then pulls on the mandrel as the rivet body is held in place. The mandrel continues to pull on the rivet shank until it bulges and forms a "head" on the blind side of the workpieces. As additional pulling pressure is applied to the mandrel, it breaks off, leaving a finished riveted joint. This procedure is illustrated in Figure 15-9.

It should be noted that there are various types and designs of blind riveters used in sheet metal work. Hand-operated riveters are used for *semihand riveting* operations. The other common expanding type riveters are pneumatic "pop" riveters frequently used in sheet metal shops and small production situations.

Removing Rivets

Because of design changes, servicing, repairs, and corrections, it sometimes becomes necessary to remove rivets. The procedures

Fig. 15-8. A "pop" rivet.

POP RIVET
CLINCHING MANDREL

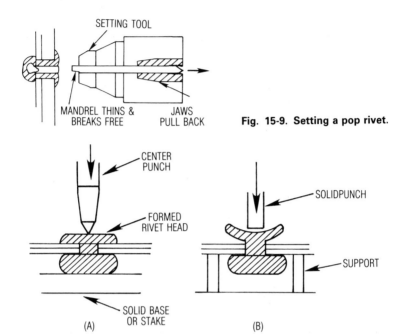

Fig. 15-9. Setting a pop rivet.

Fig. 15-10. Removing a rivet.

recommended are easy and are illustrated in Figure 15-10. Briefly, the procedures are as follows:

1. Place the rivet over a metal stake so that the formed head is facing up.

2. With a center punch, punch the center of the formed head.

3. Remove the rivet from the stake and place it on two supports so that the rivet itself is not supported.

4. Select a solid punch slightly smaller in diameter than the drilled hole and drive the rivet out with a solid blow of a riveting hammer.

THREADED FASTENERS

Another major category of mechanical fasteners used in sheet metal work includes those that use a threaded shank. These shanks may be straight, as in bolts, or tapered, as in screws. Presented in this section will be the common types of threaded fasteners used in sheet metal work.

Bolts and Nuts

Bolts are fasteners that are threaded externally and designed to hold assembled parts together. They are frequently used in combination with nuts, which are threaded internally, and are coupled with the bolt. Tightening is accomplished by applying torque (rotating force) to the nut. The two most common types of bolts and nuts are the American National Standard Square and Hexagon Bolts and Nuts (Figure 15-11).

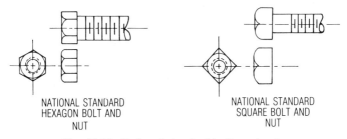

NATIONAL STANDARD HEXAGON BOLT AND NUT

NATIONAL STANDARD SQUARE BOLT AND NUT

Fig. 15-11. National standard bolts and nuts.

Screw threads standardization, used in making bolts and nuts, is maintained by the *Unified and American Screw Thread Standards* that are published by the ANSI (B1.1-1981). In the United States, standard threads, known as *series*, are used in the manufacturing of bolts and nuts. The major series found are presented as follows:

1. *Coarse Thread Series.* Noted as UNC and NC, these threaded fasteners are employed for general use, especially where rapid assembly is required.

2. *Fine Thread Series.* Identified as UNF and NF, the fine thread series are used in situations requiring greater strength.

3. *Extra Fine Thread Series.* Noted as UNEF and NEF, these fasteners are used for parts that are placed under high stresses.

4. *8 Thread Series.* Noted as 8UN and 8N, this thread is a substitute for the UNC and NC series for bolts having a diameter that exceeds 1.5 in. (3.8cm).

5. *12 Thread Series.* Identified as 12 UN and 12 N, it is an extension of the UNF and NF series for bolts with diameters exceeding 1.5 in. (3.8cm).

6. *16 Thread Series.* Also noted as 16 UN and 16N, this is a continuation of the UNEF and NEF series for diameters that exceed 2 in. (5.1cm).

Other special thread series are available, but they are seldom used in general sheet metal work. For specific information on threaded bolts and nuts, see ANSI B18.2.1-1981.

Sheet Metal and Self-Tapping Screws

Screws that were designed to meet the needs of the sheet metal industry are sheet metal and self-tapping screws. These screws were developed to fill three primary needs often faced in sheet metal work. The first is the fastening of two or more sections of thin sheet metal together by deforming the metal as the screw rotates into them. The second need occurs when thin sheet metal must be fastened to a thicker cross section of material. Fastening is achieved here by the cutting action of the screw thread (i.e., thread forming). Finally, these screws provide a fast and efficient method of fastening sections together in mass-produced products.

As might be expected, several different sheet metal and self-tapping screws are available for use in fabricating operations. The success of each type depends on the required needs of the material and the size hole available. The major categories used to identify these screws, and their uses, are illustrated in Figure 15-12 and presented as follows:

1. *Type A.* This screw is no longer recommended for sheet metal work, though it was used in a number of fabricating processes. Used for thin sheet metal, plywood that was impregnated with resin, and asbestos products, Type A screws are spaced-threaded screws with a gimlet point.

2. *Type AB.* The Type AB screw is recommended as a replacement for the Type A screw wherever possible. The spaced-thread screw has the same pitch as found in Type B screws.

3. *Type B.* A screw with a blunt point and finer screw thread than Type AB is Type B. In addition to its use with thin sheet metal, it is also recommended for fastening nonferrous castings, plastics, asbestos products, and resin-impregnated plywoods.

4. *Type BP.* This screw is the same as Type B except that it has a conical point that extends beyond the threads. Type BP screws are used in assembly operations where holes have been drilled or punched out of line.

5. *Type C.* Unlike the previous screws, Type C uses a combination of different threads and pitches. This screw incorporates machine screw-pitch combinations along with threads approximating the Unified Form. In addition, Type C screws have a blunt point. This screw should be used where high driving torques are required.

6. *Types D, F, G, and T.* These thread cutting screws have threads that are similar to machine-screw threads. Their ends are blunt and have a thread design that tapers off near the end. Fastening applications for Types D, F, G, and T screws are recommended for use in steel sheets, cast iron, brasses, plastics, and aluminum, zinc, and lead die castings.

7. *Type BF and BT.* Another group of thread cutting screws are Types BF and BT. These screws have one or more cutting grooves and are designed with a blunt end. They are used in fastening plastics, asbestos, and other similar materials.

8. *Type U.* A screw that is forced into the workpiece by pressure is Type U. This multiple-threaded drive screw has a pilot point particularly useful in both metals and plastics. Type U screws should be used where permanent fastening is required.

When ordering sheet metal and self-tapping screws, it is rec-

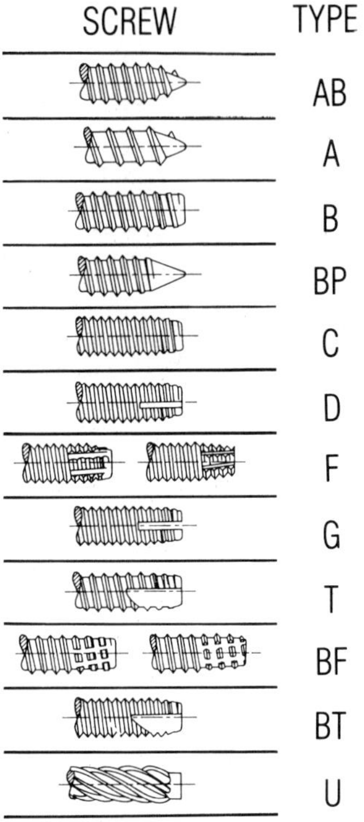

SCREW	TYPE
	AB
	A
	B
	BP
	C
	D
	F
	G
	T
	BF
	BT
	U

Fig. 15-12. Types of sheet metal and self-tapping screws.

ommended that a particular sequence of information be given. This sequential information is as follows:

1. Nominal size or equivalent number, fraction, or decimal
2. Threads per inch
3. Nominal length or equivalent fraction or decimal
4. Point type
5. Product name, which includes type of head and driving provision
6. Material
7. Protective finish, if any

Two examples of how this would be used are:

Example A: 5-20 × ¾ Type T, Type 1A Cross Recessed Pan Head Tapping Screw, Steel, Nickel Plated

Example B: ⁷⁄₁₆-10 × ⅝ Type AB, Slotted Pan Head Tapping Screw, Corrosion Resistant Steel

Presented in Tables 15-4 and 15-5 are specifications for several types of common sheet metal and self-tapping screws.

Hole Sizes for Screws

Before sheet metal and self-tapping screws can be used, it is necessary to either punch or drill a hole for them. Critical here is making these holes of the appropriate size. Several factors will

Table 15-4
Specifications for Type AB Thread Forming Tapping Screws

Nominal Size	Diameter (inch)	Threads per Inch	Minimum Screw Lengths (inch)	
			Csk Head	90° Head
0	0.0600	48	⁵⁄₃₂	⅛
1	0.0730	42	³⁄₁₆	⁵⁄₃₂
2	0.0860	32	⁷⁄₃₂	³⁄₁₆
3	0.0990	28	¼	³⁄₁₆
4	0.1120	24	⁹⁄₃₂	⁷⁄₃₂
5	0.1250	20	⁵⁄₁₆	¼
6	0.1380	20	¹¹⁄₃₂	⁹⁄₃₂
7	0.1510	19	⅜	⁵⁄₁₆
8	0.1640	18	⅜	⁵⁄₁₆
10	0.1900	16	⁷⁄₁₆	⅜
12	0.2160	14	²¹⁄₃₂	⁷⁄₁₆
¼	0.2500	14	¹⁹⁄₃₂	½
⁵⁄₁₆	0.3125	12	¾	⅝
⅜	0.3750	12	²⁹⁄₃₂	¾
⁷⁄₁₆	0.4375	10	1-¹⁄₃₂	⅞
½	0.5000	10	1-⁵⁄₃₂	1

Table 15-5
Specifications for Types B and BP Thread Cutting Tapping Screws

Nominal Size	Diameter (inch)	Threads per Inch	Minimum Screw Lengths (inch)			
			Type B		Type BP	
			Csk 90° Heads		Csk 90° Heads	
0	0.0600	48	1/8	1/8	3/16	5/32
1	0.0730	42	5/32	1/8	7/32	3/16
2	0.0860	32	3/16	5/32	9/32	1/4
3	0.0990	28	7/32	3/16	5/16	9/32
4	0.1120	24	1/4	3/16	11/32	5/16
5	0.1250	20	9/32	7/32	13/32	11/32
6	0.1380	20	9/32	1/4	7/16	3/8
7	0.1510	19	5/16	1/4	15/32	13/32
8	0.1640	18	11/32	9/32	1/2	7/16
10	0.1900	16	3/8	5/16	19/32	1/2
12	0.2160	14	7/16	11/32	21/32	9/16
1/4	0.2500	14	1/2	3/8	3/4	21/32
5/16	0.3125	12	19/32	15/32	31/32	27/32
3/8	0.3750	12	11/16	15/16	1-1/8	15/16
7/16	0.4375	10	25/32	5/8	1-1/4	1-1/8
1/2	0.5000	10	27/32	11/16	1-13/32	1-1/4

determine the size of the screw hole. These are: type of screw, screw size, type of sheet metal, and thickness of sheet metal. Presented in Tables 15-6 and 15-7 are recommended drilled hole sizes for Types AB, B, BP, and C steel thread forming screws.

SUMMARY

Mechanical fasteners are used in sheet metal work in cases where the product is too heavy or large to bend into a seam or joint, and/ or for easy servicing. The most common methods used for mechanical fastening are riveting and screwing.

Table 15-6
Hole Sizes for Steel Thread Forming Screw Types AB, B, and BP

Sheet Material	Screw Size	Material Thickness (inch)	Required Hole Size (inch)
Steel, stainless steel, Monel, and brass sheets	4	0.015	0.086
		0.018	0.086
		0.024	0.098
		0.030	0.098
		0.036	0.098
	6	0.015	0.111
		0.018	0.111
		0.024	0.111
		0.030	0.111
		0.036	0.111
	7	0.018	0.120
		0.024	0.120
		0.030	0.120
		0.036	0.120
		0.048	0.120
	8	0.018	0.136
		0.024	0.136
		0.030	0.136
		0.036	0.136
		0.048	0.136
	10	0.018	0.157
		0.024	0.157
		0.030	0.157
		0.036	0.157
		0.048	0.157
	12	0.024	0.185
		0.030	0.185
		0.036	0.185
		0.048	0.185
	¼	0.030	0.209
		0.036	0.209
		0.048	0.209

Table 15-6
Hole Sizes for Steel Thread Forming Screw Types AB, B, and BP (Cont'd)

Sheet Material	Screw Size	Material Thickness (inch)	Required Hole Size (inch)
Aluminum alloy sheets	4	0.024	0.086
		0.030	0.086
		0.036	0.086
		0 048	0.086
	6	0.024	0.111
		0.030	0.111
		0.036	0.111
		0.048	0.111
	7	0.024	0.120
		0.030	0.120
		0.036	0.120
		0.048	0.120
	8	0.024	0.136
		0.030	0.136
		0.036	0.136
		0.048	0.136
	10	0.024	0.157
		0.030	0.157
		0.036	0.157
		0.048	0.157

Riveting provides a permanent joint, and can be accomplished by either hot or cold methods. In sheet metal work, however, only cold riveting is used. A number of factors must be considered when selecting a particular riveting joint. These include spacing rivets, the type and size of rivets and holes, and the material to be riveted.

Rivets are similar in design to screws, except that they are not threaded. They do have various types of head designs, body diameters, and shank lengths. The most common types of riveting joints encountered are single riveted lap joints, double riveted lap

**Table 15-7
Hole Sizes for Type C Steel Thread Forming Screws
in Sheet Steel Material**

Screw Size	Material Thickness (inch)	Hole Size (inch)
4–40	0.037	0.094
	0.048	0.094
	0.062	0.096
	0.075	0.100
	0.105	0.102
	0.134	0.102
6–32	0.037	0.113
	0.048	0.116
	0.062	0.116
	0.075	0.122
	0.105	0.125
	0.134	0.125
8–32	0.037	0.136
	0.048	0.144
	0.062	0.144
	0.075	0.147
	0.105	0.150
	0.134	0.150
10–24	0.037	0.154
	0.048	0.161
	0.062	0.166
	0.075	0.170
	0.105	0.173
	1.134	0.177
10–32	0.037	0.170
	0.048	0.170
	0.062	0.170
	0.075	0.173
	0.105	0.177
	0.134	0.177
12–24	0.037	0.189
	0.048	0.194
	0.062	0.194
	0.075	0.199

Table 15-7
Hole Sizes for Type C Steel Thread Forming Screws (Cont'd)
in Sheet Steel Material

Screw Size	Material Thickness (inch)	Hole Size (inch)
	0.105	0.199
	0.134	0.199
¼–20	0.037	0.221
	0.048	0.221
	0.062	0.228
	0.075	0.234
	0.105	0.234
	0.134	0.236
¼–28	0.037	0.224
	0.048	0.228
	0.062	0.232
	0.075	0.234
	0.105	0.238
	0.134	0.238

joints, single riveted lap joints with inside cover plate, double riveted lap joints with inside cover plate, double riveted butt joints, and triple riveted butt joints.

One of the most traditional methods used for riveting is by hand. Here hand sets are used to "set" and form the rivet head. The other common method of riveting is expanding rivets. This procedure is more commonly known as "pop" riveting.

Bolts and nuts provide for the nonpermanent fastening of sheet metal. Screw threads are standardized by the Unified and American Screw Thread Standards, and are published by the ANSI. The major series of threads used by bolts and nuts are coarse thread series, fine thread series, extra fine thread series, 8 thread series, 12 thread series, and 16 thread series.

Screws are used to fasten two or more sheets of thin metal together by deforming the metal as the screw rotates into them. They are also used to fasten a thin section of metal to a thicker one, and provide for a fast and economical method for fastening sections together in mass production settings.

Several different screws are available for sheet metal work. The major categories of sheet metal and self-tapping screws are Types A, AB, B, BP, C, D, F, G, T, BF, BT, and U. Each is specifically designed for a particular situation. Critical to the successful use of screws is the hole size used for screwing. The specific size hole for a particular screw will vary according to its sheet material and its thickness.

REVIEW QUESTIONS

1. Explain the conditions most favorable for using mechanical fasteners in sheet metal work.

2. Briefly explain the meaning of the following terms: pitch, back or transverse pitch, diagonal pitch, and margin.

3. Explain the procedure you would use in selecting rivet sizes.

4. Identify and describe the various types of rivet joints used in sheet metal work.

5. List the procedures you would use for hand riveting.

6. What is "pop" riveting and how does it differ from hand riveting?

7. What is semihand riveting?

8. Explain the meaning of the following abbreviations: UNC, NC, UNF, NF, UNEF, NEF, 8UN, 8N, 12UN, 12N, 16UN, 16N.

9. What screw type is used for most sheet metal work? Why?

10. What factors will affect the size of a screw hole?

CHAPTER 16

Soldering and Brazing

Soldering is considered one of the oldest methods used to bond metals together and is especially effective in sheet metals such as galvanized sheet steel, tinplate, stainless steel, copper, and brass. There are two forms of soldering: soft and hard. Typically, soft soldering is accomplished at temperatures under 800°F (427°C), while hard soldering usually requires temperatures that exceed 800°F (427°C). Another name for hard soldering is brazing.

At one time, soft soldering was the primary method used in joining sheet metal, but it is infrequently used today except in the fabrication of heating and air-conditioning systems. As a replacement, brazing has become the dominant bonding process in the sheet metal shop and production setting. The reason is that brazing will produce a stronger joint, yet have the same bonding characterisitics as soft soldering. Presented in this chapter will be a discussion of both soft and hard soldering materials and operations.

SOLDERS AND FLUXES

Soft soldering is an inexpensive and efficient method that is available to the sheet metal worker for bonding two pieces of metal together. It is used to provide secure and tight joints that will not be subjected to any great stress or mechanical force. In addition, soldering can be used in combination with mechanical operations such as staking, crimping, and folding. Soldering is also used to provide a sealed joint or seam that is leakproof, to fill in crevices, and to round out the corners of sheet metal parts.

Solders

Solders are nonferrous alloyed metals that are melted to join metal pieces together. The majority of solders used are made of lead and tin compositions that vary according to application. In some cases, other alloying elements, such as antimony and silver, are added to provide specific properties.

Critical in the exact mixture of soldering alloys is the *eutectic composition*. This is the proportional mixture of metals that will result in the lowest melting temperature or *eutectic temperature*. As an example, the eutectic composition of a lead-tin solder is 37 percent lead and 63 percent tin, which has a eutectic temperature of 361°F (183°C). All other lead-tin mixtures will have a higher melting temperature.

It should also be mentioned that there will be a certain temperature range, for non-eutectic mixtures, where one metal will be liquid (liquidus) and the other metal will be solid (solidus). Above this range, both metals will be liquid, and below this range both metals will be solid. Thus, when the melting ranges of solders are specified, they will normally have two temperatures: solidus and liquidus. If both solidus and liquidus temperatures are the same, then the alloy will be a eutectic composition.

Table 16-1 lists the composition, melting ranges, and applications of common solders.

Solders are available in a variety of forms. They can be purchased as bars, cakes, wires, pigs, slabs, ingots, ribbons, segments, powders, and foils. The wire-form solder is usually employed for work on smaller parts that require the accurate control of metal flow and for machine soldering. One of the most common sizes of wire solder is ⅛ in. (3.18mm) diameter that is often found in spools ranging in size from 1 to 50 lbs. Some wire holders are manufactured with a flux core. This type, however, is primarily used in electrical soldering.

Bar solders are widely used in the construction trade and in some shop situations that require hand soldering operations. They typically weigh about 1-¼ lbs and measure 13-¼″ × ¾″ × ⅝″ (33.7 × 1.9 × 1.6cm). Pigs, ingots, and slabs are melted in soldering kettles for dip soldering operations. Ribbon, segment, powder, and foil solders are primarily designed for special applications. Cake

Table 16-1
Composition, Melting Ranges, and Applications of Solders

Tin	Lead	Antimony	Silver	Solidus	Liquidus	Applications
— Nominal Composition Percent				Melting Ranges		
70	30	—	—	361	378	Primarily used for coating metals
63	37	—	—	361	361	The eutectic composition for the alloy
						Used for hand and dip soldering
60	40	—	—	361	374	A general purpose solder considered a "fine solder"
						Often used where the temperature requirements are critical
50	50	—	—	361	421	The most popular of all solders; considered a general purpose solder.
45	55	—	—	361	441	Used in roofing seams and for automobile radiator cores
40	60	—	—	361	460	Used for soldering heating units and automobile radiator cores
						Also has applications in wiping solder for joints in lead pipes and cable sheaths
35	65	—	—	361	477	A general purpose solder
30	70	—	—	361	491	Used in torch soldering and machine soldering
25	75	—	—	361	511	Used in torch soldering and machine soldering

Table 16-1 (Cont'd)
Composition, Melting Ranges, and Applications of Solders

Nominal Composition Percent				Melting Ranges		
Tin	Lead	Antimony	Silver	Solidus	Liquidus	Applications
20	80	—	—	361	531	Used in both coating and joining metals Often applied in seam and dent filling for automobiles
15	85	—	—	440	550	Coating and joining metals, but has no practical mechanical strength at temperatures that exceed 360°F
10	90	—	—	514	570	Coating and joining metals, but has no practical mechanical strength at temperatures that exceed 360°F
5	95	—	—	518	594	Coating and joining metals
40	58	2	—	365	448	Should not be used with galvanized iron A general purpose solder
35	63.2	1.8	—	365	470	All general soldering applications, except with galvanized iron
30	68.4	1.6	—	364	482	Torch soldering and machine soldering, but not with galvanized iron
25	73.7	1.3	—	364	504	Torch and machine soldering, but not on galvanized iron

Table 16-1 (Cont'd)
Composition, Melting Ranges, and Applications of Solders

Tin	Lead	Antimony	Silver	Solidus	Liquidus	Applications
20	79	1	—	363	517	Used for metal coating and machine soldering, but not on galvanized iron
95	—	—	5	452	464	Wide applications for joining copper in electrical, heating, and plumbing work
—	97.5	—	2.5	579	579	Eutectic composition for this alloy
						Used on copper, brass, and similar metals with torch soldering
						Not recommended for use in humid or moist environments
1	97.5	—	1.5	588	588	Eutectic composition for this alloy
						Used in torch soldering on copper, brass, and similar metals

Nominal Composition Percent / Melting Ranges

solders are widely used in the plumbing industry for wiping pipe joints. Powdered solders are used where the metal's surface is constantly wet, and are applied to the joint by brush, after which it is heated for bonding.

Fluxes

Before sheet metal can be soldered, it is necessary to ensure that its surface is clean of dirt, grease, and foreign substances. In addition, care must be taken to minimize, or eliminate, oxides that form on the metal's surface. Fluxes are used to clean the surface of oxide coatings and prevent the formation of oxide films. Furthermore, fluxes lower the surface tension of the solder, which makes it flow easier and become "wetter."

Solders are generally categorized into two major groupings. The first includes noncorrosive solders, which leave no corrosive residue after soldering. The most commonly used noncorrosive solder is rosin. The second group of fluxes include all corrosive fluxes. These types are often used in sheet metal work because they penetrate oxide films much more easily than noncorrosive fluxes. The two most commonly used corrosive fluxes used are zinc chloride and ammonium chloride.

Mild fluxes useful in preventing the formation of oxide films but not very effective in removing existing oxides are rosin, tallow, and stearin. These fluxes are usually applied after the metal's surface has been cleaned by other mechanical (e.g., files, steel wool, wire brush, or emory cloth) or chemical (e.g., acid baths or dips) methods. Fluxes that readily remove surface oxides are zinc chloride and ammonium chloride (also known as sal ammoniac). Rosin flux, which is noncorrosive and nonconducting, is used for electrical soldering, on clean tinplate and copper, and for work on solder coated surfaces.

Fluxes can be purchased in various forms. These include solids, powders, pastes, and liquids. The type selected will be determined by the nature of the operation and the type of part being joined.

The residue left by corrosive fluxes can cause problems to a workpiece if not removed. Because of their "corrosive" nature, they are capable of weakening and permanently damaging the physical structure and appearance of the part. Therefore, it is essential that they be removed or neutralized. This is normally accomplished by washing the part after soldering. A common washing solution used is as follows:

- *Ferrous and Nonferrous Soldering:* 1 ounce trisodium phosphate to one gallon of water.
- *Nonferrous Soldering:* 5 ounces sodium citrate to one gallon of water.

After washing with these solutions, the part should be rinsed with clear water or with a commercial detergent that is water soluble.

SOLDERING SHEET METAL

One of the more important factors needed for successful soldering is an adequate supply of heat. Examples of heating devices are soldering coppers and irons, blowtorches, soldering furnaces, and bottled gas soldering torches. This section presents common equipment and methods used in soldering sheet metal.

Soldering Equipment

Different products are used to provide heat for soldering operations. One of the most common is the soldering iron or copper (Figure 16-1). Coppers are made of a forged copper head that is designed as either a pointed or bottom head, with sizes specified in terms of weight. Light work soldering is usually done with soldering irons that weigh up to a half pound; medium weight work use irons up to one pound; heavy weight work require irons to four pounds; and very heavy work can be accomplished with irons that weigh in excess of four pounds.

Soldering irons have no self-producing heat source and must therefore be heated in a soldering furnace or by a torch. For this reason, it is common practice to use two soldering irons at one time; one iron will be heating up while the second is in use. The advantage of the soldering furnace over the torch method is that the furnace can raise the iron's temperature more rapidly and does not require handling during the heating process. Soldering furnaces are often designed with one or two burners controlled by separate valves.

Blowtorches and bottled gas soldering (Figure 16-2) are used

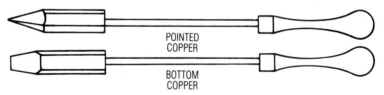

POINTED
COPPER

BOTTOM
COPPER

Fig. 16-1. Soldering coppers.

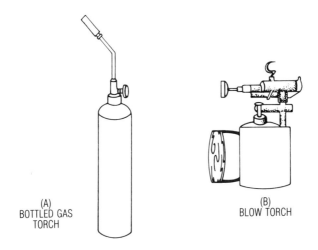

(A)
BOTTLED GAS
TORCH

(B)
BLOW TORCH

Fig. 16-2. Two types of torch heating devices.

as a direct method for providing heat to the joint area. The fuel used can be gasoline, propane, or any other fuel gas. Torch soldering is best used for larger sections requiring more heat.

Electric soldering irons (Figure 16-3) are rated in terms of electrical power or wattage. Irons rated between 25 and 100 watts are used primarily for electrical soldering. Heavier soldering operations are performed on irons up to 200 watts, and extremely rugged work is done on electric soldering irons between 350 and 550 watts.

Fig. 16-3. A small electric soldering iron.

High temperature capability is not the only critical factor in selecting the most appropriate heating device. There must also be sufficient amounts of generated heat that can be transferred to the workpiece. Remember that the heating device is not used to melt the solder, but the solder is melted when it is brought in contact with the workpiece. Thus, the workpiece must be sufficiently heated to permit free solder flow.

If the heating source is used to melt the solder directly, a *cold solder joint* will occur. What this means is that the solder will melt and deposit on the sheet metal but will not adhere well, so that any minor force will break the bond.

Soldering Operations

A good solder joint is achieved when solder flows throughout the entire section of the joint. As illustrated in Figure 16-4, the properly soldered joint has solder in all sections of the joint so that there are no gaps or air spaces. A poor joint will have solder only in small sections of the joint. Though there are a large number of applications for soldering, only a few basic operations are central to all soldering procedures. These are: tinning a soldering copper, soldering a seam or joint, sweat soldering, and dip soldering.

The tinning of a soldering copper involves preparing the iron for soldering by cleaning and coating it with a thin layer of solder. Tinning removes any unnecessary pitting and oxidation and enhances the movement of the iron over the work. The recommended procedures that should be used for this operation are given as follows:

1. Heat the copper until it is red hot and then clamp it in a vise.

2. With a mill file, file the flat sides of the copper so that all pitting and signs of oxidation are removed.

3. Re-heat the copper until its temperature is just above the melting point of the solder.

4. Remove the copper from the furnace and rub each side on a block of sal ammoniac.

(A)
PROPER SOLDERED
JOINT

(B)
IMPROPER SOLDERED
JOINT

Fig. 16-4. Joint soldering.

5. Deposit a small amount of solder on the copper and repeat the rubbing process on the sal ammoniac block. This should adequately coat the copper with a thin layer of solder.

6. If the entire surface is not coated, you may have to re-heat the copper or use more fluxing compound. If there is an excess amount of solder on the copper, wipe it off with a cloth rag.

If a noncorrosive flux is being used, such as rosin, the tip of the copper should be inserted into the powdered flux, followed by the depositing of the solder. Another technique that is sometimes used is to dip the copper head into a paste or liquid flux before the solder is applied.

When soldering a seam or joint, the sections to be joined must be securely held during the soldering operation. Try to solder all joints and seams on a surface that will not rob the heat from the sheet metal, as most metal bench tops and vises will. If two pieces of different thicknesses are to be soldered, care should be taken to apply more heat to the thicker section so that the pieces will achieve the working temperature at the same time and rate. The procedures used in soldering a seam or joint are presented as follows:

1. Clean the sheet metal surfaces to be soldered. Make sure that all dirt, grease, and foreign substances are removed from the sheet metal.

2. Select the appropriate type of heating device for the job to be done.

3. Secure the sheet metal pieces to a nonconductor top and apply flux to the seam with a brush, swab, or other appropriate implement.

4. If a soldering iron is to be used, make sure it has achieved an appropriate temperature. This can be quickly tested by touching the end of the iron with the solder. If it melts quickly, then the iron is ready; if the melt is slow, continue to heat the iron.

5. Apply heat to the sheet metal until it penetrates throughout the seam or joint.

6. "Tack" the seam or joint at various distances. This will prevent the metal from moving during the soldering process. Remember, as heat is applied, the metal will expand and move.

7. Begin at one end of the seam or joint and hold the heating device in place until the sheet metal is hot enough to melt the solder. Slowly move the heating device the length of the seam or joint, followed by the solder. See Figure 16-5.

8. Hold the sheet metal in place until the solder has solidified. If the parts are moved before this occurs, the joint or seam will be weakened.

9. Clean the sheet metal with an appropirate solution, or detergent, and rinse with clear water.

There are times when a soldering joint is desired without any sign of the solder itself. Sweat soldering is an operation used to hide the solder from view, and requires a constant and even supply of heat. The procedures used are given as follows:

1. Tin the sides of the sheet metal that are to be joined together.

2. Bring the tinned sides in contact with one another and secure in position.

3. Heat the joint with a heating device so that the heat will be transmitted through the metal and melt the solder.

4. Once the solder is melted, remove the heat source. You can tell when this occurs because the solder will tend to flow out from under the sheet metal.

5. Apply a downward, clamping pressure on the sheet metal until the solder solidifies. You can press down with a cool copper or the end of a file.

The last soldering operation to be discussed is dip soldering. In this operation, the solder is melted in soldering kettle. The part to be soldered is cleaned, fluxed, and heated at the location of the soldering joint. After adequate preparation, the sheet metal is dipped or immersed into the molten solder so that the solder alloy will flow freely into the bonding area. The part is then removed and the excess solder allowed to drain.

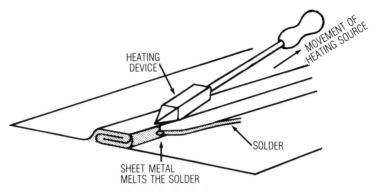

HEATING
DEVICE

MOVEMENT OF
HEATING SOURCE

SOLDER

SHEET METAL
MELTS THE SOLDER

Fig. 16-5. Soldering a seam.

DIFFICULT SOLDERING SHEET METALS

Various types of metals are not conducive for soldering and related operations. Two, however, are commonly found in sheet metal work: aluminum and stainless steel. Though other bonding techniques, such as brazing or welding, are usually employed with these metals, soldering may often prove to be more advantageous.

Aluminum Soldering

The procedures followed in soldering aluminum differ slightly from those used in conventional soldering. The reason for this is that aluminum has a very high rate of thermal conductivity. In addition, the oxide film formed on aluminum is extremely difficult to eliminate, since it forms as soon as the metal is exposed to air. Aluminum soldering occurs at temperatures ranging between 550 and 770°F as a result of its high thermal conductivity.

There are two general methods used to solder aluminum. The first is the most common and is referred to as *flow soldering*. Flow soldering consists of dissolving the flux and aluminum so that the metal will not re-form. In addition, the flux is maintained in the liquid form throughout soldering so that no oxygen is allowed to come in contact with the aluminum during the operation.

The second method employed for soldering aluminum is the

friction method. Here, the oxide film is mechanically removed by a wire brush or a special multi-tooth tool during the soldering operation. The continual action of the abrading tool as the molten solder is introduced to the sheet aluminum keeps the oxygen away from the soldered joint and the exposed metal.

The typical aluminum soldering alloy will consist of between 50 to 75 percent tin and 50 to 25 percent zinc. Aluminum metals that can be soldered are listed as follows from the easiest to the most difficult to solder:

- Commercial and high-purity aluminum (99% + pure)
- Wrought aluminum alloys that contain no more than 1 percent manganese or magnesium
- Heat-treatable aluminum alloys
- Cast and forged aluminum parts

Stainless Steel Soldering

The thermal conductivity of stainless steel is just the opposite of aluminum—it is very low. This also causes a problem for soldering by conventional methods. In addition, oxides that form on the metal's surface are very difficult to remove.

Before soldering can begin, the surface of stainless steel sheets must be thoroughly cleaned. This can be done by either mechanical abrasion or chemical immersion. The most common method is chemical immersion in an acid bath, which will turn the color of the metal white.

Common stainless steel fluxes used to remove and keep oxide films from forming are acid based. Examples of these flux mixtures are:

- Hydrochloric or muriatic acid that is saturated with zinc
- Hydrochloric or muriatic acid, saturated with zinc, plus an additional 25 percent of muriatic acid, or 10 percent additional acetic acid
- Hydrochloric or muriatic acid, saturated with zinc, and a 10 to 20 percent additional water solution of orthophosphoric acid

The solder alloy used in soldering stainless steel is a tin-lead solder. Because of the low thermal conductivity of this metal, it is important that a sufficient amount of heat is available to prepare the metal to receive the solder. If a soldering iron is the heating device, care should be taken to ensure that a large iron is used. After soldering is completed, all flux residue must be competely washed and removed with soap and water or an appropriate commercial detergent.

BRAZING FILLER METALS AND FLUXES

Brazing, or hard soldering, is a process that joins metals by using a nonferrous filler metal with a melting point below that of the base metal but above 800°F. Similar to soft soldering, the filler metal "wets" the base sheet metal when it becomes molten and adheres as it solidifies. Molten metal flow is a result of a phenomenon known as *capillary force*, which enhances the filler metal flow into close-fitting metal sections. Because of the higher strength resulting from a brazed joint and seam, brazing has replaced soldering in a number of sheet metal shop operations and production settings.

Filler Metals

Brazing filler metals have a lower melting temperature than the base sheet metal and are generally categorized into seven major groups. Each group is designated by the letter "B," to denote a brazing filler metal, followed by the chemical formula, and ending with a numerical or alphabetical code. The major filler metal groups are:

- Aluminum silicon (BAlSi)
- Copper phosphorus (BCuP)
- Silver (BAg)
- Nickel (BNi)
- Copper and copper zinc (BCu and BCuZn)
- Magnesium (BMg)
- Precious metals (BAu and BCo)

367

These codes and numbers are based on standards set by the American Welding Society (AWS). Brazing done with the silver alloy filler metal is commonly known as *silver soldering*. Presented in Table 16-2 is a listing of the AWS filler metal classification and uses.

Fluxes

Similar to soft soldering, brazing must be done on a clean surface. All dirt, oil, and oxides must first be removed before the filler metal can flow and adhere to the metal. This can be accomplished by either mechanical or chemical means. Mechanical cleaning is primarily used to remove foreign particles, while chemical methods are used to remove oils and greases. Mechanical cleaning includes the use of files, grinders, wire brushes, and machining operations. Chemical cleaning employs compounds such as trisodium phosphate, carbon tetrachloride, and trichloroethylene.

The major function of fluxes is removing and preventing the formation of oxides on the sheet metal. In addition to oxide removal, fluxes are also used to enhance the free flow of the filler metal during brazing. Depending on the type of brazing process being used, fluxes are found in a variety of forms that include powders, pastes, liquids, vapors, and gases. Some filler rods are available with a flux coating.

All fluxes will not function unless subjected to high heat. Thus, chemical activity only begins at brazing temperatures. Presented in Table 16-3 are recommended fluxes for use with different base and filler metals.

BRAZING METHODS

There are a number of different methods used in brazing metal sheets together. Presented in this section will be a discussion of the common brazing processes found in the sheet metal industry.

Torch Brazing

The most frequently used brazing method in sheet metal work is torch brazing. Also known as *blowpipe brazing*, this process uses

Table 16-2
Brazing Filler Metals
A5.8-81

AWS Classification	Uses
BAlSi-2 through BALSi-11	Suitable for joining aluminum and aluminum alloys All are useful for furnace and dip brazing BAlSi-3 through BAlSi-5 are suited for torch brazing BAlSi-6 through BAlSi-11 are used in vacuum brazing processes
BCuP-1 through BCuP-7	Suitable for joining copper and copper alloys, with limited use with silver, tungsten, and molybdenum Should not be used with iron, steel, or nickel base alloys
BAg-1 through BAg-8a, BAg-13 and -13a, and BAg-18 through BAg-28	Suitable for brazing most ferrous and nonferrous metals Not recommended for use with aluminum and magnesium These filler metals have very good brazing properties, and generally require the use of a flux
BNi-1 through BNi-8	Suitable for brazing AISI 300 and 400 series stainless steels, nickel base alloys, and cobalt base alloys
BCu-1 through BCu-2, RBCuZn-A -C, and -D, and BCuZn-D through BCuZn-H	Suitable for brazing various ferrous and nonferrous metals. Applicable in a variety of brazing processes.
BMg-1	Used for joining magnesium based metals, and in particular AZ10A, K1A, and M1A
BAu-1 through BAu-6 and BCo-1	The BAu series is used for brazing iron, nickel, and cobalt base metals, especially where resistance to oxides and corrosion is required BCo-1 is generally used where high temperature properties are required, and is compatible with cobalt base metals

Table 16-3
Brazing Metals and Flux Selection

Base or Sheet Metal Being Brazed	Filler Metal	Flux Composition	Form of Flux
Aluminum and aluminum alloys	BAlSi	Chlorides Fluorides	Powder
Magnesium alloys	BMg	Chlorides Fluorides	Powder
Aluminum-bronze alloys, and aluminum-bronzes	BCuZn BCuP	Chlorides Fluorides Borates Wetting agents	Powder Paste
Titanium and zirconium base alloys	BAg	Chlorides Fluorides Wetting agents	Powder Paste
All other brazeable alloys	All brazing filler metals except BAlSi and BMg	Boric acid Borates Fluorides Fluoroborates with fluorine compounds Wetting agents	Paste Powder Liquid
	All brazing filler metals except BAlSi, BMg, and BAg-1 through BAg-7	Borax Boric acid Borates Wetting agents	Paste powder liquid

an air-gas mixture to supply the fuel for the torch flame. Common air-gas mixtures include oxygen-acetylene, air-acetylene, and oxygen-other fuel gases. Critical here is the type of flame used. The best brazing flame should be *neutral* or slightly reducing so that the base metal does not overheat and melt. When brazing some types of bronzes, a hotter oxidizing flame is needed.

The basic procedures recommended for torch brazing are presented as follows:

1. Prepare the base metal by cleaning it thoroughly of all rust, oil, grease, and foreign substances.
2. Heat the metal with the torch and apply the flux. If a powder flux is used, heat the filler metal rod with the torch and dip it into the flux so that it will adhere to the rod.
3. Heat the metal until it just begins to glow.
4. Hold the filler rod just ahead of the flame and continue to heat until the flux and rod begin to melt.
5. As the filler metal melts, move the flame and rod the length of the joint until the braze is complete.

When torch brazing, the filler metal rod should never be melted directly by the torch. The sheet metal should be hot enough to permit the filler metal to flow over its surface.

Dip Brazing

In dip brazing, the filler metal is melted in a pot and covered with fluxing compounds. The sheet metal parts are held together in a jig and are then dipped into the molten bath for brazing. Once immersed, the filler metal flows into the joint or seam sections as a result of capillary action.

Resistance Brazing

Hot or incandescent electrodes are used to supply the heat required in resistance brazing. Heat is generated as a result of the resistance of the electrodes to the flow of electrical current. Brazing occurs when the filler metal is inserted between the electrode and base metal.

Induction Brazing

A highly specialized method of brazing is induction brazing. In this process, the sheet metal parts are placed near or inside a set of coils that carry an electrical current. Eddy current (similar to those found in electromagnets) losses are generated in the form of heat. This method is used when speed and cleanliness are important.

SUMMARY

Soldering is one of the oldest methods for joining metals. There are two basic types of soldering that the sheet metal worker can choose from. The first is known as soft solder, which is accomplished at temperatures below 800°F, and the second is hard soldering, which involves temperatures in excess of 800°F.

Solders are nonferrous alloyed metals used to bond two or more sheets of metal together. The basic composition of most solders is lead and tin. Sometimes other alloying elements are added to give the solder a unique property. Solders are available in a variety of forms that are selected because of the type of soldering operation to be accomplished.

Fluxes are chemicals incorporated into the soldering process for the purpose of cleaning off any oxide film that forms on the metal's surface. In addition, fluxes are employed to keep oxides from forming during the soldering process. The two categories of solders are corrosive and noncorrosive, with corrosive fluxes the most common in sheet metal work.

One of the most important pieces of soldering equipment is the heating device. This device supplies all the heat to the metal for soldering. Examples of heating devices are soldering coppers and irons, bottled gas torches, blowtorches, and soldering furnaces.

Soldering is accomplished by heating the sheet metal and then bringing the solder in contact with the metal. The heating device should never be used to melt the solder, otherwise a cold soldering joint might result.

There are several basic soldering operations found in many sheet metal jobs. The first is tinning a copper, which involves cleaning and depositing a thin layer of solder on the copper's head. The second operation is soldering seams and joints, and requires that the solder completely fill in all areas of the joint. The third operation is tinning, which is used to join metal when the solder is not to be seen. Finally, dip soldering involves the immersion of the workpiece into a soldering kettle that contains molten solder.

Sheet metal materials such as galvanized iron, copper, brass, and tinplate are easy to solder. Other metals, such as aluminum and stainless steel, are more difficult. The basic difference in soldering procedures between these two groups of metals is a difference in metal heating and fluxing techniques.

Brazing involves the bonding of metal by using a filler metal that becomes molten and flows as a result of capillary forces. Filler metals are coded by the American Welding Society by a letter and numbering system. Common filler metals are aluminum silicon, copper phosphorous, silver, nickel, copper and copper zinc, magnesium, and precious metals.

Fluxes are also used in brazing for the purpose of removing surface oxides. There are several basic methods used in brazing: torch brazing, dip brazing, resistance brazing, and induction brazing.

REVIEW QUESTIONS

1. Briefly explain the difference between soft and hard soldering.

2. What is meant by the terms eutectic composition and eutectic temperature?

3. What are types of good, general-purpose solders? What solder should be used where high temperatures might affect the performance of the joint?

4. What form of solder is often used by sheet metal workers on construction sites?

5. Explain the difference between a corrosive and noncorrosive flux.

6. What is the primary function of fluxes? Give examples of fluxes commonly used in sheet metal work.

7. Explain the differences between soldering with a torch and soldering iron.

8. What is a cold soldering joint and how can it be avoided?

9. How does soldering aluminum and stainless steel differ from soldering other conventional sheet metals?

10. What is meant by the term "capillary force"?

11. Explain what a filler metal is and the system used to categorize such metals.

12. What brazing filler metal should be used for joining sheet copper?

13. What forms are brazing fluxes found in?

14. Briefly describe the various types of brazing methods available to the sheet metal worker.

CHAPTER 17

Welding Sheet Metal

Welding is a generic name for a group of processes where metals are joined by fusion. Fusion is the melting of abutting or overlapping metals so that their molten material will flow together to form a single mass. Welding, like soldering, requires the use of high temperatures and can be performed with or without pressure and a filler metal. The amount of heat required for welding, however, is significantly higher than that used for soldering since the heat actually melts the base metal.

Sheet metal can be easily and economically welded as long as the appropriate process is selected for the particular type and gauged metal. Some welding processes are better suited for thicker gauged metals, while others can be performed on thin metal sections. Presented in this chapter are the common welding methods employed with sheet metals.

RESISTANCE WELDING

One of the most frequent welding processes used with sheet metal is resistance welding. This process makes use of a welding machine connected to a transformer that reduces alternating current voltage from 120 or 240 volts down to 4 or 12 volts. At the same time, the amount of current or amperage is raised, which produces the heat required for metal fusion.

The concept of resistance welding is shown in Figure 17-1. As illustrated, two electrodes apply pressure to the sheet metal sections. Electrical current is then passed through the metal, providing resistance to current flow. This resistance is the element that causes

375

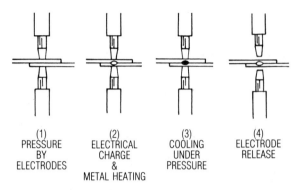

(1)	(2)	(3)	(4)
PRESSURE	ELECTRICAL	COOLING	ELECTRODE
BY	CHARGE	UNDER	RELEASE
ELECTRODES	&	PRESSURE	
	METAL HEATING		

Fig. 17-1. Principles of resistance welding.

the metal's temperature to increase. Pressure, in the area of 4,000 to 8,000 psi, is applied at the weld joint to complete the weld.

Resistance welding is used for both production and custom sheet metal work, and is one of the few welding processes employing pressure while heat is being applied. The use of pressure is important and cannot be overemphasized, for the precise controlling of pressure can lower the amount of heat needed for the weld to take place. Pressure acts as a forging mechanism between the metal sections. In all, there are five basic types of resistance welding procedures: spot, seam, flash-butt, projection, and percussion welding. See Table 17-1 for a brief description and use of the different resistance welding processes.

Spot Welding

The form of resistance welding with widest applications in sheet metal work is spot welding. This process is used to fuse together two or more sheets of metal at one time. Shown in Figure 17-2 is a diagram of a typical spot welding unit.

The welding cycle begins at the instant that the copper electrodes are brought in contact pressure with the sheet metal. This initial "squeezing" of the metal occurs before any current is allowed to flow and is known as the *squeeze time*. Next, a low-voltage current is applied to the work so that enough heat is generated to cause the metals to melt. When this critical temperature is attained,

Table 17-1
Resistance Welding Descriptions and Uses

Resistance Welding Process	Description	Uses
Spot welding	Heat is generated by electrical resistance of the workpieces as they are held under pressure between electrodes. The weld is made immediately.	Welding many different sheet metal products of various shapes and sizes. Used in the aircraft, marine, automobile, and construction industries.
Seam welding	Resistance weld is created by two circular electrodes, resulting in a continuous series of overlapping spot welds.	Same general applications as spot welding. Used in the manufacturing of containers and for joining continuous lengths of materials.
Flash-butt welding	Electrical resistance is generated between two abutting parts. Pressure is applied after heating, and causes a flash and upsetting action.	For welding metal sheets end-to-end. Primary application is in production settings.
Projection welding	Similar to spot welding except that the weld occurs at formed bumps or projections in the metal's surface.	Same general applications as in spot seam welding. Is best suited for production-type situations.
Percussion welding	An electric arc is used to provide the welding heat with percussive pressure applied to the work following the electrical discharge.	Excellent for welding tubes, pipes, and rods end-to-end.

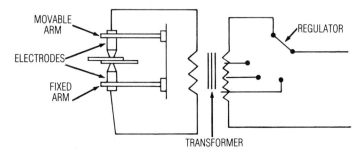

MOVABLE ARM

ELECTRODES

FIXED ARM

REGULATOR

TRANSFORMER

Fig. 17-2. Diagram of a spot welder.

additional pressure is applied by the electrodes so that the metal sheets are squeezed together to complete the weld. This second phase is known as the *weld time*, and occurs between 3 and 30 cycles per second (Hz).

After the weld time phase, current is turned off, but electrode pressure is maintained. This *hold time* allows the metal to cool and regain some of its strength. The last phase is called *off time*, and occurs when the electrode pressure is released and the workpiece is removed from the welder.

There are several types of spot welding machines. The first are known as *stationary single-spot* machines, which can be either rocker-arm or direct-pressure types. The rocker-arm spot welder is used for welding lighter gauged metals found in most sheet metal products. This machine is considered the simplest and least expensive spot welder. Direct-pressure machines are seldom used by sheet metal workers and are designed for production situations.

A second spot welder design includes the *portable spot welder*. As its name implies, this welding unit can be transported from one location to the other, and has wide acceptability in the field. The last type of spot welder is limited to production applications and is known as a *multi-spot* welder. This machine is capable of producing several spot welds at one time.

Though spot welding is the simplest of all resistance welding techniques, it is extremely effective. To produce a good weld, the sheet metal must be free of dirt, grease, and other foreign substances. If the metal's surface is insufficiently cleaned, the metal will tend to be insufficiently heated for melting and fusion.

Seam Welding

Seam welding employs two rotating electrodes that produce continuous and overlapping spot welds. Fusion occurs as a result of the heat generated by the sheet metal's resistance to current flow. Shown in Figure 17-3 is an illustration of how seam welding is done. Here, the sheet metals are held under pressure by the two circular electrodes. Since the current flow is not on a continuous basis, but at timed and regulated intervals, the weld is actually a series of spot welds. High-production seam welders who use a continuous flow of current are capable of producing one continuous weld.

The copper electrodes used in seam welding are available in different cross sections, depending on the type of weld produced. Most electrodes, however, are either slightly tapered, as shown in Figure 17-3, or have a straight side and flat welding surface. Because the electrode generates large amounts of heat, some form of cooling is required. Thus, it is not uncommon to find water used as a cooling substance in the weld area.

Seam welding is a popular resistance welding technique in shop and production settings. Examples of products manufactured by this welding process are mufflers, containers, metal cabinets, gasoline and water tanks, and automobile fenders.

Flash-Butt Welding

Flash-butt welding incorporates an electric arc to generate heat and pressure to complete the weld. As shown in Figure 17-4, the metal sheet, tubing, pipe, or rod is connected to two leads that supply the current flow. The parts are brought together so that there is a

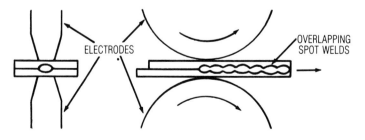

Fig. 17-3. Seam welding.

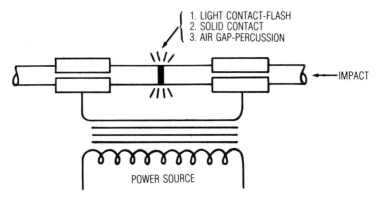

Fig. 17-4. Flash-butt welding.

very slight contact between the weld surfaces. A high voltage surge is supplied so that an arcing or flashing action occurs. This flashing continues until the metal parts increase in temperature; at the same time, additional pressure is brought into play between the two parts until the forging temperature is achieved. The weld is complete when forging pressures of 5,000 to 25,000 psi are achieved.

There are variations of flash-butt welding, including butt welding and flash welding. The first employs no electrical arcing, but makes extensive use of forging temperatures and pressures, while the second uses electrical arcing. Flash-butt welding, however, is a much more popular welding method for several reasons: first, there is less excess material to be removed around the joint; second, there is minimal atmospheric contamination; third, the process is less time consuming; and fourth, sheets can be welded end-to-end.

Flash-butt welding can be performed on most sheet metal materials, including both ferrous and nonferrous products. However, materials with a high percentage content of lead, zinc, tin, and copper are not recommended for flash-butt welding.

Projection Welding

A resistance welding process very similar to spot welding is known as projection welding. In conventional spot welding, the weld location is determined by the placement of the electrode. Projection welding, however, uses pre-formed bumps, dimples, or "projections" in the sheet metal. Thus, when the electrodes are brought in contact with the work piece, they make contact with the raised projections, and it is at that location that the weld takes place. See Figure 17-5.

The electrodes used in projection welding are in the form of copper platens attached to two arms. When the electrodes are brought into contact with the workpiece, the projections and the surface that they are in contact with heat up. Pressure is applied to the work and the weld is completed. After the work has been removed from the welding machine, the projections will have been removed (as a result of the pressing of the copper platens), and the actual weld will not be seen on the workpiece's surface—the weld is generated on the interior surfaces of the metal sheets. As might be expected, projection welding is used primarily on flat sheet materials where surface marring must be kept to a minimum.

Percussion Welding

Similar to flash-butt welding, percussion welding employs an arc effect rather than the resistance of the metal to current flow. In this process, the pieces to be welded are clamped to a stationary and a movable holder. The movable holder is connected to a spring-loaded device.

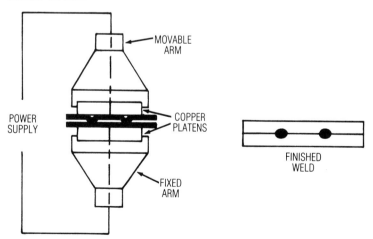

Fig. 17-5. Projection welding.

When the spring-loaded end is released, it moves along a slide. As the moving workpiece approaches the stationary part, a trip mechanism is activated so that an electrical discharge is sent through the metal, an arcing action. The electrical arc actually begins when the parts are approximately ⅟₁₆ in. (1.59mm) away from each other. The arc ceases when the two parts are forced together by a percussion-type blow.

Percussion welding is widely used to weld dissimilar metals together, such as copper to aluminum, copper to stainless steel, silver to copper, zinc to steel, and cast iron to steel. Because the process is so fast (in the area of ⅟₁₀th of a second), the metals are not significantly affected by the generated heat.

GAS WELDING

Welding processes that employ burning gases as a heating source are categorized as gas welding. In most cases, gas welding is used for joining metals up to 0.250 in. (6.35mm) thick. Because of the amount of heat generated by the welding torch, welding thinner gauged metals is extremely difficult and not often used by the sheet metal worker. Because thicker gauged materials are encountered in the field, and must often be joined by welding, it is important for the sheet metal worker to be familiar with gas welding processes.

Fuel Gases

A fuel gas is the primary gas that is used for burning. In many cases, the fuel gas acts in combination with other gases, such as oxygen and air, to obtain an optimal mixture for maximum heat. The typical arrangement used in gas welding is illustrated in Figure 17-6.

There are a variety of fuel gases available for welding. These include hydrogen, acetylene, and natural gas. Table 17-2 is a listing of the most common gas combinations, and their uses, that are found in the field.

The vast majority of welding done by sheet metal workers is oxyacetylene. When using a welding torch with this fuel, there will be two valves that control the amount of oxygen and acetylene gas flowing through the lines. Three general types of flames can be obtained:

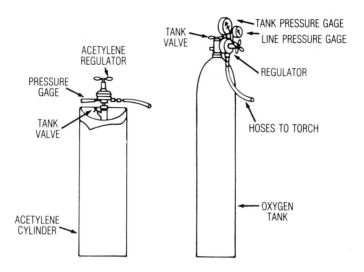

Fig. 17-6. Typical gas welding arrangement.

1. A *reducing flame* is also known as a carburizing flame. This type will have an excess amount of acetylene in the oxy-acetylene mixture, and is used in welding metals such as Monel, nickel, and some alloy steels and nonferrous metals.

2. A *neutral flame* has the widest application of the three types. This flame is made by a mixture of one part oxygen to one part acetylene (1:1). The maximum temperature of this flame is located at the tip of the luminous cone, and will range between 6,000 and 6,300°F (3,300 to 3,500°C).

3. An *oxidizing flame* is similar in appearance to the neutral flame but has an excess amount of oxygen in the mixture. Though undesirable for most welding operations, it is sometimes used to weld brass and bronze metals.

Gas Welding Procedures

Similar to any other joining process, gas welding cannot be effectively accomplished unless the workpieces have been adequately cleaned. All rust and scales must be removed, and the workpiece adequately fastened to a sturdy base. The size of the welding torch

Table 17-2
Gas Welding Descriptions and Uses

Gas Welding Process	Description	Uses
Air-acetylene	Heat is generated by burning a mixture of acetylene gas and air. Does not achieve as high a flame temperature as other gas mixtures. May use filler metals and fluxes.	Welding of lead up to 0.250 inch. Can also be used for torch brazing and soft soldering operations.
Oxyacetylene	Burning of a mixture of acetylene and oxygen gases produces heat. May incorporate pressure, filler metals, and fluxes.	For general welding of both ferrous and nonferrous metals.
Oxyhydrogen	Produces a lower flame temperature than in oxyacetylene welding. Gas mixture is oxygen and hydrogen, but no pressure is used. Filler metal is optional.	Used for welding metals with low melting temperatures, such as aluminum, lead, and magnesium. Can be employed for torch brazing.
Gas pressure	A form of oxyacetylene gas welding when pressure is used during the welding process. No filler metal is used.	Commonly used for welding various types of low and high steel alloys. Also used in welding Monel, nickel-chromium, and copper-silicon alloys.

tip is then determined and selected prior to the welding operation. In most cases, tip size will be determined by the thickness of the metal being welded (see Table 17-3).

The gas pressure is then set at both the oxygen and acetylene gas tanks. The torch valves are opened so that the correct proportion

Table 17-3
Torch Tip Sizes

Welding Tip-Number	Metal Thickness (inch)	Oxygen Pressure (psi)	Acetylene Pressure (psi)
00	$\frac{1}{64}$	1	1
0	$\frac{1}{32}$	1	1
1	$\frac{1}{16}$	1	1
2	$\frac{3}{32}$	2	2
3	$\frac{1}{8}$	3	3
4	$\frac{3}{16}$	4	4
5	$\frac{1}{4}$	5	5
6	$\frac{5}{16}$	5	5
7	$\frac{3}{8}$	7	7
8	$\frac{1}{2}$	7	7
9	$\frac{5}{8}$	7.5	7.5
10	$\frac{3}{4}+$	9	9

of gas is emitted, and it is lit with a friction lighter. Adjust the flame so that there is a neutral flame. Hold the torch so that the flame is at a 45° angle to the weld joint.

Hold the inner cone of the flame about ⅛ in. away from the metal until it begins to melt. If a filler rod is being used, insert it into the flame at this time. Move the molten puddle of metal across the sheet as you rotate the torch head in a small circular motion. As the torch moves across the sheet metal, insert the filler rod as needed.

The type of welding joint selected will be determined by the physical design of the product. Figure 17-7 is an illustration of six common weld joints.

ARC WELDING

Arc welding is a generic term used to describe a variety of processes that use an electric arc, between the workpiece and an electrode, to fuse metals together. The electrode may function as the filler

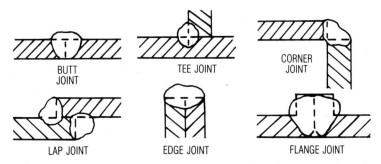

Fig. 17-7. Common welding joints.

metal. It is heated to the molten state and deposited into the workpiece. Heat is the result of an electrical circuit created between the electrode and the work, and then a slight separation of the two to form an arc. The electrical energy generated by the arc is converted to temperatures that can exceed 10,000°F (5,500°C).

Arc welding units (Figure 17-8) may be either AC or DC, with the latter the most preferred. DC units are designed with capacities up to 1,000 amperes, and have an open circuit voltage ranging from 40 to 95 volts. During the welding process, the arc voltage generated will be 18 to 40 volts. The generator is connected to wire leads—one is attached to the electrode or rod and the other to the workpiece. This connection is necessary to complete the electrical circuit and flow of current.

Electrodes

Three basic types of electrodes or rods are used in arc welding processes: bare, fluxed, and heavy coated. Bare electrodes have no coating on them and are recommended for welding mild steel metals. A fluxed rod will have a thin coating of fluxing material to enhance the flow and fusion of the metal; it also eliminates any harmful oxides and nitrides that are formed on the metal's surface. Heavy coated rods are important in that they are the most frequent type of electrode used for most commercial welding operations.

Presented in Figure 17-9 is an illustration of how a heavy coated electrode functions during arc welding. Note that a gaseous shield is generated by the fluxing compound. This shield is not only used

Courtesy The Lincoln Electric Company
Fig. 17-8. Example of arc welding unit being used on site.

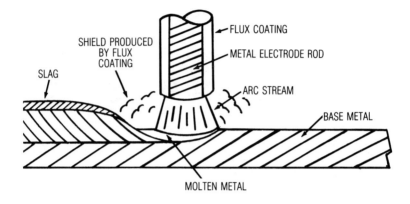

SHIELD PRODUCED BY FLUX COATING

SLAG

FLUX COATING

METAL ELECTRODE ROD

ARC STREAM

BASE METAL

MOLTEN METAL

Fig. 17-9. Functioning of a coated electrode.

to eliminate surface oxides and nitrides, but also to prevent the formation of additional oxides and nitrides.

Heavy rod coating is used for a number of purposes other than oxide and nitride removal. Examples of its other functions include:

1. Forms a protective atmosphere.

2. Produces a slag that is used to protect the liquid metal.

3. Makes it possible to execute overhead and position welding.

4. Stabilizes the welding arc.

5. Can add alloying elements to the base metal for metallurgical refining operations.

6. Increases the efficiency of the weld.

7. Removes impurities in addition to oxides and nitrides.

8. Dictate the depth of penetration and shape of the bead.

9. Reduces the rate of cooling.

The actual type of flux coating used on the welding electrode will depend on the function it is to serve. Generally, coatings will be categorized as organic or inorganic. The inorganic coatings are subdivided into fluxing and slag-forming compounds. Examples of compounds used to coat electrodes are presented in Table 17-4.

Table 17-4
Electrode Coatings

Function of the Coating	Coating Compounds
Slag formation	Silicon dioxide (SiO_2)
	Manganese dioxide (MnO_2)
	Iron oxide (FeO)
	Aluminum oxide (Al_2O_3)
Improving arc characteristics	Sodium oxide (Na_2O)
	Calcium oxide (CaO)
	Magnesium oxide (MgO)
	Titanium oxide (TiO_2)
Facilitating deoxidizing	Graphite
	Aluminum
	Wood flour
Facilitating binding	Sodium silicate ($NaSiO_4$)
	Potassium silicate ($KSiO_4$)
	Asbestos
Improvement of weld strength (alloying elements)	Vanadium
	Cesium
	Cobalt
	Molybdenum
	Aluminum
	Zirconium
	Chromium
	Nickel
	Manganese
	Tungsten

Arc Welding Processes

Similar to other types of welding procedures, arc welding incorporates several different processes. These include carbon and metal electrode arc welding, inert-gas-shielded arc welding, atomic-hydrogen arc welding, and submerged arc welding. Each of these processes incorporates the same basic concept of using an electrical arc to provide heat for metal fusion, yet requires different conditions and/or procedures.

389

Carbon and metal electrode arc welding represent perhaps the earliest forms of arc welding. Carbon electrode welding incorporates the use of a rod that is made from carbon. This electrode simply generates the heat needed to melt the metal and is considered nonconsumable. If a filler metal is required, then it must be supplied by a separate rod.

Metal electrode arc welding is the simplest of all arc welding processes. Here, the rod functions as both heat generator and filler rod. As the rod melts, most of the metal will melt into a molten pool in the base metal. Smaller amounts will vaporize and splatter along the weld joint. As the arc is moved along the weld joint, the rod is reduced in length and must be lowered for additional arcing and filler metal.

Inert-gas-shielded arc welding is used to protect the welding area from oxide and nitride formation. To accomplish this, a protective atmosphere or "shield" of inert gas is fed in and around the weld. The most common types of gases used for shielding are argon, helium, and carbon dioxide. Required here are special welding "guns" that are used to supply the rod and gas at the same time (Figure 17-10).

There are two general methods used in inert-gas-shielded arc welding. The first is known as *tungsten inert gas* (TIG) or *gas tungsten arc welding*. Here, a nonconsumable tungsten electrode is used to create the welding arc. When arcing begins, the area is protected by an atmosphere of inert gas through a water-cooled gun. Argon and/or helium are perhaps the inert gases most frequently used in the TIG welding process. DC TIG welding units are used for welding steel, cast iron, copper alloys, and stainless steel. AC TIG welding units, on the other hand, are used to weld aluminum, magnesium, cast iron, and a number of other metals.

The second method of inert-gas-shielded arc welding is known as *metal inert gas* (MIG) or *gas metal arc welding*. Unlike the TIG process, MIG welding uses a consumable electrode. This electrode is a bare wire that is fed by a wire drive mechanism. Because the electrode acts as a filler metal, the process is considered highly efficient. Again, the weld area is protected by a shield or atmosphere of inert gas. DC MIG units are generally used to weld aluminum, magnesium, copper, and steel. AC MIG welding is considered unstable, and is seldom used.

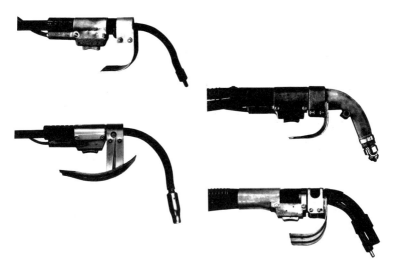

Courtesy The Lincoln Electric Company

Fig. 17-10. Various types of
welding guns.

Atomic-hydrogen arc welding employs a single phase AC arc between two tungsten electrodes. An atmosphere of hydrogen gas is created around the arc to attain exceptionally high welding temperatures. When hydrogen gas is introduced into the arc, molecules are broken down into atoms and recombine into hydrogen molecules around the arc. This makes it possible to attain welding temperatures up to 11,000°F (6,100°C). Most atomic-hydrogen arc welding is accomplished by the same processes used in inert-gas-shielded arc welding.

Submerged arc welding employs a shield that is composed of a granular, fusible flux, rather than a gas. Submerged arc welding is generally considered an automatic welding process. Here, the welding electrode is preceded by a flux feed tube as it moves along the weld joint. During the welding operation, it is critical that the tip of the electrode and arc be totally "submerged" under the granular flux. This process is limited to welding flat sheet materials, though it has been used with some success on sloping or circular joints. Most submerged arc welding is used for joining low carbon and alloy steels, but can also be used on several types of nonferrous metals.

APPROPRIATE METAL FOR WELDING

Not all welding processes can be used to weld all types of metals. Table 17-5 gives recommended welding processes that should be used with specific types of metals.

Table 17-5
Recommended Welding Processes for Metals

Metals and Alloys	Recommended	Sometimes Recommended
Low carbon steel SAE 1010, 1020	Shielded metal arc Submerged arc Flash welding Seam welding Spot welding Oxyacetylene	Atomic-hydrogen TIG MIG
Medium carbon steel SAE 1030, 1050	Shielded metal arc Submerged arc Flash welding Spot welding Oxyacetylene	Atomic-hydrogen TIG MIG Seam welding
Austenitic stainless steel AISI 301, 309, 316	Shielded metal arc Submerged arc Atomic-hydrogen TIG MIG Flash welding Seam welding Spot welding	Oxyacetylene
Other stainless steel AISI 405, 430	Shielded metal arc	Submerged arc Atomic-hydrogen TIG MIG Flash welding Seam welding Spot welding Oxyacetylene

Table 17-5
Recommended Welding Processes for Metals (Cont'd)

Metals and Alloys	Recommended	Sometimes Recommended
Aluminum	TIG MIG Spot welding	Shielded metal arc Atomic-hydrogen Flash welding Seam welding Oxyacetylene
Copper	TIG MIG	Flash welding Spot welding Oxyacetylene
Nickel	Shielded metal arc TIG MIG Spot welding	Submerged arc Atomic-hydrogen Flash welding Seam welding Oxyacetylene
Magnesium	TIG	MIG Spot welding
Silver	Atomic-hydrogen TIG Oxyacetylene	MIG Flash welding
Gold and platinum	Atomic-hydrogen TIG Oxyacetylene	MIG Flash welding Spot welding

SUMMARY

Welding consists of a number of different processes used to join metal by fusion. It is not as widely used for joining sheet metal as other processes because of the extreme heat needed to melt the metal for fusion. However, some welding processes are suited for sheet metals.

One of the welding processes most frequently used for joining sheet metal is resistance welding. Resistance welding employs two copper electrodes that pass electrical current through the metal as pressure is being applied. The combination of heat and pressure then causes the metal to fuse together. Common resistance welding processes encountered in sheet metal work are spot welding, seam welding, flash-butt welding, projection welding, and percussion welding.

Gas welding is a process that uses a welding torch and some mixture of fuel gas. It is normally employed on metals up to 0.250 in. thick. Fuel gases commonly found in gas welding are hydrogen, acetylene, and natural gas. Of these, acetylene, in combination with oxygen, is the most frequently used mixture and is referred to as oxyacetylene welding.

Arc welding is a generic term used to describe a variety of processes that use an electrical arc between the workpiece and electrode for fusing metals together. The electrode may serve as a filler metal and is often coated with a fluxing material. This flux is used to remove any harmful oxide or nitride film that may form on the metal's surface. Arc welding processes often encountered include inert-gas-shield welding, carbon and metal electrode arc welding, atomic-hydrogen arc welding, and submerged arc welding.

REVIEW QUESTIONS

1. Briefly explain how welding differs from soft and hard soldering.
2. Explain the principle involved in resistance welding.
3. What is spot welding and how is it accomplished?
4. Briefly explain the differences between seam, flash-butt, projection, and percussion welding.
5. What is meant by the expression "fuel gas"?
6. Explain the relationship between oxyacetylene welding requirements and the thickness of the metal to be welded.
7. What is arc welding?
8. Explain what MIG and TIG welding are and how they differ.

9. What are the three different types of electrodes used in arc welding?

10. What is the advantage of submerged arc welding over other arc welding processes?

PART V

FINISHING SHEET METAL PRODUCTS

CHAPTER 18

Surface Preparation and Finishes

The standards demanded for consumer products have improved significantly over the years. The requirements for increased reliability, quality, and product appearance have placed a new awareness on sheet metal workers. Much of the success of many sheet metal products is directly related to the surface preparation and type of finish applied. This chapter is specifically designed to provide information to the sheet metal worker to help deal with problems associated with surface preparation and finishing.

SHEET METAL SURFACE PREPARATION

The appropriate selection of sheet materials must be carefully handled when choosing a surface preparation and product finish. Consideration must be given to such factors as corrosion, wear, chemical conductivity, reflectivity, electrical conductivity, absorption, and decorative coating. It is therefore important to understand how sheet metal products are prepared and processed to achieve a particular type of finish.

Central to the vast majority of product finishes is surface preparation. Basically, this involves the cleaning and removal of contaminants and foreign materials from the metal's surface. This may appear to be simple at first, but it involves the proper selection of cleaning compounds or methods as they relate to the type of finish desired.

Selecting a Surface Preparation Process

One factor to consider when selecting a surface preparation process is the type of soil to be removed. Soils usually appear in the form of grease, oil, grit, paint, and other undesired foreign substances. Soils must be evaluated in terms of how they will affect the desired finish. Their characteristics can be generally categorized into four major groups:

1. Pigmented drawing soils
2. Unpigmented oil and grease
3. Chips and cutting fluids
4. Polishing and buffing compounds

The exact process selected for cleaning each of these soils will depend on the type of finish selected. Table 18-1 lists cleaning processes, for specific finishes, that are typically used in sheet metal shops. Note that the surface preparation varies according to the type of soil present and the finish desired.

In large production settings, detailed consideration is given to the chemical and physical properties of soils. This, however, is beyond the scope of work encountered by most sheet metal workers.

Characteristics of the Product

The size and shape of the sheet metal product are basic considerations in surface preparation selection. For example, the product may be so large that it would be impossible to immerse it in a tank for cleaning, and it might require the use of a high-pressure hot detergent and water spray machine. Some sheet metal parts are more easily hand wiped with a solvent or sprayed with an emulsifiable solvent.

Another consideration given to surface prepration is the type of metal used in the product. Steel, which is fairly resistant to many cleaning chemicals, will rust if the rinsing operation is not handled properly. Strong alkali solutions should not be used to clean aluminum because they can dissolve the metal and cause pitting in the metal's surface. Brass will tarnish when exposed to strong alkaline

Table 18-1
Cleaning Processes

Type of Soil	Types of Surface Preparation for		
	Painting	Plating	Phosphating
Pigmented drawing compounds	Acid cleaning. Alkaline spray or soak followed by hot rinse. Vapor-slush degrease followed by hand wipe. Boiling alkaline dip followed by blow off and hand wipe.	Hot alkaline soak, followed by hot rinse and hand wipe. Hot emulsion soak, followed by hot rinse, electrolytic alkaline soak, and hot rinse.	Alkaline soak followed by hot rinse, alkaline spray, and hot rinse. Hot emulsion hand slush followed by spray emulsion hot rinse, and hand wipe.
Unpigmented oil and grease	Phosphoric acid clean. Vapor degrease.	Emulsion soak, rinse, electrolytic alkaline, rinse, hydrochloric dip, and rinse. Vapor degrease, electrolytic alkaline, rinse, hydrochloric dip, and rinse.	Emulsion dip or spray and rinse. Vapor degrease. Acid cleaning.
Chips and cutting fluids	Solvent dip. Alkaline dip or spray and emulsion surfactant.	Alkaline dip, rinse, electrolytic alkaline, rinse, acid dip, and rinse.	Alkaline dip and emulsion surfactant. Solvent dip and emulsion surfactant.
Polishing and buffing compounds	Emulsion soak and rinse. Surfactant alkaline spray and rinse.	Surfactant, rinse, and electroclean. Surfactant alkaline soak, rinse, and electrolytic alkaline.	Surfactant and rinse. Emulsion soak and rinse. Emulsion spray and rinse.

cleaners and galvanized metals are very sensitive to cleaning agents. Hence, care must be taken in selecting an appropriate cleaner.

The last consideration includes the physical properties of the metal. In addition to chemical properties, careful thought must be given to how the metal will behave if exposed to mechanical cleaning such as is found in abrasion or mechanical methods. Materials that dent or fracture easily are sometimes cleaned with a foamy cleaner that is used as a cushion for the moving parts.

Chemical Cleaning

Chemical cleaning is one of the most widely accepted methods used for surface preparation and perhaps one of the best methods available for preparing a surface for subsequent finishing by painting, electroplating, and other processes. These procedures are usually limited to sheet metal products that are either custom made or produced in low volumes in sheet metal shops.

The success of chemical cleaning will depend on the type of chemical or solvent used to clean the metal and the type of soil present. Because chemical cleaning processes rely on chemical reactions, it is common practice to raise the temperature of the cleaning solution to facilitate cleaning. Chemical cleaning processes are divided into two major categories. The first is a *precleaning* process that uses alkali, petroleum, and chlorinated solvents, or emulsions, to remove solid or caked-on soil. The second category of cleaning employs alkaline and acid baths, electropolishing, and bright dipping for the removal of metal oxides, scales, and contaminants.

There are numerous chemical cleaning processes that are used in manufacturing settings. Not all are suitable for small-scale operations, yet several procedures can be used by the sheet metal worker for individual or low volume products. These cleaning processes are presented as follows:

1. *Chemical Dipping.* Also known as *soak tank* or *tank immersion* cleaning, chemical dipping is a simple method that can be used to clean sheet metal products. This process consists of dipping or immersing the product into a tank that contains a cleaning solution and removing it when all the soil

has been eliminated. Dipping is then followed by some form of rinsing. This process is recommended for low volume production of smaller products.

Critical in this process is the correct selection of cleaning chemical. As an example, a mild alkaline or solvent is used to remove light shop soil and oil from parts, while heavy greases and shop oils are dissolved with strong alkaline and solvent solutions. Immersion time will vary from 30 seconds to 2 minutes for light cleaning, and 15 to 30 minutes for heavy duty cleaning.

2. *Chemical Spraying.* The process known as chemical spraying usually involves a high pressure stream of cleaning solution. The temperature of the solution will normally be around 212°F (100°C). Here, the force of the spray, coupled with the chemical action of the solution, wets, penetrates, and cleans the metal's surface. Again, products that are chemically sprayed must be rinsed before final finishing. Chemical spraying is recommended for high volume production and/or products that are too large for immersion in chemical dipping tanks.

3. *Solvent Cleaning.* Solvent cleaning is normally defined in terms of the type of solvent used to remove soil. There are basically four types of solvents used to clean sheet metals: straight solvents chlorinated solvents, emulsion cleaners, and diphase solvents. Examples of each type of solvent are presented in Table 18-2.

4. *Alkaline Cleaning.* The most widely used industrial cleaners are alkaline cleaners. These detergents are used to remove shop soils, oil, and grease, but are not effective in removing rust or scale. Examples of alkaline cleaners are sodium hydroxide, sodium metasilicate, orthosilicate, sodium carbonate, sodium tetraborate, and trisodium phosphate.

5. *Pickling.* Pickling is a surface preparation treatment used to remove oxides, scales, stains, discolorations, and dirt from metal. The most common solutions used here are diluted sulfuric acid (approximately 10 to 25 percent of full strength), commercial hydrochloric acid, and phosphoric acid. Most

pickling operations take place in tanks lined with stainless steel or some other acid-proof material. All pickling operations should be followed by a thorough rinse.

6. *Vapor Degreasing.* This process is limited primarily to large production settings. Briefly, vapor degreasing physically removes solvent-soluble soils by bringing them in contact with a hot solvent vapor. The vapor condenses on the part's surface to form a liquid, which flows to wash away the soil.

An operation that is important to most chemical cleaning operations is rinsing. The type of rinse employed will be determined by the type of material used to clean the metal, the metal used, and the finishing to be applied. Generally, most rinsing operations will use clear water. Because most waters will contain compounds such as chlorides, sulfates, and carbonates, it is advisable to use a water softening system to avoid problems in finishing operations such as plating.

Table 18-2
Cleaning Solvents

Solvent Category	Examples	Applications
Straight solvents	Kerosene Naphtha Carbon tetrachloride	Used full strength where water would be harmful to the product, such as for electrical parts, control panels, and chassis.
Chlorinated solvents	Chlorothene Trichloroethylene Perchloroethylene	Employed to dissolve oils, waxes, grease, and dirt.
Emulsion cleaners	Solvent-emulsion	Used as a mixture in water to dissolve and react with oils.
Diphase solvents	Layers of solvent covered by water	Employed where economy of cleaning solvent is important.

Non-Chemical Cleaning

Most sheet metal cleaning will involve non-chemical methods. In addition to manual methods employing steel wool, emery cloth, files, and machining operations, a number of other non-chemical procedures are available in the sheet metal field. These methods are presented as follows:

1. *Dry Blast Cleaning.* The dry blast cleaning process consists of blowing abrasive materials through the nozzle of any air gun, at high velocities, onto the surface of the metal. This technique is used to remove soil other than grease and oil. The primary uses for this process include removing contaminants, oxides, corrosion, and mill scale; preparing the surface to better accept a paint bonding; eliminating burrs, scratches, paint, and dry surface material; and producing a matte finish on the metal.

2. *Wet Blasting.* A blasting process that uses an abrasive slurry is known as wet blasting. It avoids unnecessary dust, produces a fine abrasive finish, and prevents immediate oxidation. Here, the abrasive grain is mixed with water, rust inhibitors, wetting agents, and anticlogging agents. In situations where the metal may corrode, as a result of exposure to the water mix, a petroleum distillate can be substituted.

3. *Power Driven Brushes.* In many sheet metal shops, power driven brushes are used to remove soil. These brushes are mounted onto a wheel that is attached to a motor driven unit. As the brush rotates, the workpiece is brought in contact with it. The major uses for power driven brushes are for removing oxides, weld scales, and burrs.

4. *Polishing and Buffing.* Polishing is a process that removes small amounts of metal to produce a luster. Buffing, on the other hand, produces a luster without material removal. Both techniques can be used with either wheels or belts—both work equally well.

PLATING PROCESSES

One of the most well-known methods of metal finishing is plating or electroplating. Considered a decorative finish, plating is also used for improving the solderability of metals, building up of machine parts, protecting from corrosive materials, and improving electrical contacts. The most frequently used plating metal found today is cadmium, followed by tin, zinc, nickel, and silver.

Most electroplating is accomplished in a series of plating operations. An example of this would be a copper, nickel, chromium sequence. Depending on the base metal, this sequence would vary from product to product. Examples of different metals used in electroplating are presented in Table 18-3.

Electroplating Process

Electroplating is a process where metal atoms (metallic ions) are deposited on the surface of a base metal as an electrical current flows through a liquid solution known as an *electrolyte*. DC current is used to make the metallic ions flow from the anode (positive) to cathode (negative) end of the circuit. The metal that is to be coated

Table 18-3
Electroplating Metals

Electroplating Metals	Application
Nickel	Build-up of machine parts
Tin	Improve the solderability of the base metal Food handling equipment and containers
Tin-lead alloys	Improve the solderability of the base metal
Cadmium	Protection from marine and exterior environmental conditions
Zinc	Protective coatings in an industrial environment
Gold	Electrical contacts

is always the cathode, and the metal doing the coating is the anode. This is illustrated in Figure 18-1.

As an example of electroplating, consider the use of copper as plating material for a product that must provide electrical conductivity, with its base metal a poor conductor. Here, a strip of copper metal, usually pure copper, is hooked up to the positive end of a DC power supply, making it the anode. The base metal to be coated is connected as the cathode to the negative side of the power unit. Both anode and cathode are then immersed in a tank filled with an electrolyte—in this case a solution of copper sulfate ($CuSO_4$).

When the direct current is allowed to flow through the electrolyte, the copper ions move through the solution and plate the sheet of base metal. Any impurities that might be present in the copper strip (e.g., zinc and cadmium) would not move as easily in the electrolyte and would tend to hold their position around the anode end.

Metal Specifications

The thickness of the plating and the type of metals used in the process are determined by many different factors. The primary ones, however, are the base metal, plating metal, corrosion protection, and conditions that the finished product will encounter.

The three most frequent base metals used in electroplating operations are steel, brass, and zinc. Brass is commonly plated with nickel plus chromium for both protective and decorative applica-

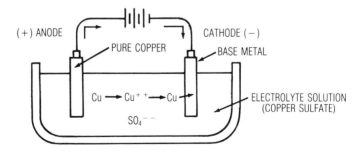

Fig. 18-1. Electroplating with copper.

tions. Steel is commonly coated with either nickel or zinc, while zinc is plated with copper-nickel-chromium.

Generally, the more expensive the plating metal, the thinner the coating. In this case, metals such as silver, gold, and platinum provide for the thinnest coatings. Zinc, cadmium, and copper are used for intermediate thickness coatings, while nickel is often used for thick coatings.

As a rule of thumb, the greater the product's exposure to a corrosive environment, the thicker the required plating. In most situations, the level of exposure will be rated in terms of mild, moderate, and severe. A sign of plating failure here occurs when the base metal begins to corrode.

The conditions that the finished product will encounter relate to its functional use. Products employed for industrial use will often require additional specifications compared to those found in domestic situations. These specifications are generally given in terms of plating thickness.

PAINTS: ORGANIC COATINGS

Organic coatings, or paints, provide sheet metal workers with an almost unlimited number of surface finishes and characteristics that can be used for a given product. These coatings are used for both decorative and protective effects, and are perhaps the most common finishes used in the field. In these cases, organic coatings are selected to obtain aesthetic effects such as color, texture, and sheen; they must also be protective and withstand the effects of detergents, acids, salt water, alkalis, and solvents.

Several methods are used to classify organic coatings (in most cases, coatings will use many of these classifications) and are listed as follows:

1. Function that the coating is to serve
2. Appearance of the organic film
3. Composition of the vehicle
4. Method of application or curing

All paints are made up of constituent parts. One of the most important is known as the *binder*. Examples of binders are oleoresinous varnish, alkyd varnish, epoxy, vinyl, or nitrocellulose. If the binder is not a liquid, the paint cannot be applied. Another component found in paints is its liquid portion, known as the *vehicle*. Vehicles are made of all oil, solutions of various binders, water emulsions, or dispersions such as vinyl organosols.

Compounds known as *fillers* are used to lower the cost of the paint, improve the covering ability of the coating, and provide other desirable properties. To cover or hide a base metal, paints must have color. *Pigments* are used in combination with fillers to give the paint color. A type of filler that does not provide color is known as an *extender*. Extenders are used almost exclusively to build up the body of paints. The last compounds found in paints are *additives*, which contribute to speeding up the drying time and aid in wetting the pigment

Preparing for Painting

At first it may appear that "painting" is a simple process that does not require much information or skill. This, however, is completely untrue. One of the most important factors that must be considered is the proper preparation of the metal surface before paint is applied. Without adequate preparation, even the best paints will last for only a short period of time.

Before painting can take place, all dirt, grease, scaling, rust, dust, and other foreign substances must be removed from the metal. The common mechanical methods of scraping, chipping, wire brushing, and blasting do well with most steel and galvanized sheet materials. When blasting is used, a rough surface is produced. This allows for a good mechanical bonding between the paint and metal. However, if a thin paint is applied, care must be taken to ensure that an adequate amount is applied to cover the area.

Chemical cleaning, as discussed earlier in this chapter, can also be employed. Common methods in the field are solvent and alkali washing and the use of commercial and emulsion cleaners. It must be emphasized that these procedures are excellent in removing soluble or loose materials, but are not too effective in removing rust or scale from the metal.

Undercoats

There are many times when an undercoat must be applied to the metal before the finished paint can be added. Undercoats are painted layers that function as a surface onto which the paint is applied. The major functions of undercoats are:

1. To provide for a stronger bonding between the metal and second coat
2. To supply additional protection against corrosion
3. To cover minor surface defects or irregularities
4. To provide a smooth surface on which the paint can be applied if the metal's surface has been blasted or sanded

A *primer* functions in any one or all of these areas, and is the first coat applied to sheet metal in many finishing operations. For metals that have unusually deep markings or roughness, the primer should be highly pigmented to fill in these marks. Many times, these marks require the application of two or more coats of primer. A *primer surfacer* is a single undercoat that serves as a primer and surfacer.

There are certain pigments added to primers that function as corrosion inhibitors. Examples of these are red lead, lead chromate, and zinc chromate. Other special pigments are the following:

- *Zinc oxide* is used to prevent the formation of mildew, as well as to control temperature.
- *Cuprous oxide* is a marine antifouling coating used to prevent barnacles and other life matter from forming.
- *Calcium carbonate, silica, talc, and China clay* are used to reduce the cost of the primer.

Topcoats

The undercoat, by itself, does not necessarily look good or weather well. Thus, a topcoat of paint must be applied to provide these characteristics. Together with a proper undercoat, topcoats will produce an attractive appearance, be resistant to weathering and abrasion, possess toughness, and have other desirable properties.

Numerous topcoat paints are available on the market, and to discuss each would be beyond the scope and purpose of this chapter. Examples of some special types of topcoat paints are given here:

- Polychromatic metallic paints produce a smooth surface but give the appearance of a peen-hammer finish. A technique used on some office equipment (e.g., metal cabinets, business machines, and vacuum cleaners) that gives a rough texture is the application of a polychrome layer of paint that is then sprayed with a mist of water before it dries.

- Polyurethane paints are usually applied to wooden floors that are subjected to abrasion and other physical wear. However, polyurethanes are finding more use in painting sheet metals that require the same resistance to wear.

- Silicones are used on small sheet metal products that must resist high temperatures and on materials that will not accept other types of paint. Silicone paints pigmented with aluminum are used to coat cooking pans, boilers, and jet fantails.

- Epoxy paints are made of a thermosetting plastic, and are used to protect sheet metal containers from chemical corrosion and adhesions.

- Acrylics are very resistant to detergents, stains, chemicals, and grease, and are recommended for products such as appliances and building components of aluminum and galvanized metal.

- Vinyl paints that are organosols and plastisols are widely used to coat sheet metal products such as window frames, steel container linings, sheet metal trim, and racks.

Application Methods

The selection of an appropriate paint application method is important for the coating material to perform properly. No matter what method is chosen, care must be taken to ensure that when the coating is applied a uniform layer of film is painted throughout the job—avoiding thick and thin layers.

Structural, construction, and maintenance painting are normally accomplished by using a hand brush or spraying method. While brushing is simple, it is considered slow and tedious and requires a great deal of skill and competence. The material that the brush bristles are made of can play a significant role in the success of the brushing operation. For best results, it is recommended that the individual use a combination of long and short natural bristles with the tips split into finer ends. This construction is referred to as *flagged* ends. Flagging is used to permit the brush to hold more paint and leave fewer brush marks in the finish.

Air spraying is only recommended for larger structures and in mass production situations. Here, the paint is supplied through a pressurized container that will hold up to 100 psi of pressure. When pressure is applied, the paint is forced through a hose and air gun and is sprayed as a thin, flowing stream. The hand-held unit is moved back and forth over the surface to be coated so that no pattern is generated. When using the air spraying method, care must be taken to avoid applying paint to other sections of the building or structure that are not to be covered.

In the sheet metal shop situation, other methods are available for paint application. These include:

- *Dip coating* completely immerses the part in an open tank of liquid coating material. The part is then withdrawn, allowed to drain completely, and either dried or cured.

- *Flow coating* handles the part on a conveyor and carries it through an enclosed unit. Here, a series of nozzles connected to a pump that supplies the paint are positioned so that the part will be thoroughly covered. Excess paint flows from the part and is recycled through the pump.

- *Curtain coating* is a specialized technique in which the part moves under a constant curtain of paint. The paint is literally poured as a sheet, resembling a wall. The surface(s) to be painted are then exposed to the paint, allowed to drain, and then dried or cured.

SUMMARY

The demands made by consumers and the standards of the industry have made the sheet metal worker more aware of surface preparation and finishing techniques. The appropriate selection of sheet materials must be carefully considered when determining a surface preparation and product finish. Normally, this involves selecting a method for cleaning and preparing the metal for finishing, then applying a particular finish.

Surface preparation frequently deals with the removal of soils, such as oil, grit, dirt, grease, rust, and scale. The cleaning method used will depend on the type of soil found on the metal. In addition, the characteristics of the product, such as size, shape, and material properties, will have a role in determining cleaning methods and compounds.

Chemical cleaning is widely used in small shop and production settings. Here, chemicals such as solvents, alkali, and acids are used to remove surface soil. Examples of common chemical cleaning processes used are chemical dipping, chemical spraying, solvent cleaning, alkaline cleaning, pickling, and vapor degreasing.

Non-chemical cleaning refers primarily to mechanical methods of soil removal. In addition to the manual methods such as steel wool, emery cloth, and files, other techniques are employed. These include dry blast cleaning, wet blasting, power driven brushes, and polishing and buffing.

Plating is a finishing procedure in which a metal coating is applied to a base metal. Direct current passes metallic ions from a pure metal to the base metal through a chemical solution known as an electrolyte. Plating is used as both an aesthetic and protective finish.

Painting, or organic coating, is one of the most common methods of finishing used by sheet metal workers. Paints are made of six types of compounds: binders, vehicles, fillers, pigments, extenders, and additives.

Preparing the metal for painting basically consists of removing all surface dirt, rust, grease, scales, oil, and other foreign materials. Undercoats are used as an intermediate paint coating between the metal and finished coat. These paints provide a stronger mechanical bonding between the paint and metal, additional protection against corrosion, cover for minor surface defects, and a smooth surface on which the final finish can be applied.

Topcoats are the final layers of paint applied to the product. Examples of paints commonly used for this purpose are polychromatic metallic paints, polyurethanes, silicones, epoxies, acrylics, and vinyls. Within the sheet metal field, the most common methods used to apply paints are by brush and hand spray. Other techniques such as dipping, flow coating, and curtain coating are used in small production settings.

REVIEW QUESTIONS

1. Why is surface preparation so important in sheet metal finishing?

2. Identify and describe the four major groups of soils.

3. Identify those factors that would determine what surface preparation method would be used for finishing a sheet metal project.

4. What is the difference between chemical and non-chemical cleaning? Which is more commonly used in the sheet metal trades?

5. Identify and describe the common methods used in chemical and non-chemical cleaning.

6. What is electroplating? List its major functions.

7. Name and give examples of the major components of paint.

8. What is an undercoat and why is it important for finishing?

9. What is the relationship between an undercoat and topcoat? Briefly give the characteristics of a good topcoat.

10. Briefly describe the two methods most commonly used to apply paint in most sheet metal jobs.

PART VI

PRODUCTION WORK

CHAPTER 19

Production Processes

To this point, all operations and procedures have been presented in terms of producing single item or low volume products. Though the majority of the work encountered by sheet metal workers will be of custom or low volume in nature, it is important that some understanding of production processes is obtained. These processes are used to manufacture large numbers of sheet metal products.

Sheet metals that are converted into useful parts can be worked by either hot or cold processing. Most work in the sheet metal field, however, incorporates cold processing methods. This chapter presents a discussion of related sheet metal processes commonly found in manufacturing industries.

PRODUCTION CONSIDERATIONS

Most manufacturing processes used in sheet metal work can be divided into three major areas—material preparation, deformation and fabrication, and finishing. The starting point of most processes is a prepared piece of metal, known as a blank. Blanks are carefully designed so that a large number can be produced from a single strip of metal with minimum waste. In addition, properly designed and cut blanks can reduce the number of forming and finishing operations. The factors closely examined in blank design are pattern layout, quality of design, and processing cost.

Deformation refers to the forming, bending, and shaping of the metal. The vast majority of metal deformation accomplished in high-volume work is executed on large presses that are equipped with dies. These dies can be designed to accommodate a variety of cutting and forming operations.

Product fabrication is the assembling, fastening, and joining phase of production. It consists of those processes that usually precede finishing, though some finishing operations can be accomplished beforehand. Examples of fabricating operations are bolting, screwing, welding, brazing, soldering, and gluing.

The last aspect of consideration concerns product finishing. Here, special procedures have been developed to apply finishes best suited for the part (e.g., plating, anodizing, painting, galvanizing, etc.). Care is taken to select the best type of finishing process for specific types of metals demanded by consumers.

CUTTING AND SHEARING

Sheet materials used in large production settings are supplied in coil or roll form, rather than in individual sheets. As a result, the sheet stock must first be cut into workable sizes—though some operations are designed to work directly from coiled and rolled metal. The precutting of metal is done on cutting and shearing equipment similar to that found in small sheet metal shops. The primary differences involve design and shearing capacity.

Types of Shears

There are four broad categories of shears used for production situations. The first shear category includes various types of *squaring shears* (Figure 19-1). It should be noted that squaring shears are powered by mechanical and hydraulic drive systems. For this reason, each system is considered as a different type of shear.

"Squaring shears" are also known by a variety of terms, including *resquaring*, *guillotine*, and *gate shears*. Their primary function is to produce straight-sided blanks. In some cases, squaring shears are also used for trimming and producing notches and slits.

Production-type mechanical squaring shears are available in a wide variety of sizes and designs. Their most common application, in terms of volume, is for cutting sheets of metal to length as they are unrolled from coils or as they are produced from continuous mills. Because closer tolerances are held in production work, care must be taken when cutting straight-sided blanks with shears. This is usually accomplished with the use of *jigs* and *fixtures*. Fixtures

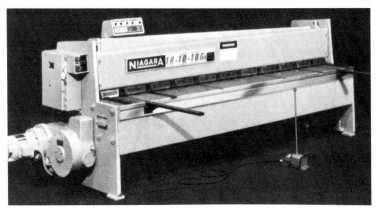

Courtesy Niagara Machine and Tool Works
Fig. 19-1. Power shears.

are holding or clamping devices that hold the metal as it is being cut, while jigs are used to move the metal into the blades of the shears.

One reason for the wide use of squaring shears is that they are among the most economical pieces of equipment available for producing straight-sided cuts. In addition, squaring shears can also be used to cut different types of sheet materials with different thicknesses. Most power squaring shears will have a maximum cutting capacity up to 1.500 in. (3.81cm) of mild steel plate, and can handle lengths ranging from 2 (61cm) to over 20 (6.1m) feet.

The second major category of shears includes all *hydraulic squaring shears.* Hydraulic shears use a cylinder that fills with oil to drive a ram. The ram is connected to the shear's blade; therefore, when it moves in the cylinder, it will move the blade for shearing.

Hydraulic shears also have the unique characteristic of being able to change the angle of cut of the upper blade. This ability increases the cutting capacity of the machine (e.g., with a higher angle of cut, the shear can increase its cutting capacity from plate thickness of ½ in. to ¾ in. (12.7 to 19.1mm).

Hydraulic shears are primarily used for shearing plate material. Unlike mechanical shears, this type cannot be overloaded, otherwise they will simply stop. For this reason, hydraulic shears are not widely found in job shops. The major advantage of using hydraulic shears is that they have a longer stroke and can perform long, stroking cuts more efficiently and economically than a mechanical shear.

The third category of shears is known as *alligator shears*. The cutting action of these shears is similar to that of a pair of scissors. Alligator shears are used to cut bars, rods, plates, and special shaped metals. Their use, however, is limited since they can only generate a short cutting stroke. Hence, long cuts are normally beyond their capability.

The last type of shear used for production purposes is the *rotary shear*. This machine is used to produce circular and irregular shaped parts from plate material. With some adjustments, rotary shears can also be used to make straight cuts.

Most rotary machines have a maximum cutting thickness of approximately 1 in. Two circular blades are mounted onto rotating heads in such a way as to offer no restriction to the metal's movement. Thus, it is possible to cut a wide variety of shapes, in addition to beveled cuts. For production work, holding fixtures are often used as both a support and guide for the workpiece.

Shearing Guidelines

There are several factors that are analyzed for production shearing. The first is *shearing speed*. Simply, this refers to the number of strokes per minute (spm) (i.e., cuts per minute) performed by the machine. The optimum spm used for most shears will range between 30 and 300 spm, with the high end limited to cut-to-length operations on coiled sheet stock.

Depending on the type of cut being made, the spm specified can vary greatly. Other factors influencing the spm are material thickness, length of cut, motor horsepower, and type of metal. A common-sized sheet metal used on squaring shears will range between 10 gauge and 0.250 in. (6.35mm). Here, the maximum rate of cutting will be in the area of 60 spm.

Another important shearing factor is *shearing accuracy*. Today, shearing operations are often called on to hold cutting accuracies to within 0.005 in. (.127m). To accomplish this, blades, back gauges, and the workings of the machine must be periodically and properly maintained.

Other Cutting Operations

In addition to the more traditional forms of shearing, other cutting operations are performed. The first is known as *slitting*. This process cuts narrow widths of coiled metal into smaller widths. The cutting is accomplished by a set of circular blades mounted on two rotating arbors. Slitting widths are established by using steel spacers that are slipped onto the arbor and held in place by a key.

A common slitting operation will handle coils of metal between 36 and 60 in. (91.4 and 152.4cm) in width, and thicknesses of 0.020 to 0.125 in. (.51 to 3.18mm). In some cases, it is possible to use rotary slitting on coil widths over 100 in. (254cm). The length of the coil will normally have no bearing on the slitting operation.

Another cutting process found in industry is *gas cutting*. This process is commonly used to cut various shapes out of plate material 1.500 in. (38.1mm) or thicker. Compared to shearing, gas cutting will not produce as clean an edge, but is very versatile. In fact, it is possible to gas cut several plates with varying thicknesses at one pass—this procedure is known as *stack cutting*.

PRESSWORK

There is probably nothing more significant than presswork in differentiating high production and low volume sheet metal work. Power presses are frequently used in manufacturing to cut, shape, and form sheet metal. These machines subject the metal to specific amounts of stresses and forces, at specific locations and directions, so that the operation will be performed in a minimum period of time. Thus, what might normally take up to an hour to hand form can spend but a few seconds on a production press.

Power presses provide the mechanical or hydraulic *force* necessary for metal processing. Actual cutting and forming are accomplished by special tooling known as dies. The basic types of cutting operations performed with dies are blanking, punching, perforating, notching, lancing, trimming, slugging, piercing, and parting. Noncutting or forming dies, by comparison, can perform bending, forming, drawing, bulging, and contouring operations.

Cutting Dies

Cutting dies incorporate shearing forces onto sheet material with a mating punch and die. The punch is used to stress the metal between it and the die. Though there are a large number of die cutting operations, blanking and punching are perhaps the most basic. The difference between these two operations is given in terms of the function that the metal cutout will serve. If the cutout is used in other processes, then the operation is known as blanking; if it is scrap, then the process is punching.

A number of important factors must be considered when working with cutting dies. One of the more significant is *clearance*—the distance between the die and punch. Proper clearance allows the metal to fracture cleanly and with minimal distortions. The exact amount of clearance required will depend on the type of metal being cut, its temper, and thickness.

Clearance is usually expressed in terms of the percentage of stock thickness. As an example, the clearance for a round hole will be expressed as one-half the difference between the punch and die diameters.

When specifying the amount of clearance for a punch and die, consideration is given to the type of die cut edge to be generated. This second factor is critical in many close-tolerance parts. The classifications used to identify die cut edges are given as follows:

1. *Type I* edges are used in structural metalwork products where the primary function is to produce a hole in a wide variety of thicknesses with a coarse finish.
2. *Type II* edges produce a general purpose hole with a medium finish.
3. *Type III* edges are burr free and are perhaps the most desired production hole produced.
4. *Type IV* edges are characterized by their finished appearance.
5. *Type V* edges are clean and vertical. They are primarily found on softer metals such as aluminum, copper, brass, and lead.

Examples of die clearances and edge types are presented in Table 19-1.

422

Table 19-1
Die-Punch Clearances for Die-Cut Edges of Different Metals

Blanking Metal	Clearance (% of blank thickness)				
	Type I	Type II	Type III	Type IV	Type V
Aluminum (250)	17	9	7	3	1
Brass (hard)	24	10	7	4	0.80
Brass (soft)	21	9	6	2.5	1
Copper (hard)	25	11	8	3.5	1.25
Copper (soft)	26	8	6	3	0.75
Lead	22	9	7	5	2.5
Magnesium	16	6	4	2	0.75
High carbon steel	26	18	15	12	
Stainless steel	23	13	10	4	1.5
Mild steel (1020)	21	12	9	6.5	2

The third factor critical to cutting dies is the amount of *punching pressure* required. This is figured out by using mathematical formulas that take into account four measures: shear strength of the material in psi (S), sheared length (L), diameter (D), and thickness of the material (T). The formulas used are:

- Pressure for any shape: $P = SLT$.
- Pressure for round holes: $P = \pi SDT$.

In addition to these calculations, other factors such as the characteristics of the sheet and die materials must also be considered. As an example, silicon steels and high carbon steels often require equipment with 50 percent greater tonnage to provide punch pressure.

The last major factor considered with cutting dies is the *design of the blank*. All blanks are cut from either a flat or pre-formed piece of stock material. Flat blanks will typically involve a larger number of additional forming and/or cutting operations than pre-formed pieces. Examples of products made from pre-formed blanks are transformer and motor laminations, flywheels, and padlock cases.

Blank design is limited in size only by the width of the sheet material. To obtain exceptionally wide products, sheets are sometimes welded together, though this is not a common practice. One of the largest sheet metal blanks is used in the automotive industry, where large sheet metal panels are cut and formed to shape.

Forming Dies

The second type of die used in industrial presswork includes all kinds of forming dies. These dies are used to bend, form, and shape sheet material. What this involves is the shaping of metal by applying stresses that are beyond its yield strength, but below its fracture strength. Hence, the deformity (bend) is permanent.

The appropriate selection of sheet materials is important when using forming dies. The property that is most often sought in sheet materials that are worked in forming dies is *formabililty*. Formability is usually specified in terms of yield strength and tensile characteristics. Table 19-2 contains examples of several types of steels used in bending operations. An excellent metal with good formability properties is a steel alloy with a tensile strength of 70,000 psi and yield strength of 50,000. These properties would be expressed as a high-tensile, medium-yield steel.

There are many different types of dies and presses used in forming and shaping sheet metal. Shown in Figures 19-2 and 19-3 is a press brake used for forming metal, along with examples of simple bending dies. When simple shapes are made (such as channels, ribs, and corrugations), relatively higher press tonnage is recommended. As a guide, Table 19-3 presents general load requirements for offset bending.

The number and types of bends that can be performed with press dies are staggering. Some involve simple straight line bends, while others incorporate complex contouring. Most, however, can

Table 19-2
Formability of Steels

Material	Tensile Strength (psi)	Yield Strength (psi)
Mild steel	55,000–65,000	35,000–45,000
High-tensile, low-yield steel	80,000–90,000	30,000–40,000
Medium-tensile, medium-yield steel	60,000–75,000	45,000–55,000
High-tensile, high-yield steel	105,000–135,000	90,000–100,000

be categorized into 18 basic designs. These product die designs are presented as follows:

1. *Right Angle Forming Dies.* One of the most common types of forming dies found is the 90° forming die. These designs require a radius at the bend point and employ a V-die opening.

2. *Acute Angle Dies.* Also known as *air-forming dies*, this design type is used to make angle bends less than 90°. When accuracy is not critical, the acute angle die can also be used to make obtuse and 90° bends.

3. *Gooseneck Dies.* Another name for this design is the *return-flanging die*. These V-bend dies provide for flanging clearances.

4. *Z-Dies.* A Z-die design is capable of making two right angle or acute angle bends. Sometimes called *offset dies*, these dies must be used with care since they usually require exceptionally high press loads that could fracture the metal.

5. *Hemming Dies.* As their name implies, hemming dies are used to provide a hem on a product. This can be accomplished in two operations: acute angle bend followed by flattening.

6. *Seaming Dies.* There are numerous seaming dies used in the fabrication of sheet metal products. Because of the variety of seam designs, seaming dies have no single type of design.

7. *Radius Dies.* Dies that are used to produce a curved radius on products are known as radius dies. This type of tooling, however, is not usually incorporated unless the radius exceeds the thickness of the metal by at least four times.

8. *Beading Dies.* Beads are formed on flat and curved stock by beading dies. There are two general types of beading dies: one that is used for open beads that run from one edge to another, and the second for closed or blind beads that appear and disappear in the sheet.

9. *Curling Dies.* All curling dies are used where long, continuous lengths of sheet metal are generated. Their primary function is to "curl" the metal into a coil or roll.

10. *Tube and Pipe Forming Dies.* A modification of the curling die includes dies that are used to form tubing and pipes. Instead of curling the metal along the width, curling is accomplished along the length of the sheet material.

11. *Four-Way Dies.* These dies are used for smaller production runs. Here, the male portion, or punch, of the die is used in all operations; what changes is the female impression area. The female die has an impression on four separate sides of the die block. As the production demands, the die block is rotated to the appropriate side and the metal is formed by the stroke of the punch.

12. *Channel Forming Dies.* A simple die design is one used for channel forming. The channel-shaped die is usually equipped with a set of *strippers* that remove the metal from the punch after forming.

13. *U-Bend Dies.* The U-bend die is another form of channel die, except that the bottom of the channel has a radius.

14. *Box-Forming Dies.* The fabrication of box-shaped products presents a series of unique problems, though the bends required are simple. Of importance is the sequence of bends

to be made. To solve this problem, box-forming dies are used.

15. *Corrugating Dies.* Corrugated sheet products are economically made with the aid of corrugating dies. These dies are available in a variety of corrugated shapes and sizes.

16. *Multiple Bend Dies.* A large production die design is the multiple bend die. Here, a series of bends is executed in one stroke of the press. Because of the high expense involved in machining these dies, they are not used for small production purposes.

17. *Rocker Dies.* Products that require bending in directions in addition to the vertical axis must utilize a rocker die design. Here, "rocker" inserts move the die sections to increase the number of bends produced.

18. *Cam Driven Dies.* Complex forms are made with the aid of cam driven dies. In these designs, the die is equipped with "mini-dies" that are activated by cams when the die is closed.

COLD ROLL FORMING

The processes discussed so far can also be accomplished by traditional hand methods. Cold roll forming, however, is a production process that is used to make products not found in low volume manual production. Basically, cold roll forming is a process whereby sheets or strips of metal are formed into various shapes having a uniform cross section. This is accomplished by feeding the stock through a series of forming rolls, each progressively forming the metal until the final form is produced.

Products made by this process can be held to close tolerances; in fact, it is not uncommon to find smaller shapes made to within 0.002 in. (.051mm). The primary advantage of cold roll forming is that it can produce products of any length. The only limitation is the length of the metal fed into the rolls.

Cold roll forming is a high volume process that can generate a finished product at a rate of 50 to 300 linear feet (152 to 914m) per minute. Here, the metal is formed with minimal handling. The only

Courtesy Niagara Machine and Tool Works
Fig. 19-2. Press brake.

human contact normally made is in loading the coil or roll of metal prior to processing.

Tooling requirements for the process are initially expensive. However, because of its ability to produce a large volume of finished products, the overall cost is low. Since the product is formed in one pass, care must be taken to ensure that not too radical a bend is made from one roll to the next. Products that have unusually deep bends often require a larger number of rollers. Examples of sheet metal products made by this process are gutters, downspouts, tubing, and channels.

Roll Design

The number of rolls required for a product cannot be determined by a quick rule of thumb formula. The primary method used is to sketch each sequence of bends and count the number of sketches

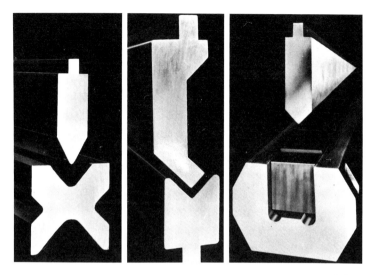

Courtesy Niagara Machine and Tool Works
Fig. 19-3. Simple bending dies.

Table 19-3
Recommended Load Requirements for Offset Bending

Material Thickness	Press Tonnage (tons/foot)
20 gauge	10–30
18 gauge	10–30
16 gauge	15–35
14 gauge	20–40
12 gauge	25–50
10 gauge	30–60
0.1875 in.	35 (forming) 65 (setting)
0.2500 in.	45 (forming) 60 (setting)

to determine the number of rolls. This drawing procedure not only gives an indication of how many rolls are required, but also shows the amount of bending achieved at each roll. This procedure is illustrated in Figure 19-4.

The amount of bend made at each roll should not be too great. Guidelines governing maximum bends will vary from product to product and material to material. Many cold roll formed products,

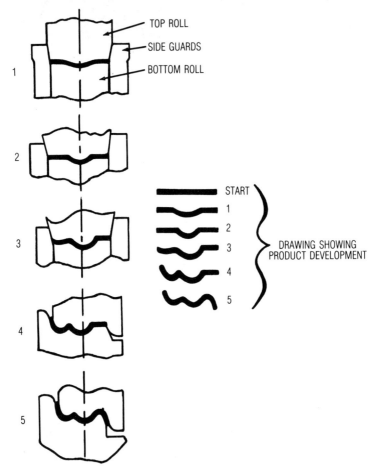

TOP ROLL
SIDE GUARDS
BOTTOM ROLL

START
1
2
3
4
5

DRAWING SHOWING
PRODUCT DEVELOPMENT

Fig. 19-4. Drawn cross section showing development of a product through forming rolls.

however, are made with no more than a 15° bend at one time, otherwise problems such as crimping and folding may occur. Too few rolls can therefore cause production problems and material defects. Conversely, too many rolls can increase the cost of the product.

Rolls are designed as one and multiple piece rolls. The more complex the form, the larger the number of pieces. In some situations, extremely large rolls would be difficult to handle (for mounting and maintenance), and are designed in several sections for easy handling. Roll designers, however, try to minimize the number of pieces used to make up a roll because of the added costs associated with its machining.

Rolls are made of a variety of materials. The specific one selected will depend on the sheet metal to be formed. Example of roll materials are:

- Cast iron and soft machine steel rolls are used for small runs.

- Alloy steel and oil or air hardened tool steels are recommended where long wear under severe conditions is required.

- High carbon, high chromium steel rolls are often used in the roll forming close toleranced parts.

- Aluminum bronze rolls are used because of the superior frictional qualities that are required in forming deep sections.

- Hot rolled steel, high carbon, high chrome tool steels are used in rolls that must be resistant to abrasion.

- Hardwood and plastic rolls are used in the roll forming of light gauged metals.

Tube and Pipe Rolling

Cold roll forming is also used in the manufacturing of welded tube and pipe products. Specifications for welded tubing will range from 0.250 to 24 in. (.635 to 60.96cm) in diameter, with wall thickness between 0.015 and 0.750 in. (.381 and 19.05mm). Tube and pipe rolling are manufactured in *mills* that form strips of metal into tubular shapes, followed by a welding unit for seaming, a cooling unit, and a sizing and straightening unit.

Illustrated in Figure 19-5 is the typical sequence of tube and pipe rolling found in industry. Here, the metal is passsed through a series of rolls that are designed with one radius per roll pass. In this way, the radius of the material will decrease with each roll until the final pass is made. In most cases, the final roll passes are used to align the tubing's edges so that they can be accurately welded.

Welding is accomplished on tubing and pipes so that the outside diameter is slightly larger than the finished diameter. Once cooled,

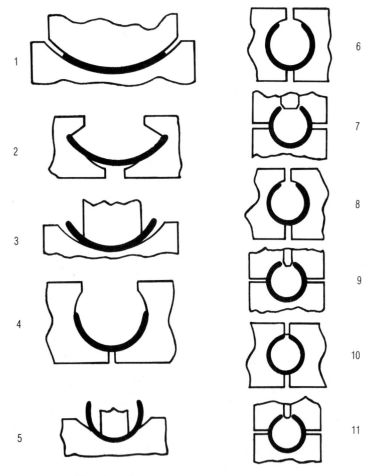

Fig. 19-5. Sequence of roll forming for tubing.

the tubing and pipe are passed through a series of sizing and straightening rolls consisting of three driven roll passes. With each pass through the rolls, the diameter of the tubing decreases until the final dimension is achieved.

STRETCH FORMING

The process known as stretch forming is used to produce contours in sheet metal by bending it over a stretch die. This process requires the opposite edges of the metal to be gripped and pulled in a "stretching" manner over a die that is also known as a *stretch form*. The die is then raised and pushed against the taut metal. The metal is stretched to conform to the die. Not only is this process used with sheet metal, but it is often employed with rods, bars, tubing, and extruded sections.

Not all metals are suited for stretch forming operations. Those commonly used in this process are aluminum alloys (24S and 75S), stainless steel (302, 321, and 347), and low carbon steel. Care must be taken when working with aluminum, since it will have a tendency to fracture at the jaw inserts. This, however, is avoided by shielding the metal with a soft cloth or rubber insert.

In all, there are four basic types of stretch forming operations. These are presented as follows:

1. *Stretch Wrapping.* The most basic form of stretch forming is known as stretch wrapping. Here, one end of the sheet material is clamped in a jaw that is attached to a rotating table. The other end is also clamped to a jaw, but it is connected to a hydraulic cylinder pivot mounted to the machine's frame. The metal is first stretched when the cylinder is activated. The *form block* (stretch die) is then rotated into the metal, which causes additional stretching and metal contouring.

2. *Compression Forming.* In compression forming, one end of the metal is attached to a table gripper. With the use of a hydraulic cylinder, a *wiper shoe* is forced up against the metal so that it is stretched against the form block. At this time, the form block rotates into the metal, causing it to stretch and take on the die's contour.

3. *Spiral Forming.* Spiral forming is similar to compression forming, except that the wiper shoe continues to apply pressure in a vertical direction. This forces the metal in a downward direction. As the form block rotates, a spiral form is produced.

4. *Radial Draw Forming.* A procedure that combines the advantages of both stretch wrapping and compression forming is radial draw forming. Here, the metal is first arranged as for stretch wrapping. When the form block is rotated into the metal, a wiper shoe is forced into it by a hydraulic cylinder. The primary use of this technique is in forming offsets in parts.

SUMMARY

In terms of total volume, more sheet metal products are made by production processes than by hand or manual procedures. Sheet metal manufacturing processes are divided into three major areas: material preparation, deformation and fabrication, and finishing.

Since most of the sheet material supplied for production processing comes in coil or roll form, cutting it to size becomes critical. Pre-cutting sheet stock to size is usually accomplished on cutting and shearing equipment similar to that found in smaller job and sheet metal shops.

There are four general types of shears used in industry: mechanical squaring shears, hydraulic squaring shears, alligator shears, and rotary shears. Of these, rotary shears are capable of generating the greatest volume of stock. When using any cutting or shearing equipment, there are two major factors that must be accounted for: shearing speed and shearing accuracy. Other cutting operations used in industry are slitting and gas cutting.

Presswork is probably the biggest difference between production and manual sheet metal work. Power presses are used in manufacturing industries to generate the force necessary for cutting and forming sheet material. The tools used in presses are called dies and are of two types. The first are cutting dies, which use shearing forces to punch or cut material. The second type of die is known as a forming die. Forming dies are used to bend, form, shape, and contour sheet metal to specification.

Cold roll forming is primarily limited to production work. This is a process where sheets or strips of metal are formed into various shapes that have a uniform cross section. Pipes, tubing, gutters, and other similar products are made by this process.

Stretch forming is another production process with wide application in sheet metal work. Here, the sheet metal is stretched by grippers and forced against a die or stretch form. In most cases, the die is raised, rolled, or forced into the sheet stock as it is being held taut. The basic stretch forming operations used are stretch wrapping, compression forming, spiral forming, and radial draw forming.

REVIEW QUESTIONS

1. What is the major difference between construction type sheet metal work or sheet metal shop work and production techniques?
2. Identify and briefly describe the three major areas of production work.
3. Describe the different types of production shears and their primary applications.
4. What are cutting dies and how do they function?
5. What is meant by the specification "Cut Edge Type Number"?
6. What are the primary functions of forming dies; how do these dies differ from cutting dies?
7. Identify the major types of forming dies and products they are used to produce.
8. Describe what cold forming is, and how tubing is produced in this process.
9. What is stretch forming?

Appendix

Table A-1
Decimal Equivalents of Fractions

Fractions	Decimal
$1/64$	0.015625
$1/32$	0.03125
$3/64$	0.046875
$1/16$	0.0625
$5/64$	0.078125
$3/32$	0.09375
$7/64$	0.109375
$1/8$	0.125
$9/64$	0.140625
$5/32$	0.15625
$11/64$	0.171875
$3/16$	0.1875
$13/64$	0.203125
$7/32$	0.21875
$15/64$	0.234375
$1/4$	0.250
$17/64$	0.265625
$9/32$	0.28125
$19/64$	0.296875
$5/16$	0.3125
$21/64$	0.328125
$11/32$	0.34375
$23/64$	0.359375
$3/8$	0.375
$25/64$	0.390625
$13/32$	0.40625

Table A-1
Decimal Equivalents of Fractions (Cont'd)

Fractions	Decimal
$27/64$	0.421875
$7/16$	0.4375
$29/64$	0.453125
$15/32$	0.46875
$31/64$	0.484375
$1/2$	0.500
$33/64$	0.515625
$17/32$	0.53125
$35/64$	0.546875
$9/16$	0.5625
$37/64$	0.578125
$19/32$	0.59375
$39/64$	0.609375
$5/8$	0.625
$41/64$	0.640525
$21/32$	0.65625
$43/64$	0.671875
$11/16$	0.6875
$45/64$	0.703125
$23/32$	0.71875
$47/64$	0.734375
$3/4$	0.750
$49/64$	0.765625
$25/32$	0.78125
$51/64$	0.796875
$13/16$	0.8125
$53/64$	0.828125
$27/32$	0.84375
$55/64$	0.859375
$7/8$	0.875
$57/64$	0.890625
$29/32$	0.90625
$59/64$	0.921875
$15/16$	0.9375
$61/64$	0.953125
$31/32$	0.96875
$63/64$	0.984375
1	1.000

Table A-2
English Weights and Measures

Linear Measures

 1 mile = 1760 yards = 5280 feet
 1 yard = 3 feet = 36 inches
 1 foot = 12 inches
 1 mil = 0.001 inch
 1 fathom = 2 yards = 6 feet
 1 rod = 5.5 yards = 16.5 feet
 1 hand = 4 inches
 1 span = 9 inches

Area Measures

 1 square mile = 640 acres = 6400 square chains
 1 acre = 10 square chains = 4840 square yards = 43,560 square feet
 1 square chain = 16 square rods = 484 square yards. = 4356 square feet
 1 square rod = 30.25 square yards = 272.25 square feet = 625 square links
 1 square yard = 9 square feet
 1 square foot = 144 square inches

Diameter Measures

 1 circular inch = area of circle having a diameter of 1 inch = 0.7854 square
 inch
 1 circular inch = 1,000,000 circular mils
 1 square inch = 1.2732 circular inch

Cubic Measures

 1 cubic yard = 27 cubic feet
 1 cubic foot = 1728 cubic inches

Liquid Measures

 1 U.S. gallon = 0.1337 cubic foot = 231 cubic inches = 4 quarts = 8 pints
 1 quart = 2 pints = 8 gills
 1 pint = 4 gills
 1 British Imperial Gallon = 1.2009 U.S. gallon = 277.42 cubic inches

Dry Measures

 1 bushel = 1.2445 cubic foot = 2150.42 cubic inches
 1 bushel = 4 pecks = 32 quarts = 64 pints

Table A-2
English Weights and Measures (Cont'd)

1 peck = 8 quarts = 16 pints
1 quart = 2 pints
1 heaped bushel = 1.25 struck bushel
1 cubic foot = 0.8036

Commercial Weights

1 gross or long ton = 2240 pounds
1 net or short ton = 2000 pounds
1 pound = 16 ounces = 7000 grains
1 ounce = 16 drachms = 437.5 grains

Table A-3
Metric Weights and Measures

Linear Measures

1 centimeter (cm) = 10 millimeters (mm)
1 decimeter (dm) = 10 centimeters
1 meter (m) = 10 decimeters
1 kilometer (km) = 1000 meters

Area Measures

1 square centimeter = 100 square millimeters
1 square decimeter = 100 square centimeters
1 square meter = 100 square decimeters
1 are (a) = 100 square meters
1 hectare (ha) = 100 ares
1 square kilometer = 100 hectares

Cubic Measures

1 cubic centimeter = 1000 cubic millimeters
1 cubic decimeter = 1000 cubic centimeters
1 cubic meter = 1000 cubic decimeters

Liquid and Dry Measures

1 centiliter (cl) = 10 milliliters (ml)
1 deciliter (dl) = 10 centiliters

Table A-3
Metric Weights and Measures (Cont'd)

1 liter (l) = 10 deciliters
1 hectoliter (hl) = 100 liters

Weight Measures

1 centigram (cg) = 10 milligrams (mg)
1 decigram (dg) = 10 centigrams
1 gram (g) = 10 decigrams
1 dekagram (dag) = 10 grams
1 hectogram (hg) = 10 deckagrams
1 kilogram (kg) = 10 hectograms
1 metric ton (t) = 1000 kilograms

Table A-4
Conversion Table

Linear Measures

1 kilogram = 0.6214 mile
1 meter = 39.37 inches = 3.2808 feet = 1.0936 yards
1 centimeter = 0.3937 inch
1 millimeter = 0.03937 inch

1 mile = 1.609 kilometers
1 yard = 0.9144 meter
1 foot = 0.3048 meter = 304.8 millimeters
1 inch = 2.54 centimeters = 25.4 millimeters

Area Measures

1 square kilometer = 0.3861 square mile = 247.1 acres
1 hectare = 2.471 acres = 107,639 square feet
1 are = 0.0247 acre = 1076.4 square feet
1 square meter = 10.764 square feet
1 square centimeter = 0.155 square inch
1 square millimeter = 0.00155 square inch

1 square mile = 2.5899 square kilometers
1 acre = 0.4047 hectare = 40.47 ares

Table A-4
Conversion Table (Cont'd)

1 square yard = 0.836 square meter
1 square foot = 0.0929 square meter
1 square inch = 6.452 square centimeters = 645.2 square millimeters

Cubic Measures

1 cubic meter = 35.315 cubic feet = 1.308 cubic yards
1 cubic meter = 264.2 U.S. Gallons
1 cubic centimeter = 0.061 cubic inch
1 liter = 0.0353 cubic foot = 61.023 cubic inches
1 liter = 0.2642 U.S. gallon = 1.0567 U.S. quarts

1 cubic yard = 0.7646 cubic meter
1 cubic foot = 0.02832 cubic meter = 28.317 liters
1 cubic inch = 16.38706 cubic centimeters
1 U.S. gallon = 3.785 liters
1 U.S. quart = 0.946 liter

Weight Measures

1 metric ton = 0.9842 ton (long) = 2204.6 pounds
1 kilogram = 2.2046 pounds = 35.274 ounces
1 gram = 0.03527 ounce
1 gram = 15.432 grains

1 long ton = 1.016 metric ton = 1016 kilograms
1 pound = 0.4536 kilogram = 453.6 grams
1 ounce = 28.35 grams
1 grain = 0.0648 gram
1 calorie (kilogram calorie) = 3.968 Btu

INDEX

INDEX

448

**Over a Century of Excellence
for the Professional
and
Vocational Trades and the Crafts**

**Order now from your local bookstore
or use the convenient order form at
the back of this book.**

AUDEL

These fully illustrated, up-to-date guides and manuals mean a better job done for mechanics, engineers, electricians, plumbers, carpenters, and all skilled workers.

Contents

Fractional Horsepower Electric Motors

Rex Miller and Mark Richard Miller
5½ x 8¼ Hardcover 436 pp. 285 illus.
ISBN: 0-672-23410-6 $15.95

Fully illustrated guide to small-to-moderate-size electric motors in home appliances and industrial equipment: • terminology • repair tools and supplies • small DC and universal motors • split-phase, capacitor-start, shaded pole, and special motors • commutators and brushes • shafts and bearings • switches and relays • armatures • stators • modification and replacement of motors.

Electrical

House Wiring sixth edition
Roland E. Palmquist
5½ x 8 ¼ Hardcover 256 pp. 150 illus.
ISBN: 0-672-23404-1 $14.95

Rules and regulations of the current National Electrical Code® for residential wiring, fully explained and illustrated: • basis for load calculations • calculations for dwellings • services • nonmetallic-sheathed cable • underground feeder and branch-circuit cable • metal-clad cable • circuits required for dwellings • boxes and fittings • receptacle spacing • mobile homes • wiring for electric house heating.

Practical Electricity fourth edition
Robert G. Middleton; revised by L. Donald Meyers
5½ x 8¼ Hardcover 504 pp. 335 illus.
ISBN: 0-672-23375-4 $14.95

Complete, concise handbook on the principles of electricity and their practical application: • magnetism and electricity • conductors and insulators • circuits • electromagnetic induction • alternating current • electric lighting and lighting calculations • basic house wiring • electric heating • generating stations and substations.

Guide to the 1984 Electrical Code®
Roland E. Palmquist
5½ × 8¼ Hardcover 664 pp. 225 illus.
ISBN: 0-672-23398-3 $13.95

Authoritative guide to the National Electrical Code® for all electricians, contractors, inspectors, and homeowners: • terms and regulations for wiring design and protection • wiring methods and materials • equipment for general use • special occupancies • special equipment and conditions • and communication systems. Guide to the 1987 NEC® will be available in mid-1987.

Mathematics for Electricians and Electronics Technicians
Rex Miller
5½ × 8¼ Hardcover 312 pp. 115 illus.
ISBN: 0-8161-1700-4 $14.95

Mathematical concepts, formulas, and problem solving in electricity and electronics: • resistors and resistance • circuits • meters • alternating current and inductance • alternating current and capacitance • impedance and phase angles • resonance in circuits • special-purpose circuits. Includes mathematical problems and solutions.

Electric Motors
Edwin P. Anderson; revised by Rex Miller
5½ x 8¼ Hardcover 656 pp. 405 illus.
ISBN: 0-672-23376-2 $14.95

Complete guide to installation, maintenance, and repair of all types of electric motors: • AC generators • synchronous motors • squirrel-cage motors • wound rotor motors • DC motors • fractional-horsepower motors • magnetic contractors • motor testing and maintenance • motor calculations • meters • wiring diagrams • armature windings • DC armature rewinding procedure • and stator and coil winding.

Home Appliance Servicing fourth edition
Edwin P. Anderson; revised by Rex Miller
5½ x 8¼ Hardcover 640 pp. 345 illus.
ISBN: 0-672-23379-7 $15.95

Step-by-step illustrated instruction on all types of household appliances: • irons • toasters • roasters and broilers • electric coffee makers • space heaters • water heaters • electric ranges and microwave ovens • mixers and blenders • fans and blowers • vacuum cleaners and floor polishers • washers and dryers • dishwashers and garbage disposals • refrigerators • air conditioners and dehumidifiers.

Television Service Manual

fifth edition

Robert G. Middleton; revised by Joseph G. Barrile

5¹⁄₂ x 8¹⁄₄   Hardcover   512 pp.   395 illus.
ISBN: 0-672-23395-9 $15.95

Practical up-to-date guide to all aspects of television transmission and reception, for both black and white and color receivers: • step-by-step maintenance and repair • broadcasting • transmission • receivers • antennas and transmission lines • interference • RF tuners • the video channel • circuits • power supplies • alignment • test equipment.

Electrical Course for Apprentices and Journeymen

second edition

Roland E. Palmquist

5¹⁄₂ x 8¹⁄₄   Hardcover   478 pp.   290 illus.
ISBN:0-672-23393-2 $14.95

Practical course on operational theory and applications for training and re-training in school or on the job: • electricity and matter • units and definitions • electrical symbols • magnets and magnetic fields • capacitors • resistance • electromagnetism • instruments and measurements • alternating currents • DC generators • circuits • transformers • motors • grounding and ground testing.

Questions and Answers for Electricians Examinations eighth edition

Roland E. Palmquist

5¹⁄₂ x 8¹⁄₄   Hardcover   320 pp.   110 illus.
ISBN: 0-672-23399-1 $12.95

Based on the current National Electrical Code®, a review of exams for apprentice, journeyman, and master, with explanations of principles underlying each test subject: • Ohm's Law and other formulas • power and power factors • lighting • branch circuits and feeders • transformer principles and connections • wiring • batteries and rectification • voltage generation • motors • ground and ground testing.

Machine Shop and Mechanical Trades

Machinists Library

fourth edition   3 vols

Rex Miller

5¹⁄₂ x 8¹⁄₄   Hardcover   1,352 pp.   1,120 illus.
ISBN: 0-672-23380-0 $44.85

Indispensable three-volume reference for machinists, tool and die makers, machine operators, metal workers, and those with home workshops.

Volume I, Basic Machine Shop
5¹⁄₂ x 8¹⁄₄   Hardcover   392 pp.   375 illus.
ISBN: 0-672-23381-9 $14.95

• Blueprint reading • benchwork • layout and measurement • sheet-metal hand tools and machines • cutting tools • drills • reamers • taps • threading dies • milling machine cutters, arbors, collets, and adapters.

Volume II, Machine Shop
5¹⁄₂ x 8¹⁄₄   Hardcover   528 pp.   445 illus
ISBN: 0-672-23382-7 $14.95

• Power saws • machine tool operations • drilling machines • boring • lathes • automatic screw machine • milling • metal spinning.

Volume III, Toolmakers Handy Book
5¹⁄₂ x 8¹⁄₄   Hardcover   432 pp.   300 illus.
ISBN: 0-672-23383-5 $14.95

• Layout work • jigs and fixtures • gears and gear cutting • dies and diemaking • toolmaking operations • heat-treating furnaces • induction heating • furnace brazing • cold-treating process.

Mathematics for Mechanical Technicians and Technologists

John D. Bies

5¹⁄₂ x 8¹⁄₄   Hardcover   392 pp.   190 illus.
ISBN: 0-02-510620-1 $17.95

Practical sourcebook of concepts, formulas, and problem solving in industrial and mechanical technology: • basic and complex mechanics • strength of materials • fluidics • cams and gears • machine elements • machining operations • management controls • economics in machining • facility and human resources management.

Millwrights and Mechanics Guide

third edition

Carl A. Nelson

5¹⁄₂ x 8¹⁄₄   Hardcover   1,040 pp.   880 illus.
ISBN: 0-672-23373-8 $24.95

Most comprehensive and authoritative guide available for millwrights and mechanics at all levels of work or supervision: • drawing and sketching

• machinery and equipment installation • principles of mechanical power transmission • V-belt drives • flat belts • gears • chain drives • couplings • bearings • structural steel • screw threads • mechanical fasteners • pipe fittings and valves • carpentry • sheet-metal work • blacksmithing • rigging • electricity • welding • pumps • portable power tools • mensuration and mechanical calculations.

Welders Guide third edition

James E. Brumbaugh

5¹⁄₂ x 8¹⁄₄   Hardcover   960 pp.   615 illus.
ISBN: 0-672-23374-6 $23.95

Practical, concise manual on theory, operation, and maintenance of all welding machines: • gas welding equipment, supplies, and process • arc welding equipment, supplies, and process • TIG and MIG welding • submerged-arc and other shielded-arc welding processes • resistance, thermit, and stud welding • solders and soldering • brazing and braze welding • welding plastics • safety and health measures • symbols and definitions • testing and inspecting welds. Terminology and definitions as standardized by American Welding Society.

Welder/Fitters Guide

John P. Stewart

8¹⁄₂ x 11   Paperback   160 pp.   195 illus.
ISBN: 0-672-23325-8 $7.95

Step-by-step instruction for welder/fitters during training or on the job: • basic assembly tools and aids • improving blueprint reading skills • marking and alignment techniques • using basic tools • simple work practices • guide to fabricating welds • avoiding mistakes • exercises in blueprint reading • clamping devices • introduction to using hydraulic jacks • safety in weld fabrication plants • common welding shop terms.

Sheet Metal Work

John D. Bies

5¹⁄₂ x 8¹⁄₄   Hardcover   456 pp.   215 illus.
ISBN: 0-8161-1706-3 $19.95

On-the-job sheet metal guide for manufacturing, construction, and home workshops: • mathematics for sheet metal work • principles of drafting • concepts of sheet metal drawing • sheet metal standards, specifications, and materials • safety practices • layout • shear cutting • holes • bending and folding • forming operations • notching and clipping • metal spinning • mechanical fastening • soldering and brazing • welding • surface preparation and finishes • production processes.

Power Plant Engineers Guide

third edition
Frank D. Graham; revised by Charlie Buffington
5½ x 8¼   Hardcover   960 pp.   530 illus.
ISBN: 0-672-23329-0 $27.50

All-inclusive question-and-answer guide to steam and diesel-power engines: • fuels • heat • combustion • types of boilers • shell or fire-tube boiler construction • strength of boiler materials • boiler calculations • boiler fixtures, fittings, and attachments • boiler feed pumps • condensers • cooling ponds and cooling towers • boiler installation, startup, operation, maintenance and repair • oil, gas, and waste-fuel burners • steam turbines • air compressors • plant safety.

Mechanical Trades Pocket Manual

second edition
Carl A. Nelson
4 × 6   Paperback   364 pp.   255 illus.
ISBN: 0-672-23378-9 $10.95

Comprehensive handbook of essentials, pocket-sized to fit in the tool box: • mechanical and isometric drawing • machinery installation and assembly • belts • drives • gears • couplings • screw threads • mechanical fasteners • packing and seals • bearings • portable power tools • welding • rigging • piping • automatic sprinkler systems • carpentry • stair layout • electricity • shop geometry and trigonometry.

Plumbing

Plumbers and Pipe Fitters Library third edition 3 vols

Charles N. McConnell; revised by Tom Philbin
5½x8¼   Hardcover   952 pp.   560 illus.
ISBN: 0-672-23384-3 $34.95

Comprehensive three-volume set with up-to-date information for master plumbers, journeymen, apprentices, engineers, and those in building trades.

Volume 1, Materials, Tools, Roughing-In
5½ x 8¼   Hardcover   304 pp.   240 illus.
ISBN: 0-672-23385-1 $12.95

• Materials • tools • pipe fitting • pipe joints • blueprints • fixtures • valves and faucets.

Volume 2, Welding, Heating, Air Conditioning
5½ x 8¼   Hardcover   384 pp.   220 illus.
ISBN: 0-672-23386-x $13.95

• Brazing and welding • planning a

---

heating system • steam heating systems • hot water heating systems • boiler fittings • fuel-oil tank installation • gas piping • air conditioning.

Volume 3, Water Supply, Drainage, Calculations
5½ x 8¼   Hardcover   264 pp.   100 illus.
ISBN: 0-672-23387-8 $12.95

• Drainage and venting • sewage disposal • soldering • lead work • mathematics and physics for plumbers and pipe fitters.

Home Plumbing Handbook third edition

Charles N. McConnell
8½ x 11   Paperback   200 pp.   100 illus.
ISBN: 0-672-23413-0 $13.95

Clear, concise, up-to-date fully illustrated guide to home plumbing installation and repair: • repairing and replacing faucets • repairing toilet tanks • repairing a trip-lever bath drain • dealing with stopped-up drains • working with copper tubing • measuring and cutting pipe • PVC and CPVC pipe and fittings • installing a garbage disposals • replacing dishwashers • repairing and replacing water heaters • installing or resetting toilets • caulking around plumbing fixtures and tile • water conditioning • working with cast-iron soil pipe • septic tanks and disposal fields • private water systems.

The Plumbers Handbook seventh edition

Joseph P. Almond, Sr.
4 × 6   Paperback   352 pp.   170 illus.
ISBN: 0-672-23419-x $10.95

Comprehensive, handy guide for plumbers, pipe fitters, and apprentices that fits in the tool box or pocket: • plumbing tools • how to read blueprints • heating systems • water supply • fixtures, valves, and fittings • working drawings • roughing and repair • outside sewage lift station • pipes and pipelines • vents, drain lines, and septic systems • lead work • silver brazing and soft soldering • plumbing systems • abbreviations, definitions, symbols, and formulas.

Questions and Answers for Plumbers Examinations second edition

Jules Oravetz
5½ x 8¼   Paperback   256 pp.   145 illus.
ISBN: 0-8161-1703-9 $9.95

Practical, fully illustrated study guide to licensing exams for apprentice, journeyman, or master plumber: • definitions, specifications, and regulations set by National Bureau of Standards and by various state codes

---

• basic plumbing installation • drawings and typical plumbing system layout • mathematics • materials and fittings • joints and connections • traps, cleanouts, and backwater valves • fixtures • drainage, vents, and vent piping • water supply and distribution • plastic pipe and fittings • steam and hot water heating.

HVAC

Air Conditioning: Home and Commercial second edition

Edwin P. Anderson; revised by Rex Miller
5½ x 8¼   Hardcover   528 pp.   180 illus.
ISBN: 0-672-23397-5 $15.95

Complete guide to construction, installation, operation, maintenance, and repair of home, commercial, and industrial air conditioning systems, with troubleshooting charts: • heat leakage • ventilation requirements • room air conditioners • refrigerants • compressors • condensing equipment • evaporators • water-cooling systems • central air conditioning • automobile air conditioning • motors and motor control.

Heating, Ventilating and Air Conditioning Library second edition 3 vols

James E. Brumbaugh
5½ x 8¼   Hardcover   1,840 pp.   1,275 illus.
ISBN: 0-672-23388-6 $47.95

Authoritative three-volume reference for those who install, operate, maintain, and repair HVAC equipment commercially, industrially, or at home. Each volume fully illustrated with photographs, drawings, tables and charts.

Volume I, Heating Fundamentals, Furnaces, Boilers, Boiler Conversions
5½ x 8¼   Hardcover   656 pp.   405 illus.
ISBN: 0-672-23389-4 $16.95

• Insulation principles • heating calculations • fuels • warm-air, hot water, steam, and electrical heating systems • gas-fired, oil-fired, coal-fired, and electric-fired furnaces • boilers and boiler fittings • boiler and furnace conversion.

Volume II, Oil, Gas and Coal Burners, Controls, Ducts, Piping, Valves
5½ x 8¼   Hardcover   592 pp.   455 illus.
ISBN: 0-672-23390-8 $15.95

• Coal firing methods • thermostats and humidistats • gas and oil controls and other automatic controls •

ducts and duct systems • pipes, pipe fittings, and piping details • valves and valve installation • steam and hot-water line controls.

Volume III, Radiant Heating, Water Heaters, Ventilation, Air Conditioning, Heat Pumps, Air Cleaners
5 1/2 x 8 1/4   Hardcover   592 pp.   415 illus.
ISBN: 0-672-23391-6 $17.95
• Radiators, convectors, and unit heaters • fireplaces, stoves, and chimneys • ventilation principles • fan selection and operation • air conditioning equipment • humidifiers and dehumidifiers • air cleaners and filters.

Oil Burners fourth edition
Edwin M. Field
5 1/2 x 8 1/4   Hardcover   360 pp.   170 illus.
ISBN: 0-672-23394-0 $15.95

Up-to-date sourcebook on the construction, installation, operation, testing, servicing, and repair of all types of oil burners, both industrial and domestic: • general electrical hookup and wiring diagrams of automatic control systems • ignition system • high-voltage transportation • operational sequence of limit controls, thermostats, and various relays • combustion chambers • drafts • chimneys • drive couplings • fans or blowers • burner nozzles • fuel pumps.

Refrigeration: Home and Commercial second edition
Edwin P. Anderson; revised by Rex Miller
5 1/2 x 8 1/4   Hardcover   768 pp.   285 illus.
ISBN: 0-672-23396-7 $17.95

Practical, comprehensive reference for technicians, plant engineers, and homeowners on the installation, operation, servicing, and repair of everything from single refrigeration units to commercial and industrial systems: • refrigerants • compressors • thermoelectric cooling • service equipment and tools • cabinet maintenance and repairs • compressor lubrication systems • brine systems • supermarket and grocery refrigeration • locker plants • fans and blowers • piping • heat leakage • refrigeration-load calculations.

Pneumatics and Hydraulics

Hydraulics for Off-the-Road Equipment second edition
Harry L. Stewart; revised by Tom Philbin
5 1/2 x 8 1/4   Hardcover   256 pp.   175 illus.
ISBN: 0-8161-1701-2 $13.95

Complete reference manual for those who own and operate heavy equipment and for engineers, designers, installation and maintenance technicians, and shop mechanics: • hydraulic pumps, accumulators, and motors • force components • hydraulic control components • filters and filtration, lines and fittings, and fluids • hydrostatic transmissions • maintenance • troubleshooting.

Pneumatics and Hydraulics fourth edition
Harry L. Stewart; revised by Tom Philbin
5 1/2 x 8 1/4   Hardcover   512 pp.   315 illus.
ISBN: 0-672-23412-2 $19.95

Practical guide to the principles and applications of fluid power for engineers, designers, process planners, tool men, shop foremen, and mechanics: • pressure, work and power • general features of machines • hydraulic and pneumatic symbols • pressure boosters • air compressors and accessories • hydraulic power devices • hydraulic fluids • piping • air filters, pressure regulators, and lubricators • flow and pressure controls • pneumatic motors and tools • rotary hydraulic motors and hydraulic transmissions • pneumatic circuits • hydraulic circuits • servo systems.

Pumps fourth edition
Harry L. Stewart; revised by Tom Philbin
5 1/2 x 8 1/4   Hardcover   508 pp.   360 illus.
ISBN: 0-672-23400-9 $15.95

Comprehensive guide for operators, engineers, maintenance workers, inspectors, superintendents, and mechanics on principles and day-to-day operations of pumps: • centrifugal, rotary, reciprocating, and special service pumps • hydraulic accumulators • power transmission • hydraulic power tools • hydraulic cylinders • control valves • hydraulic fluids • fluid lines and fittings.

Carpentry and Construction

Carpenters and Builders Library
fifth edition 4 vols
John E. Ball; revised by Tom Philbin
5 1/2 x 8 1/4   Hardcover   1,224 pp.   1,010 illus.
ISBN: 0-672-23369-x $43.95
Also available in a new boxed set at no extra cost:
ISBN: 0-02-506450-9 $43.95

These profusely illustrated volumes, available in a handsome boxed edition, have set the professional standard for carpenters, joiners, and woodworkers.

Volume 1, Tools, Steel Square, Joinery
5 1/2 x 8 1/4   Hardcover   384 pp.   345 illus.
ISBN: 0-672-23365-7 $10.95
• Woods • nails • screws • bolts • the workbench • tools • using the steel square • joints and joinery • cabinetmaking joints • wood patternmaking • and kitchen cabinet construction.

Volume 2, Builders Math, Plans, Specifications
5 1/2 x 8 1/4   Hardcover   304 pp.   205 illus.
ISBN: 0-672-23366-5 $10.95
• Surveying • strength of timbers • practical drawing • architectural drawing • barn construction • small house construction • and home workshop layout.

Volume 3, Layouts, Foundations, Framing
5 1/2 x 8 1/4   Hardcover   272 pp.   215 illus.
ISBN: 0-672-23367-3 $10.95
• Foundations • concrete forms • concrete block construction • framing, girders and sills • skylights • porches and patios • chimneys, fireplaces, and stoves • insulation • solar energy and paneling.

Volume 4, Millwork, Power Tools, Painting
5 1/2 x 8 1/4   Hardcover   344 pp.   245 illus.
ISBN: 0-672-23368-1 $10.95
• Roofing, miter work • doors • windows, sheathing and siding • stairs • flooring • table saws, band saws, and jigsaws • wood lathes • sanders and combination tools • portable power tools • painting.

Complete Building Construction
second edition
John Phelps; revised by Tom Philbin
5 1/2 x 8 1/4   Hardcover   744 pp.   645 illus.
ISBN: 0-672-23377-0 $19.95

Comprehensive guide to constructing a frame or brick building from the footings to the ridge: • laying out building and excavation lines • making concrete forms and pouring fittings and foundation • making concrete slabs, walks, and driveways • laying concrete block, brick, and tile • building chimneys and fireplaces • framing, siding, and roofing • insulating • finishing the inside • building stairs • installing windows • hanging doors.

Complete Roofing Handbook
James E. Brumbaugh
5½ x 8¼   Hardcover   536 pp.   510 illus.
ISBN: 0-02-517850-4 $29.95

Authoritative text and highly detailed drawings and photographs,on all aspects of roofing: • types of roofs • roofing and reroofing • roof and attic insulation and ventilation • skylights and roof openings • dormer construction • roof flashing details • shingles • roll roofing • built-up roofing • roofing with wood shingles and shakes • slate and tile roofing • installing gutters and downspouts • listings of professional and trade associations and roofing manufacturers.

Complete Siding Handbook
James E. Brumbaugh
5½ x 8¼   Hardcover   512 pp.   450 illus.
ISBN: 0-02-517880-6 $23.95

Companion to *Complete Roofing Handbook*, with step-by-step instructions and drawings on every aspect of siding: • sidewalls and siding • wall preparation • wood board siding • plywood panel and lap siding • hardboard panel and lap siding • wood shingle and shake siding • aluminum and steel siding • vinyl siding • exterior paints and stains • refinishing of siding, gutter and downspout systems • listings of professional and trade associations and siding manufacturers.

Masons and Builders Library
second edition   2 vols
Louis M. Dezettel; revised by Tom Philbin
5½ x 8¼   Hardcover   688 pp.   500 illus.
ISBN: 0-672-23401-7 $27.95

Two-volume set on practical instruction in all aspects of materials and methods of bricklaying and masonry: • brick • mortar • tools • bonding • corners, openings, and arches • chimneys and fireplaces • structural clay tile and glass block • brick walks, floors, and terraces • repair and maintenance • plasterboard and plaster • stone and rock masonry • reading blueprints.

Volume 1, Concrete, Block, Tile, Terrazzo
5½ x 8¼   Hardcover   304 pp.   190 illus.
ISBN: 0-672-23402-5 $13.95

Volume 2, Bricklaying, Plastering, Rock Masonry, Clay Tile
5½ x 8¼   Hardcover   384 pp.   310 illus.
ISBN: 0-672-23403-3 $12.95

Woodworking

Woodworking and Cabinetmaking
F. Richard Boller
5½ x 8¼   Hardcover   360 pp.   455 illus.
ISBN: 0-02-512800-0 $18.95

Compact one-volume guide to the essentials of all aspects of woodworking: • properties of softwoods, hardwoods, plywood, and composition wood • design, function, appearance, and structure • project planning • hand tools • machines • portable electric tools • construction • the home workshop • and the projects themselves – stereo cabinet, speaker cabinets, bookcase, desk, platform bed, kitchen cabinets, bathroom vanity.

Wood Furniture: Finishing, Refinishing, Repairing second edition
James E. Brumbaugh
5½ x 8¼   Hardcover   352 pp.   185 illus.
ISBN: 0-672-23409-2 $12.95

Complete, fully illustrated guide to repairing furniture and to finishing and refinishing wood surfaces for professional woodworkers and do-it-yourselfers: • tools and supplies • types of wood • veneering • inlaying • repairing, restoring, and stripping • wood preparation • staining – shellac, varnish, lacquer, paint and enamel, and oil and wax finishes • antiquing • gilding and bronzing • decorating furniture.

Maintenance and Repair

Building Maintenance second edition
Jules Oravetz
5½ x 8¼   Hardcover   384 pp.   210 illus.
ISBN: 0-672-23278-2 $9.95

Complete information on professional maintenance procedures used in office, educational, and commercial buildings: • painting and decorating • plumbing and pipe fitting

• concrete and masonry • carpentry • roofing • glazing and caulking • sheet metal • electricity • air conditioning and refrigeration • insect and rodent control • heating • maintenance management • custodial practices.

Gardening, Landscaping and Grounds Maintenance
third edition
Jules Oravetz
5½ x 8¼   Hardcover   424 pp.   340 illus.
ISBN: 0-672-23417-3 $15.95

Practical information for those who maintain lawns, gardens, and industrial, municipal, and estate grounds: • flowers, vegetables, berries, and house plants • greenhouses • lawns • hedges and vines • flowering shrubs and trees • shade, fruit and nut trees • evergreens • bird sanctuaries • fences • insect and rodent control • weed and brush control • roads, walks, and pavements • drainage • maintenance equipment • golf course planning and maintenance.

Home Maintenance and Repair: Walls, Ceilings and Floors
Gary D. Branson
8½ x 11 Paperback   80 pp.   80 illus.
ISBN: 0-672-23281-2 $6.95

Do-it-yourselfer's step-by-step guide to interior remodeling with professional results: • general maintenance • wallboard installation and repair • wallboard taping • plaster repair • texture paints • wallpaper techniques • paneling • sound control • ceiling tile • bath tile • energy conservation.

Painting and Decorating
Rex Miller and Glenn E. Baker
5½ x 8¼   Hardcover   464 pp.   325 illus.
ISBN: 0-672-23405-x $18.95

Practical guide for painters, decorators, and homeowners to the most up-to-date materials and techniques: • job planning • tools and equipment needed • finishing materials • surface preparation • applying paint and stains · decorating with coverings • repairs and maintenance • color and decorating principles.

Tree Care second edition
John M. Haller
8½ x 11 Paperback 224 pp. 305 illus.
ISBN: 0-02-062870-6 $16.95

New edition of a standard in the field, for growers, nursery owners, foresters, landscapers, and homeowners: • planting • pruning • fertilizing • bracing and cabling • wound repair • grafting • spraying • disease and insect management • coping with environmental damage • removal • structure and physiology • recreational use.

Upholstering
updated
James E. Brumbaugh
5½ x 8¼ Hardcover 400 pp. 380 illus.
ISBN: 0-672-23372-x $14.95

Essentials of upholstering for professional, apprentice, and hobbyist: • furniture styles • tools and equipment • stripping • frame construction and repairs • finishing and refinishing wood surfaces • webbing • springs • burlap, stuffing, and muslin • pattern layout • cushions • foam padding • covers • channels and tufts • padded seats and slip seats • fabrics • plastics • furniture care.

Automotive and Engines

Diesel Engine Manual fourth edition
Perry O. Black; revised by William E. Scahill
5½ x 8¼ Hardcover 512 pp. 255 illus.
ISBN: 0-672-23371-1 $15.95

Detailed guide for mechanics, students, and others to all aspects of typical two- and four-cycle engines: • operating principles • fuel oil • diesel injection pumps • basic Mercedes diesels • diesel engine cylinders • lubrication • cooling systems • horsepower • engine-room procedures • diesel engine installation • automotive diesel engine • marine diesel engine • diesel electrical power plant • diesel engine service.

Gas Engine Manual third edition
Edwin P. Anderson; revised by Charles G. Facklam
5½ x 8¼ Hardcover 424 pp. 225 illus.
ISBN: 0-8161-1707-1 $12.95

Indispensable sourcebook for those who operate, maintain, and repair gas engines of all types and sizes: • fundamentals and classifications of engines · engine parts • pistons • crankshafts • valves • lubrication, cooling, fuel, ignition, emission

control and electrical systems • engine tune-up • servicing of pistons and piston rings, cylinder blocks, connecting rods and crankshafts, valves and valve gears, carburetors, and electrical systems.

Small Gasoline Engines
Rex Miller and Mark Richard Miller
5 ½ x 8¼ Hardcover 640 pp. 525 illus.
ISBN: 0-672-23414-9 $16.95

Practical information for those who repair, maintain, and overhaul two- and four-cycle engines – with emphasis on one-cylinder motors – including lawn mowers, edgers, grass sweepers, snowblowers, emergency electrical generators, outboard motors, and other equipment up to ten horsepower: • carburetors, emission controls, and ignition systems • starting systems • hand tools • safety • power generation • engine operations • lubrication systems • power drivers • preventive maintenance • step-by-step overhauling procedures • troubleshooting • testing and inspection • cylinder block servicing.

Truck Guide Library 3 vols
James E. Brumbaugh
5½ x 8¼ Hardcover 2,144 pp. 1,715 illus.
ISBN: 0-672-23392-4 $45.95

Three-volume comprehensive and profusely illustrated reference on truck operation and maintenance.

Volume 1, Engines
5½ x 8¼ Hardcover 416 pp. 290 illus.
ISBN: 0-672-23356-8 $16.95

• Basic components · engine operating principles • troubleshooting • cylinder blocks • connecting rods, pistons, and rings • crankshafts, main bearings, and flywheels • camshafts and valve trains • engine valves.

Volume 2, Engine Auxiliary Systems
5½ x 8¼ Hardcover 704 pp. 520 illus.
ISBN: 0-672-23357-6 $16.95

• Battery and electrical systems • spark plugs • ignition systems, charging and starting systems • lubricating, cooling, and fuel systems • carburetors and governors • diesel systems • exhaust and emission-control systems.

Volume 3, Transmissions, Steering, and Brakes
5½ x 8¼ Hardcover 1,024 pp. 905 illus.
ISBN: 0-672-23406-8 $16.95

• Clutches • manual, auxiliary, and automatic transmissions • frame and suspension systems • differentials and axles, manual and power steering • front-end alignment • hydraulic, power, and air brakes • wheels and tires • trailers.

Drafting

Answers on Blueprint Reading
fourth edition
Roland E. Palmquist; revised by Thomas J. Morrisey
5½ x 8¼ Hardcover 320 pp. 275 illus.
ISBN: 0-8161-1704-7 $12.95

Complete question-and-answer instruction manual on blueprints of machines and tools, electrical systems, and architecture: • drafting scale • drafting instruments • conventional lines and representations • pictorial drawings • geometry of drafting • orthographic and working drawings • surfaces • detail drawing • sketching • map and topographical drawings • graphic symbols • architectural drawings • electrical blueprints • computer-aided design and drafting. Also included is an appendix of measurements • metric conversions • screw threads and tap drill sizes • number and letter sizes of drills with decimal equivalents • double depth of threads • tapers and angles.

Hobbies

Complete Course in Stained Glass
Pepe Mendez
8½ x 11 Paperback 80 pp. 50 illus.
ISBN: 0-672-23287-1 $8.95

Guide to the tools, materials, and techniques of the art of stained glass, with ten fully illustrated lessons: • how to cut glass • cartoon and pattern drawing • assembling and cementing • making lamps using various techniques • electrical components for completing lamps • sources of materials • glossary of terminology and techniques of stained glasswork.

Macmillan Practical Arts Library
Books for and by the Craftsman

World Woods in Color
W.A. Lincoln
7 × 10   Hardcover   300 pages
300 photos
ISBN: 0-02-572350-2 $38.41

Large full-color photographs show the natural grain and features of nearly 300 woods: • commercial and botanical names • physical characteristics, mechanical properties, seasoning, working properties, durability, and uses • the height, diameter, bark, and places of distribution of each tree • indexing of botanical, trade, commercial, local, and family names • a full bibliography of publications on timber study and identification.

The Woodworker's Bible
Alf Martensson
8 × 10   Paperback   288 pages   900 illus.
ISBN: 0-02-011940-2 $13.95

For the craftsperson familiar with basic carpentry skills, a guide to creating professional-quality furniture, cabinetry, and objects d'art in the home workshop: • techniques and expert advice on fine craftsmanship whether tooled by hand or machine • joint-making • assembling to ensure fit • finishes. Author, who lives in London and runs a workshop called Woodstock, has also written. *The Book of Furnituremaking.*

Cabinetmaking: The Professional Approach
Alan Peters
8½ × 11   Hardcover   208 pages   175 illus.
(8 pp. color)
ISBN: 0-02-596200-0 $28.00

A unique guide to all aspects of professional furniture making, from an English master craftsman: • the Cotswold School and the birth of the furniture movement • setting up a professional shop • equipment • finance and business efficiency • furniture design • working to commission • batch production, training, and techniques • plans for nine projects.

The Woodturner's Art: Fundamentals and Projects
Ron Roszkiewicz
8 × 10   Hardcover   256 pages   300 illus.
ISBN: 0-02-605250-4 $28.80

A master woodturner shows how to design and create increasingly difficult projects step-by-step in this book suitable for the beginner and the more advanced student: • spindle and faceplate turning • tools • techniques • classic turnings from various historical periods • more than 30 types of projects including boxes, furniture, vases, and candlesticks • making duplicates • projects using combinations of techniques and more than one kind of wood. Author has also written *The Woodturner's Companion.*

Cabinetmaking and Millwork
John L. Feirer
7⅛ × 9½   Hardcover   992 pages
2,350 illus. (32 pp. in color)
ISBN: 0-02-537350-1 $47.50

The classic on cabinetmaking that covers in detail all of the materials, tools, machines, and processes used in building cabinets and interiors, the production of furniture, and other work of the finish carpenter and millwright: • fixed installations such as paneling, built-ins, and cabinets • movable wood products such as furniture and fixtures • which woods to use, and why and how to use them in the interiors of homes and commercial buildings • metrics and plastics in furniture construction.

Carpentry and Building Construction
John L. Feirer and Gilbert R. Hutchings
7½ × 9½   hardcover   1,120 pages
2,000 photos (8 pp. in color)
ISBN: 0-02-537360-9 $50.00

A classic by Feirer on each detail of modern construction: • the various machines, tools, and equipment from which the builder can choose • laying of a foundation • building frames for each part of a building • details of interior and exterior work • painting and finishing • reading plans • chimneys and fireplaces • ventilation • assembling prefabricated houses.

Just select your books, fill out the card, and mail today.

Money-Back Guarantee

BUSINESS REPLY MAIL

FIRST CLASS   PERMIT NO. 348   NEW YORK, NY

POSTAGE WILL BE PAID BY ADDRESSEE

Macmillan Publishing Company
Audel® Library
866 Third Avenue
New York, NY 10022

Attention: Special Sales Department

NO POSTAGE
NECESSARY
IF MAILED
IN THE
UNITED STATES